C000201641

Design in Britain

DESIGN MUSEUM

Design in Britain

Big ideas (small island)
General Editor Deyan Sudjic

First published in 2009 by
Conran Octopus Ltd
a part of Octopus Publishing Group
2–4 Heron Quays, London E14 4JP
www.octopusbooks.co.uk

An Hachette Livre UK Company
www.hachettelivre.co.uk

Distributed in the United States
and Canada by Octopus Books USA
c/o Hachette Book Group USA
237 Park Avenue, New York
NY 10017 USA
www.octopusbooksusa.com

British Library Cataloguing-in-
Publication Data. A catalogue
record for this book is available
from the British Library.

Publisher: Lorraine Dickey
General Editor: Deyan Sudjic
Managing Editor: Sybella Marlow
Editor: Robert Anderson
Art Director: Jonathan Christie
Design: Untitled
Picture Researcher:
Anne-Marie Hoines
Production Manager:
Katherine Hockley

ISBN: 978 1 84091 542 6
Printed in China

Design in Britain

One of the many exhibitions staged in quick-fire succession in the early days of the Design Museum, in its first incarnation as the Boilerhouse Project in the basement of the Victoria and Albert Museum, was an engaging attempt to get to grips with the concept of national identity in design. The exhibition was laid out as a checkerboard, comparing product categories from a random shuffle of nations. So, in the car row, the Mini occupied the British slot, the 2CV filled it for France, and the VW Beetle did the same, unsurprisingly enough, for Germany. What could be more British than a Mini, as portrayed in *The Italian Job*, endorsed by Michael Caine and Noël Coward? Alongside the cars, there were comparisons between typefaces, consumer electronics and, in a bolder exploration of national psyche, the differing configurations of the toilet bowl as favoured by the Anglo-Saxons, the Teutons and the French.

National identity and design

The exhibition posited an arresting idea, and made a clear point, but it did not really come to terms with the way in which national identity is itself a carefully constructed artifact, dependent on a wide range of self-conscious design skills, rather than the organic and inevitable outcome of race memory or national temperament. A little later the conservative historian Correlli Barnett, in his acidly unsentimental book *The Audit of War: The Illusion and Reality of Britain as a Great Nation* (1986), attempted to demolish another of the great icons of British design – the Spitfire. This is a machine in which a huge amount of patriotic, not to say nostalgic, emotion has been invested: the summation of British engineering brilliance, and a model of elegance and grace, it was the tool that allowed the heroes of the Royal Air Force to turn back the totalitarian hordes. The Spitfire was the best of British, and looked it too. Except that Barnett's calculations suggested that, contrary to

the myth, the Spitfire was actually a war-*losing* machine, not a war-winning one – at least when set beside the brutish-looking, technically less sophisticated, but far easier to maintain and build Messerschmitt flown by the Germans. Attrition in the air could not overcome supremacy in the factory. For all the effectiveness of the more agile British fighter pilot, when you compare the man-hours and money it took the Germans and British to make their respective iconic fighter planes, in the long run Britain was going to lose. The blunt instrument would eventually triumph over the well-crafted rapier. You could say much the same about the Concorde, a brilliant answer to the wrong question.

In the past ten years, British Prime Ministers Tony Blair and Gordon Brown have invested considerable amounts of political capital in the exploration of the concept of 'Britishness' as a shared identity – both in the interests of civic and national harmony and in the pursuit of a kind of national tone of voice that the state should adopt in its dealings with its citizens. Yet there must be a question mark over the very idea of what constitutes Britishness in British design, just as there is doubt that one could define clearly what it is that makes American design an entity distinct from Japanese or French or Chinese design.

Take for example that quintessential icon of British design – the Mini. The original category-defining small car was dependent on the brilliance of Alec Issigonis (1906–88), an automotive engineer who was born in an ethnic Greek enclave on the Turkish coast and who was forced to move to Britain as a refugee. Though built in Britain, the new Mini is German-owned and was designed by a team lead by an American who then left to try to work the same nostalgic magic for the Italian automotive company Fiat by bringing back the Cinquecento. The 'British' luxury brand Bentley,

Introduction
Deyan Sudjic

too, belongs to another German-owned carmaker, and its head of exterior styling, Raul Pires, is a Brazilian, whose previous job was working for the Czech manufacturer Škoda. On the other hand, Apple Inc. designer Jonathan Ive (1967–) was certainly born and educated in Britain, but to claim on that basis that the iPhone and the MacBook are examples of British design would invite only derision.

Made in Britain

When you look at the names of the designers and architects whose work the Design Museum has showcased in recent years, while many may be based in Britain, it quickly becomes clear that they are British by choice rather than by birth.

That is why this book explores the impact of contemporary design in Britain, rather than describing it as British. There are of course certain characteristics that designers working in the UK share. For example, it's not hard to see the impact of the country's educational system, which, at least until recently, has been a kind of state-licensed archipelago of dissent, in the shape of the art school tradition. Then there is also the effect of a constant anxiety about the place of British manufacture in the world. The Royal College of Art and the Victoria and Albert Museum are both institutions that were originally established as part of a state-sponsored effort to give British manufacturers lessons in how to beat back their foreign competitors. In the mid-nineteenth century the competition was from Prussia, France and Austria-Hungary. Now it is from China, Korea and India, and in neither case has the effort been conspicuously successful.

And yet it is not hubristic to suggest that Britain in the first decade of the twenty-first century has become an important focus for contemporary design. Britain may be far from being the fabled 'workshop of the world', but for all the talk of industrial decline, it is still a country with an important manufacturing base. The car factories in Britain may be owned by Indian, Chinese, Japanese, American, French and German businesses, but they still support an intricate network of components suppliers and engineering expertise, and so still provide a grounding in the friction of reality that industrial designers need to be credible. It may not be British design, but designers based in Britain are certainly producing a body of work that is an essential element of the international landscape of contemporary design.

Locked as we are inside the bubble of the present, it is never easy to characterize convincingly the mood of a moment in any cultural form or economic strategy – and design is both of these. But we can certainly see a neurotic fluctuation between design as a form of self-expression and as a utopian attempt to democratize the world of objects; between the commercial engineering of desire and the careful attempt to minimize waste. It is certainly in Britain that these extremes have been most fully described, and where the rhetoric has been most passionately explored. Design in Britain has been spectacularly successful at salesmanship, too. It is the focus for sophisticated advertising, for the voodoo magic of packaging design. It is also one of the places in the world with the best-developed sense of the *cultural* qualities of design, and it is a place where these two apparently contradictory streams coincide.

Britain in the World, the World in Britain

It's a culture that has produced the work of the industrial designer Ron Arad (1951–) whose creations belong in galleries and museums but which are also brilliantly conceived objects designed to be made in very large numbers with carefully crafted economy of means. It's a culture that has formed the graphic work of Neville Brody (1957–), an artist in graphics who fiercely guards his independence and yet who understands what his role in the economic cycle as a designer really is.

This is a book that covers the full range of design, just as the Design Museum itself does. Fashion is not a frivolous sideshow as is often implied; it is the most visible side of a huge worldwide industry. And designers in Britain lead it. And while most architects based in Britain complain that they are under-appreciated on their own turf, they are undoubtedly a global force in their discipline. Britain leads, too, in the virtual, dematerialized world of the screen.

In industrial design, it's possible to see the influence of those who were educated or born in Britain across the world – from the Milanese enclave of British designers, to the impact of Jasper Morrison (1959–) in Japan and Korea, to that of Jonathan Ive in California. At the same time, the world comes to Britain. It's to Britain that they come to study design, and to establish their studios, whether it is individuals such as the Australian Marc Newson (1963–) or global conglomerates such as Nissan or Ford. And behind these individuals, there is another generation ready to take their place ... and behind them yet another.

This is a key moment for design in Britain. Its importance is recognized everywhere. Its quality is admired. And yet it is also only too apparent that design has become an endlessly mobile process. There is no *British* design; there is only design *in Britain*. For 20 years, it has been an extraordinarily fruitful place to be. But there is nothing to guarantee that it will go on being so. But even as I write these words, I understand it is that sense of self-doubt, that suspicion of complacency, that is the most essential quality of what it is that shapes design in Britain.

Can Britain Still Make It?

Product
Daniel Charny

At the start of 2009, when pressed for some good news in the face of the rather bleak prospects predicted for the British economy, politicians from both left and right could come up with just two bright spots. The first was the declining value of the pound, which had the potential to reinvigorate domestic manufacturing and to give it a better chance in export markets. The other was to talk up the creative industries as a potential saviour for the economy, standing ready to fill the gap left by the vaporization of the financial services sector.

It is a tough burden for design, architecture, advertising and fashion to carry, yet it is true none the less that the reputation of industrial design, from and in Britain, has never stood higher. Designers based or trained in the UK dominate the field of commercial product design, while leading manufacturing brands from Apple to Nissan look to Britain both for top creative talent and as a vantage point from which to identify the trends that will shape their future business. Beyond the purely pragmatic, Britain is also a place in which critical debate and research into the multifarious nature of design have flourished, and this despite the country's reputation for a brisk, matter-of-fact approach, especially when set beside the more formally poetic character of, say, its Italian counterpart.

This essay explores the diversity of industrial, product and furniture design in contemporary Britain. Looking at how this cultural ecology has come about, and why it has had so much impact internationally, is also to question whether it can be sustained in the context of the new challenges that Britain and the rest of the world face in the future, and whether the factors that brought it into being in the first place are still relevant and whether they can still provide sufficient energy to drive it.

Cole v Morris – the duality of British design

In December 1852 the great Victorian educator and art patron Sir Henry Cole (1808–92) gave a lecture in which he assessed the impact of the Great Exhibition of 1851, the first real 'world fair', sponsored by Prince Albert and the Royal Society of Arts. As the chief organizer of the exhibition, Cole was proud of having started what he considered 'a promising and vital international dialogue, which would foster international competition and free trade'. He described the 'readiness of acceptance, confidence in production, and public awareness' raised by government-supported exhibitions, and the way that the British, unlike their French counterparts, accepted the strategic change from national to international exhibitions. Cole heralded the start of organized education in design for industry and described the dramatic improvements in the freedom of communication that came through the establishment of an international postal system and the 'wonderful morality' of what was to become international patent protection. He noted the emergence of a non-national style: 'a likeness that pervades ... that is the Spirit of the Age'.

Looking back from today's perspective, it's interesting to see how closely Cole's blueprint for the future has been realized, and how it set in train the creation of what we now understand as 'British' design. An international perspective, self-confidence and openness to new ideas, technology and an understanding of the importance of communication are still at the heart of successful industrial design. Even back then, Cole was worried how British industrial hegemony might be threatened by competition from France, Prussia and Austria-Hungary. Now the concern is about China, India, South Korea, Taiwan and Brazil, and is not just about manufacturing but design as well.

Daniel Charny

Top and middle: The Great Exhibition, held in the Crystal Palace in London's Hyde Park in 1851, showed off Britain's design culture to the world. The exhibition, which also featured a treasure trove of objects from around the globe, signalled the country's embrace of innovation and openness to outside influence. British design was to be determinedly cosmopolitan.

Left: Morris & Co.'s textile workshops at Merton Abbey (now southwest London), first opened in 1881. Morris was deeply suspicious of mass production and proposed an alternative, humanized aesthetic characterized by the handmade and by social responsibility. Morris's values still resonate in British design today.

11

There were other voices, though, that have been equally important to the direction taken by design in Britain. The socialist designer and writer William Morris (1834–96) expressed a widespread nostalgia for the individual, the handmade and the artisanal, and a rising disquiet about the fast pace of industrial change. Even as an adolescent, when taken to the Crystal Palace – the venue for the Great Exhibition – Morris had refused to set foot inside, so convinced was he that he would find nothing in it but meretricious machine-made junk. From Morris, then, came another sensibility, the one that led to the Arts and Crafts Movement and a critical view of mass production and the culture of consumption that is, if anything, even more pertinent today. The duality represented by Cole and Morris – an embrace of industry versus a deep suspicion of its effects, while on both sides also coupled with a deep appreciation of knowledge and skills – remains an essential element in the landscape of design in Britain today.

Fast forward to 1946

The Victoria and Albert Museum, the first museum of design in the world, was undoubtedly one of the most extraordinary outcomes of the Great Exhibition. It may since have turned into a museum of decorative arts, but in 1946, in the aftermath of the World War II, it was the venue for an enormously important exhibition whose significance can be compared with that of the Great Exhibition of 1851. Before the V&A's permanent collection – moved out of London for safekeeping during the Blitz – was reinstalled, the entire museum was devoted to a morale-boosting celebration of what British industry and design were capable of. Close to 1.5 million people came to see 'Britain Can Make It' (BCMI). Given the harsh rationing regime then in force, it's perhaps not surprising that the public quickly redubbed the show 'Britain Can't Have It' – indeed, many of the products on display were available only for export as the country desperately tried to attract foreign currency.

On one level, the BCMI exhibition represented an opening-up of what had hitherto seemed, at least in the public mind, an arcane and remote profession – industrial design. A key exhibit was called 'The Birth of an Eggcup?', put together by yet another great supporter of design innovation and education in Britain, the Azerbaijan-born Misha Black (1910–77), from the Design Research Unit – the first substantial British industrial design consultancy. It was an attempt to encapsulate for a non-specialist audience 'What industrial design means' and 'How the industrial designer works'; it showed the problems and how these could be overcome by fruitful collaboration between designers and manufacturers. Design had been harnessed by the state in the drive for national reconstruction, but at the same time the designers involved in BCMI were able to make big steps in changing the public's perception of what designers actually did. Fundamental was the idea that designers think of the users and industry before their own artistic interests. In her book *Did Britain Make It?* (Design Council, 1986) the influential design historian Penny Sparke commented on the moral, even utopian vision that underpinned the 1946 exhibition:

'Britain Can Make It' projected a bright image of a future in which design would play an important part in establishing Britain as a world manufacturing force, raising the level of public taste and improving the quality of everyday life in Britain. Viewed as a thematic forerunner to the Festival of Britain, for which the idea of design as an intrinsic part of civilization was developed, Britain Can Make It presented design as an indivisible moral concept to be applied to society using the terminology of what was most practical, most fitting for its purpose.

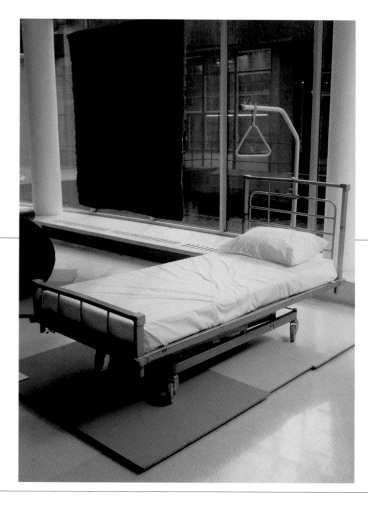

Top left: The Jaguar E-Type, manufactured between 1961 and 1974, encapsulated two of the key strands of design in Britain – innovative engineering and consummate craftsmanship. The designer of what Enzo Ferrari called 'the most beautiful car ever made' was Malcolm Sayer (1916–70).

Top right: The New British Standard hospital bed, designed by a team led by Bruce Archer. The concise engineering and user-centric design have remained the strengths of industrial design in Britain to this day.

Left: The red double-decker Routemaster was another triumph of postwar British engineering and design. Made by the Associated Equipment Company (AEC) between 1955 and 1967, it rapidly established itself as a London icon.

Above: The ZX Spectrum home computer, released by Sinclair in 1982. It was a huge commercial success and is credited with having launched Britain's IT industry. Its designer was the British maverick entrepreneur Clive Sinclair (1940–).

This page: The 1950s and 60s were an especially rich period for British design, as designers played their role in the postwar recovery. The Trimphone (left), designed by Martyn Rowland in 1964, featured an innovative electronic ringer and is widely considered to be the first modern telephone.

Main picture: Ercol furniture such as this Butterfly chair, first produced in 1951 (main picture), became a popular staple in aspirational middle-class homes across the UK.

Top: In 1965 the Department of the Environment commissioned the industrial designer David Mellor – better known as a cutler and silversmith – to redesign Britain's traffic lights. His clean-lined designs are still in use today.

Above: The mass-produced injection-moulded Polyprop chair, designed by Robin Day in 1962 and launched the following year. This low-cost, high-volume chair has become near invisible owing to its ubiquity but it is an outstanding, innovative design for all that.

Needless to say, the ethos of the BCMI era – in which designers believed in problem solving, in combining industry and engineering with academic research and social concerns – still has potency today.

The impact on designers of 'Britain Can Make It' and, subsequently, the Festival of Britain (1951) can scarcely be overestimated. Bruce Archer (1922–2005), who would later become Professor of Design Research at the RCA, claimed of BCMI: 'I was saved. I heard of industrial design. I could be an artist and an engineer at one and the same time.' Archer led the design research of those responsible for what was perhaps the ultimate expression of the BCMI ethos – the King's Fund British Standard hospital bed. This now-classic piece of design, in which the users' experience – not just the patients' but also that of medical staff – was as critical to the design as the consideration of the limitations of manufacturing technologies, served to define a certain strand in no-nonsense innovation that has characterized British design ever since. Even though it has been overlaid by brand strategy, commercial packaging, or by aesthetic values, it is still a defining characteristic today. (And that NHS bed may even explain why it is that so many airlines to this day look to British designers to work on their flat-bed sleeper seats.)

The post-war optimism surrounding British design cascaded down the subsequent decades. It was encapsulated in the Routemaster double-decker bus, which dates back to 1954, and the E-Type Jaguar, first produced in 1961, and it underpinned the success of manufacturers such as Morphy Richards and Russell Hobbs. It radiated from designers such as David Ogle (1922–62), Ernest Race (1913–64), Robin Day (1915–) and David Mellor (1930–2009), and it defined the work of Kenneth Grange (1929–), perhaps Britain's most prolific industrial designer. Grange, who is still active as an independent designer today, was a founder member of Pentagram, the interdisciplinary design consultancy, and during his long career has worked for Kodak, Parker, London Transport and British Railways. His Kenwood Chef mixer of 1964 demonstrates his ability to refine and domesticate technology with a contemporary sense of taking part in both commercial and domestic environments.

The approach defined by 'Britain Can Make It' – of mixing wit with insight (typified by the eggcup design presentation), of a marriage between Coles-style down-to-earth pragmatism and a Morrisian concern with craftsmanship and societal well-being – can be seen as the matrix of contemporary British industrial design. With the addition of the critical approach of the 1980s, all the elements of the qualities that constitute 'Britishness' in design are in place.

The 1980s – new directions

To anyone who, like me, studied industrial design in the 1980s, it was increasingly obvious that by that time both the professionals and the education systems were losing their grasp on any clear definition of what an industrial designer should be doing. Marketing and branding had taken over the foreground. Manufacturing was in decline; developments in technology meant that engineering was increasingly flexible; consumer markets had matured. A postmodern and post-industrial culture made anything seem possible, but the end result was confusion. Designers in search of direction gravitated towards the certainty of such fields as ergonomics. Art was another important pull, as was craft and making. And there were other, fresh directions, such as experience design or user-centred design. Semantics, sociology and engineering also pulled the profession in new and disparate directions.

Above: Elegance and ergonomics – the aluminium-and-black-leather Supporto office chair, designed by Frederick Scott (1942–2001) in 1976. Once again, Scott brought together the two leitmotifs of British design – industrial innovation and consummate craftsmanship. No wonder, then, that the California studio of Apple design maestro Jonathan Ive is kitted out with this enduring classic.

This page and opposite: A founding-partner of the multidisciplinary design consultancy Pentagram, Kenneth Grange (1929–) has always been concerned that products should be 'a pleasure to use'. His elegant, functional approach has been associated with new types of objects such as the Kodak 130 camera (left), the Intercity 125 train (above) and the famous Kenwood Chef food mixer (opposite, left).

This page, main picture: The Book Worm bookshelf (1993) is in many ways typical of Ron Arad's sculptural approach to design. Initially, this signature piece was made in steel as a one-off, but became a mass-produced best-seller in a plastic version by Kartell.

This was the period in which the Israeli-born Ron Arad (1951–), fresh from studies at the Architectural Association, produced the Rover Chair (1981) – the furniture equivalent of a readymade – and his Concrete Stereo (1983); the period in which the Argentine-born Daniel Weil (1953–) at the Royal College of Art designed his famous Bag Radio. Both pieces have come to be seen as signifying the new directions of that period, but what did they really signify for industrial design?

Let's concentrate on Weil's radio, which, I think, marked the first seismic shift from the pragmatism of the past. Working from a specific change in technology – the possibility of a printed digital circuit –Weil discarded the big box, the radio shell, and put everything in a bag (you can see all the components, thrown together inside). It was a complete break with past typologies. But it was more than that – it spoke about the classic industrial designed product and it demonstrated an alternative. It was a critical response to industrial design and offered another way of thinking about industrial design objects. This in itself was so new; in this move we can see the most significant representative of the birth of the whole conception of critical design.

A new beginning it certainly was, but the Bag Radio didn't *end* anything. To this day the cleanly designed radios and clocks by Sam Hecht (1969–) or Naoto Fukosawa (1956–) continue to subscribe successfully to the shell and are perfect examples of a continuing design tradition. And, intriguingly, Daniel Weil was the industrial designer that Ken Grange invited to join Pentagram, where he continues to be based.

Furniture design
The course taken by furniture design in the latter half of the twentieth century can be seen as emblematic of the broader fortunes of industrial design. It's a course, too, that shows how what were previously discrete design disciplines, with radically different, even contradictory, cultures, have tended to cross-pollinate and sometimes even fuse.

Previously, of course, furniture was scarcely considered as 'industrial' design at all – it belonged, at least in name if not in practice, to the hallowed sphere of the craftsman-designer. The crossover of furniture from artisan to industrial design, indeed, had started in Britain long before World War II, but was accelerated by the war itself, when timber rationing prompted the state-led development of Utility Furniture, with its pared-back, utilitarian aesthetic. Furniture featured largely, too, in the 'Britain Can Make It' exhibition. Most notable, perhaps, were the mass-produced bentwood furniture designs of Ercol, a company originally set up in 1920 by the Italian-born designer Lucian Ercolani (1888–1976). Ercol's modern-meets-traditional designs were to prove enormously popular and influential over the following decades.

With the 1960s came an understanding that furniture designers working in contract environments must be as attentive to industrial production as to marketing. This development is well represented by entrepreneur designers who crossed over into production and retail – for example Terence Conran (1931–), Rodney Kinsman (1943–) and, more recently, Tom Dixon (1959–) and Matthew Hilton (1957–). In the 1980s the furniture pieces that had the most impact on perceptions of design were those that combined industrial process or off-the-shelf elements – as can be seen in the early work of both Jasper Morrison (1959–) and Ron Arad. Radically different as these two designers' work was, both were reacting to the vicissitudes of the economic climate and reflected ways of thinking that went far beyond the mere utility of the product.

Above: The Durabeam torch – created by Nick Butler (1942–) in 1986–87 and manufactured by Duracell – is a design classic, combining no-nonsense engineering with innovative plastic technology, all while offering a new, user-friendly typology.

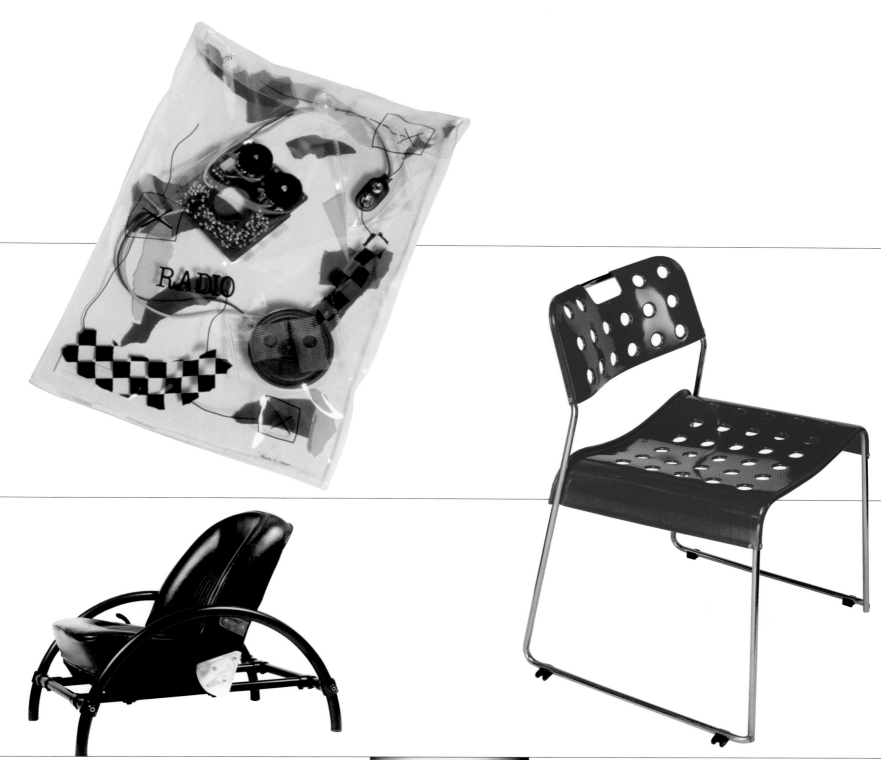

Top left and middle left: The 1980s witnessed a new critical spirit in British design. Daniel Weil's Bag Radio (1983) broke radically with industry conventions by discarding the shell, while Ron Arad's Rover chair (1981) was an anarchic fusion of design and the ready-made.

Left: In 1986 the design studio Seymour Powell developed the world's first cordless kettle for Tefal. The kettle – still an industry paradigm for user-friendly, mass-market design – represents the triumph of functionalism.

Above: The OMKSTAK stacking chair (1971) by Rodney Kinsman (1943–). With its pressed-steel or epoxy seat and back and continuous tubular-steel frame, the OMKSTAK combined modernist rationalism with a Pop sensibility. This became *the* chair of 1970s Britain.

This page: The spirit of William Morris lives on… Matthew Hilton (1957–) produces a range of luxurious yet individual furniture using low-tech casting techniques. Shown here are the Antelope table and the Balzac chair and ottoman made by SCP.

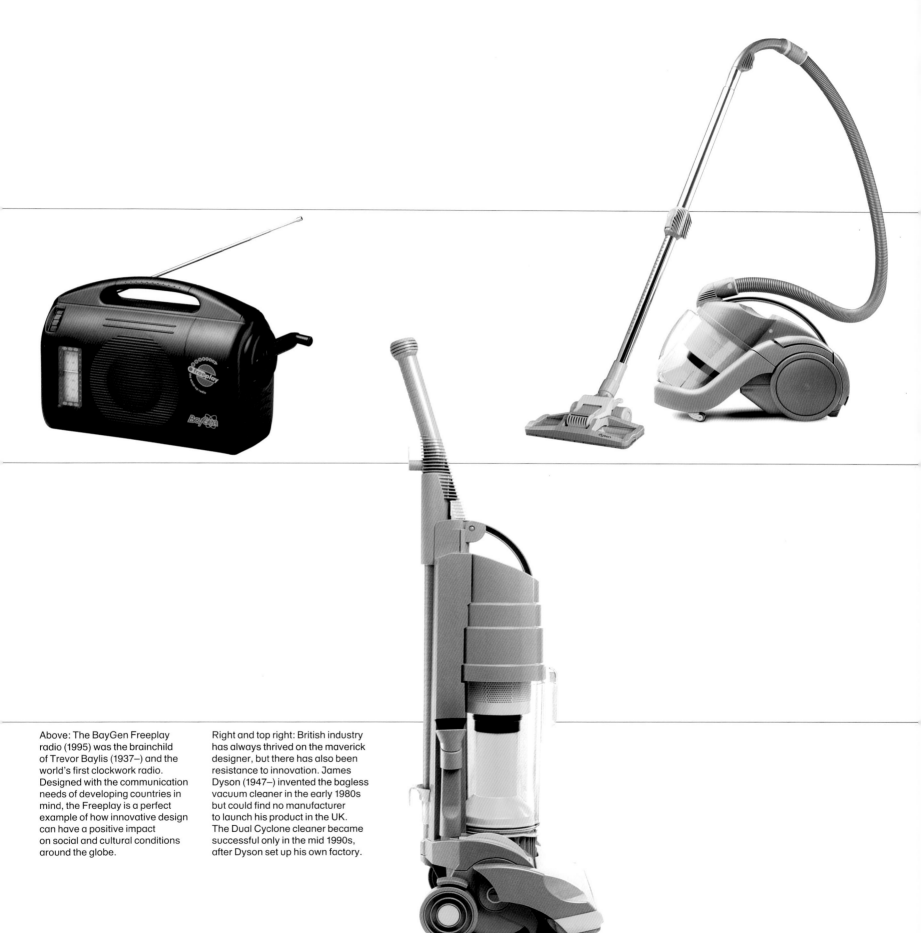

Above: The BayGen Freeplay radio (1995) was the brainchild of Trevor Baylis (1937–) and the world's first clockwork radio. Designed with the communication needs of developing countries in mind, the Freeplay is a perfect example of how innovative design can have a positive impact on social and cultural conditions around the globe.

Right and top right: British industry has always thrived on the maverick designer, but there has also been resistance to innovation. James Dyson (1947–) invented the bagless vacuum cleaner in the early 1980s but could find no manufacturer to launch his product in the UK. The Dual Cyclone cleaner became successful only in the mid 1990s, after Dyson set up his own factory.

The most substantial change, however, was the internationalization, then globalization, of furniture design. In Italy, family-run furniture companies, led by strong creative directors, were acquiring an appetite for working with British-based or -trained designers. Some of these – notably Perry King (1938–) and James Irvine (1958–) – settled in Milan. Charles (died 1992) and Jane Dillon (1943–) worked across Europe and in the United States and had a particular impact on Spanish companies, later in the 1990s also opening a studio in Girona. In the past two decades, EU countries have opened up to British-based designers in a major way, and even the strongly inward-looking Nordic industries now work at creative director levels with designers such as Tom Dixon or the British-trained duo El Ultimo Grito. The United States, too, has discovered an innovative streak in designers such as Ross Lovegrove (1959–), and has learned to appreciate the user-centric innovations of the industrial design and consultancies Pearson Lloyd and Industrial Facility.

The career paths of designers such as Ross Lovegrove, who initially trained in industrial design, encapsulate one of the most significant changes in the practice of design over the past two decades – the all but complete dissolution of the gap between furniture and industrial design. It has resulted in a striking infusion of cultural and critical practice into industrial design, and a transformation from furniture conceived as the outcome of a craft tradition into an activity dependent on industrial mass production. Furniture designers needed to understand industrial processes and materials – initially composites and plastics – and to be able to work with contract and system furniture. Industrial designers, however, have been drawn into the expressive and cultural aspects of the objects that they work with, a shift that required the sensibilities of art and craft training that used to be the preserve of furniture designers.

Left: Bottle developed by Ross Lovegrove for the Welsh mineral water company Ty Nant in 1999–2002. Its fluid, asymmetrical form is not just a matter of aesthetics – the bottle is easy to grasp as well as to crush for disposal.

Above: The Cobi chair (2009), designed by PearsonLloyd in partnership with the US office furniture manufacturer Steelcase. No furniture type can remain static – the Cobi is designed specifically for the modern collaborative office.

Right: The lightweight, stackable Air One chair and Air Two stool (both 2000), designed by Ross Lovegrove for the Italian manufacturer Edra. Lovegrove's ethical, minimalist approach to design typically produces pieces that are at once visually disconcerting and practical.

Top: Compass Table from Dunne & Raby's 2001 Placebo Project. In this project the experimental design duo explored users' private relationships with technology. In the Compass Table, the compasses spin and twitch when an electronic item is placed upon the table or brought nearby.

Above and top right: PearsonLloyd's 2003 designs for Virgin Atlantic's Upper Class service manage to satisfy the long-haul requirement for both comfort and privacy. The seating unit transforms into a completely flat bed, but without the usual visual complexity and layering associated with aircraft seating.

Right: In their 1994–7 project Hertzian Tales, Dunne & Raby imagined products that might enable people to take shelter from a supersaturated technological and intelligent environment. The Faraday chair offers a cocoon, safe from the bombardment of telecommunication and electronic radiation.

Left: Ron Arad's stackable Tom Vac chair (1999) for Vitra comprises a ridged, shell-like polypropylene seat with a tubular-steel base.

Above: Jasper Morrison's one-piece polypropylene Air chair for Magis (1999) is an exercise in productional and functional minimalism.

Above: Industrial Facility, the consultancy started by Sam Hecht and Kim Colin, works on consumer electronics as well as furniture, such as this desk for Herman Miller, the American office furniture manufacturer.

Above: The MacBook Air (2008) is another in the succession of sleek, minimalist Apple designs produced by the British designer Jonathan Ive. Earlier designs include the iMac (original version, 1998) and the iPod (2001). Apple, of course, is a quintessentially Californian company, so does, one may wonder, this slimline beauty really count as 'British' design? Probably not…

Alongside them, too, were the engineers who discovered furniture design and developed refined levels of consumer-facing product details and communication.

This direction became part of the new generation of designers, whose training heritage it is harder and mostly irrelevant to pinpoint, as they are comfortable with product and furniture design as one discipline. These include Konstantin Grcic, Michael Marriott, Sebastian Bergne, AZUMI Studio's Shin and Tomoko Azumi, Michael Young, El Ultimo Grito's Roberto Feo and Rosario Hurtado, Jerszy Seymour, Michael Sodeau, and duo Edward Barber and Jay Osgerby, to name only some of the more interesting practitioners – with British design education or practice background – working currently across both sectors, with most also active in the cultural and critical arena as well.

Industrial design now

What is it, then, that characterizes British or British-influenced industrial design today? There is diversity of activity and multiplicity of motivations and approaches, but there are common features. It is characterized by a strong sense of observation. It is humanistic and respects human behaviour. It is interested in wit and individuality and character. But there is also an analytical tendency. There is a special kind of ingenuity based on a cultural heritage mixing arts and crafts genealogy and industrial engineering. It has a special interest in making and improving tools. It often pushes manufacturing clients beyond their expectations and immediate comfort. This may sound incoherent. But it's working and it's popular.

The pre-1980s industrial designer developed in response to a critical engagement within the design disciplines, as we have seen, but he or she also responded to fashion, art, music, craft and business. More recently, the discipline has been

This page: The 'Jonathan Ive' aesthetic of transparency, minimalism and technological accessibility has been hugely influential on contemporary industrial design. Sebastian Bergne's calculator (1998) for Authentics (top) and Michael Young's Apple-compatible I24R3 wireless speakers (2008–9) are cases in point.

This page: The design team BarberOsgerby, founded in 1996, offers another example of the convergence between furniture and industrial design. This die-cast and pressed- aluminium chair was commissioned by the De La Warr Pavilion, Bexhill on Sea (right, now a contemporary arts centre) in 2005 and was manufactured by Established & Sons.

Can Britain Still Make It?_Product

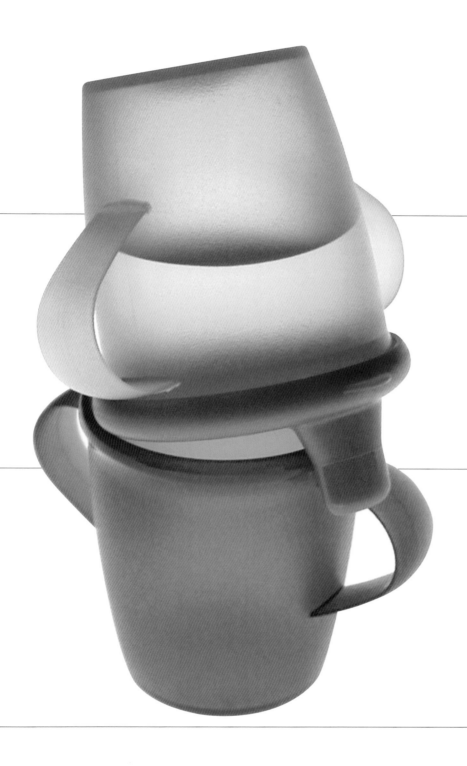

Above left: In 1997 Sebastian Conran was commissioned to redesign the Anywayup Cup, the brainchild of the British inventor Mandy Haberman. Some 10 million of the toddlers' cups are sold every year and in 1999 it was named as one of Britain's millenium Products.

Above: El Ultimo Grito's post-disciplinary approach is typical of many youthful design studios. The GUAU wall light (2008) for Arturo Alvarez is typical of the studio's playful yet practical aesthetic – the light can be manipulated to create a range of atmospheric effects.

exposed to new media and publications; it has been interpreted by museums and cultural institutes, nurtured by government departments and loosened up by education. And all the while it has retained an entrepreneurial spirit and disciplined heart, which means that developments in technology and industry are embraced and enable brave moves. The result is a diversity in industrial design practice that is very hard to rival. Types of designer and interest groups persist, of course: the no-nonsense mechanical engineer; the artisan maker with social and community interests; the inventor-innovator; and the entrepreneurial strand that cuts through all of the above. But commercial design for mass production no longer dominates. Academic and research-led design, though typically experimental in character, has become increasingly influential and stretches the field in cultural terms. And critical design, though still effectively an umbrella term covering a broad field of activity, is significant in developing the discipline. Interestingly, unlike in the 1980s, there is no apparent conflict in this diversity – the commercial, the cultural and the critical all enrich one other.

Commercial design for mass production is sometimes referred to in the industry as 'hardcore industrial design'. Agencies, consultancies and signature design studios provide industrial design services to global brands and innovation-led entrepreneurial ventures. Broadly speaking, this means the development of objects that fit the vision and production capabilities of the clients, although the usual ideal is to surprise the client through brilliant innovation and enable them to expand their activities.

Medical and grooming, sport and leisure, agricultural and gardening, military and offshoot products, transport and travel, office systems and accessories, home and personal entertainment devices, communication and mobile handsets: industrial design is a substantial step in the process of making all these products take part in everyday life. Design groups dominant in this field often expand their services beyond the end product development, from strategy to point of sale, full retail environments and staff training programmes, and often include what borders on management consultancy and brand development. Increasingly, innovation-led companies are attracted to working with British-based or -trained designers.

Academic and research-led design – positively represented as blue-sky thinking or more sceptically as the product of an ivory tower – is an environment where industrial design is treated to lab conditions, often without practical considerations to guide or hinder the exploration of ideas and potential products. These environments are increasingly common in industry, and increasingly prominent in academia. Industry collaborations with educational institutions, where students get to experience real-world considerations and in which companies get to challenge their own practice, are a way of combining interests and are of increasing value to all parties, and not only for the few occasions that a product makes it to market or when a student is brought in-house. Research projects, whether in industry or academia, typically have longer-term agendas and are of a more exploratory nature, the briefs often concerned with the analysis of an issue – perhaps social or environmental change or, more traditionally, a material or technology.

Generally the lab environment rarely produces products that reach the public or professional spheres, and so it is initially surprising that it has significant influence on the perception of the quality and value of British design. But British design schools, in particular at postgraduate and research levels, are international hubs, attracting worldwide interest. Work done

Above: Stack storage drawer, designed by the Israeli-born RCA graduate Shay Alkalay for Established and Sons. Intriguing and sculptural, the piece breaks from the usual typology of the chest of drawers to celebrate the joyous jumble of everyday life.

Top left: The importance of the Royal College of Arts as a generator of design talent in Britain cannot be overestimated. Peter Marigold (1978–) graduated from the RCA in 2006 – his Make/Shift shelving system shows his flexible, sculptural approach to domestic furniture.

Above and top right: The British penchant for eccentricity can sometimes breed brilliant ideas. The Omlet eglu – or chicken house – is a vibrant, practical solution to the growing demand for sustainable, ecological living, even at the heart of the city.

This page: The work of Thomas Heatherwick blurs the boundaries between public sculpture and industrial design. The Rolling Bridge (2004) at Paddington Basin is both a beautiful piece of engineering and an elegant addition to this London canalside development.

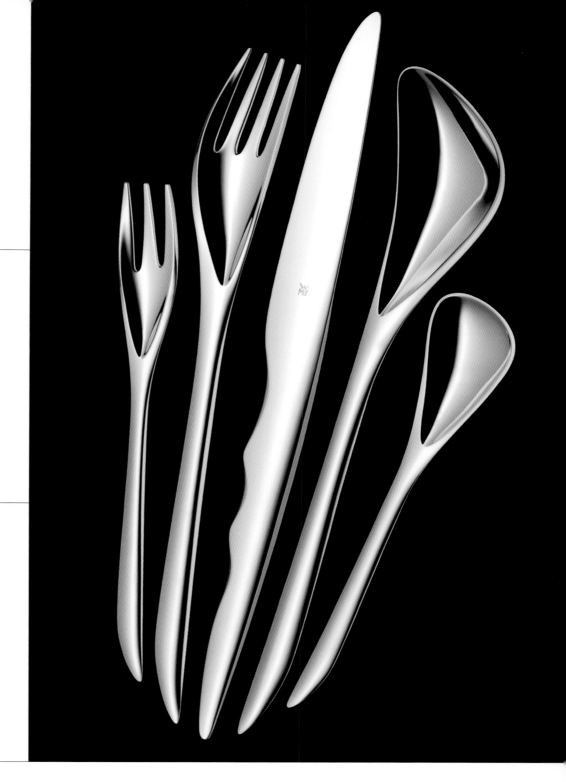

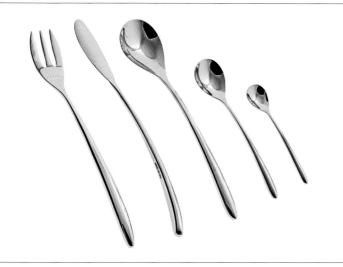

Above: The asymmetrical cutlery, curiously designed for the left-handed user, designed by Architect Jan Kaplicky of Future Systems as part of recently launched Bettina table service for Italian brand Alessi. Above right: The renowned Iraqi-born architect Zaha Hadid also applies her organic, dynamic aesthetic to the small scale – here an unorthodox stainless-steel cutlery set (2007) for WMF.

in these institutions commands attention, and students and graduates become part of a successful international network of designers who share a common culture and sensibility. Beyond this, research-led design projects are typically of an experimental, expressive and non-commercial character, and emerge from the labs to a limited audience at exhibitions or in publications, only on occasion making it to the status of commercial product.

How much of this impacts directly on mainstream industrial design in a tangible way? It's sometimes hard to tell. But the point of these projects is to work outside the pressures of the commercial world, so that potential and prospects for change in that very commercial world can be examined and imagined. Things such as impact, ethics or user behaviour can be interrogated in a meaningful way, which, even if it isn't apparent on the shelves, might become so in the sourcing or manufacturing process or in the brand strategy. Commercial companies are very serious about these projects – they're about the future, a future in which these companies are determined to play an important part. And beyond the direct impact there is also the influence of exposure to these projects, the methods and spirit of a critical approach that the design leaders of the future take with them when they graduate from the education system and make their way increasingly to board-level positions.

A key and hugely influential creative research environment in the UK is academic design education, of which the Royal College of Art in London is a recognized centre of excellence. The RCA brings together a wide spectrum of international staff and students, both in its various Masters programmes and in its research environments. In this institution, as in others such as Central Saint Martins, University College for the Creative Arts

This page: Industrial Facility's Second Telephone (2003) for Muji eschews the contemporary phone set's complexity for unadorned simplicity. The phone is intended to spend most of its time unused.

Above: Another of Industrial Facility's pared-back designs for Muji – this perfectly cylindrical, unobtrusive coffee maker (2006). Industrial Design was founded in 2002 by Sam Hecht and Kim Colin.

Top: The Apollo Torch (1997), by the industrial designer Marc Newson (1963–) for Flos. Newson's elegantly futuristic designs have included everything from a private jet plane to a concept car for Ford.

Above: The computer plays an increasingly important role in product and furniture design. The complex surfaces of the MIURA bar stool (2005), designed by Konstantin Grcic for Plank, is exemplary.

This page: The future of design in Britain will have to take account of sustainability in the face of mounting environmental pressures and rapidly diminishing resources. SolarLab is a leading London-based sustainable design agency, founded by the German-born product designer Christoph Behling (1970–) in 2006.

Among SolarLab's outstanding creations has been the Solar Shuttle (2006; right, above and below), a pollution-free boat that ferries passengers across Hyde Park's Serpentine in London. Behling has also worked extensively for industry, designing innovative high-end products such as the Merediist cell phone (2008; above) for TAG Heuer.

Can Britain Still Make It?_Product

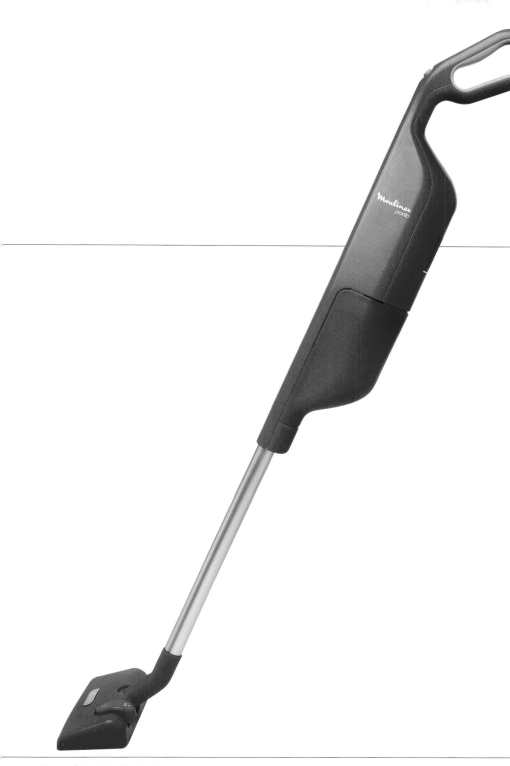

(UCCA) and London Metropolitan University, students and researchers are encouraged to explore cultural and critical contexts to their work. At this level of study they are expected to interrogate their own identity as designers, in pursuit of which they set their own briefs and explore a unique open-ended methodology for achieving results.

In addition to designing, they will be thinking *about* design, will be reacting *to* design and generating commentary *on* design. They are not encouraged solely to target results but also to develop their creative process. To anyone involved with industry this is clearly a high-risk approach, but supported within the academic environment it is a unique situation where industrial design is considered critically. And as before, while the work rarely directly translates to market, publications, exhibitions and media interest mean that this kind of work is seen by significant numbers of people from industry and beyond.

It's worth noting that this is a very British approach to design education, and is certainly not shared by all institutions that teach design around the world. Elsewhere, briefs and contents are often much more controlled; design management and marketing take the foreground as designers are directed to face business rather than industry; and the technical discipline of the profession is often valued over the critical. Good design is often reduced to a recipe and creativity is packaged as commodity rather than an attitude.

Critical design – or cultural design – uses industrial design knowledge to produce high-value products. These might be mass-produced, might be limited edition or small-batch production, or might not even be objects. What they hold in common is a value beyond their tangible form, whether that be cultural or critical significance, comment or expression.

Above: Sebastian Bergne's Pronto vacuum cleaner (2005) for Moulinex. Cordless, bagless, quiet and lightweight, the Pronto responds to the need for fast and efficient household cleaning without the need to resort to cumbersome equipment.

This page: New materials
continue to inspire new products.
The cantilever chair is one of the
classic typologies of twentieth-
century modernism. In the MYTO
chair (2008), created for Plank,
Konstantin Grcic exploited Ultradur
High Speed – a material developed
by the plastics manufacturer BASF –
to create a strong, stackable and
visually striking chair for outdoor use.

Can Britain Still Make It?_Product

There are two distinct groups of work in this area. The first, commonly if only recently referred to as critical design, is made up of projects that comment about design or that harness design to discuss other matters. Often in this group the designed object is not the point. The design results in installations, exhibitions, or publications in which unique objects take part in creating the whole picture. The more theoretical and academic proponents of this work are almost exclusively based in Britain, and their research into the impact and future impacts of the industrial and the design world on people's lives often play out in science-fiction-like scenarios. While sounding obscure, they command attention and interest in the highest levels of industry and government.

The second is predominantly made up of highly expressive design pieces that are strongly associated with influences and individuals and, often as not, the art world. They cross free creative artistic expression with industrial design. A variant of this group is large-scale public-space installations that use industrial design processes and industrially produced components. The British designer Thomas Heatherwick (1970–) is perhaps the best-known exponent of this last tendency.

Future directions
With industrial designers influencing so many aspects of all our lives, and so many companies now facing reassessment (not only in respect of *how* they do things but of *what* they do), is the role of the industrial designer in need of change? Is the technical training backed by cultural studies or cultural ambition backed by technical abilities a sufficient balance for the necessary diversity and challenges facing the manufacturing and consuming world?

Industrial design training has often led people to the forefront of newer disciplines. This was very evident in the 1990s when interaction design and sustainable design became, for a while, independent streams of work. What are the new streams that are breaking out now? How will critical design, design activism, speculative design, green thinking, user-driven design and transformative design make their mark?

Beyond these thoughts of possible new directions, the more pertinent, current and significant question is to do with the impact we can hope industrial designers may have on the changing global, commercial, social and cultural climates of our immediate and longer-term futures. This is particularly interesting for contemporary Britain, with its unique design heritage. The big question that we now face – one that perhaps design education may be best suited to pose and start answering – is: will the characteristics that have worked so well, so far, be sufficient enough to hold fast beyond the comfort zones and respond effectively to the more radical and more challenging creativity now required?

Building in a Cold Climate

Architecture
Deyan Sudjic

The Design Museum building has its own, albeit modest, place in the highly political recent history of British architecture. The museum's sharply delineated white walls, its stacked cube form, contained between stair towers incised with slots of glass bricks, clearly make it a cut-down and knowing tribute to Walter Gropius's Bauhaus. Richard Doon, of Conran & Partners, was the architect responsible for the transformation of a former banana warehouse built in the 1950s, and of little distinction, into its present incarnation.

Back in 1989 the museum planned a gala opening and its founders went to see the Prince of Wales to invite him to officiate at the ceremony, taking with them a model of the project. Terence Conran and Stephen Bayley were quickly disillusioned. Why, he asked them, does it have to have a flat roof? They might have expected nothing else – their conversation took place at a time when Britain was still locked in the style wars triggered by the Prince's onslaught on modernism in all its incarnations. In 1984 he had used his invitation from the Royal Institute of British Architects (RIBA) to present the Royal Gold Medal for Architecture at Windsor Castle to suggest that Britain's architects had done the country more damage than the Luftwaffe. The Prince was determined to turn the tide against contemporary architecture and engineer a return to what he believed were the traditional values of building. In the Prince's view, flat roofs were anything but traditional, and he had no intention of endorsing something so provocative as a celebration of the Bauhaus on the Thames. And so the museum ended up being opened by the more accommodating Prime Minister of the day, Margaret Thatcher.

It was a remarkable period. Architectural taste had become headline news, and Britain's architects were polarized between those who saw themselves as persecuted modernists and those who joined the Prince in his quixotic campaign for brick, a rediscovery of the rural vernacular, and even a return to classicism.

'A monstrous carbuncle'

The initial flash point between the two camps was the scheme to build an extension to the National Gallery in Trafalgar Square to house its Italian Renaissance collection.

While Richard Rogers' new Lloyd's building was emerging from its scaffolding and Canary Wharf was still derelict, the Prince of Wales was driven to Hampton Court to start a revolution. The RIBA was celebrating its 150th anniversary with fireworks, champagne, a court masque and a more than adequate supply of self-congratulation. Shortly before the Prince rose to make his speech as guest of honour, a ripple of dismay spread through the palace as hints of what he was going to say began to circulate. It was going to be anything but the anodyne address his audience was expecting.

'Some planners and architects have consistently ignored the feelings and wishes of the mass of ordinary people in this country,' the Prince began. He went on to name names. With Peter Palumbo, the developer battling to create a new square at Mansion House and build Mies van der Rohe's elegant tower, in the audience, the Prince continued: 'It would be a tragedy if the character and skyline of our capital city were to be further ruined and St Paul's dwarfed by yet another giant glass stump.' Peter Ahrends, whose firm, ABK, had recently been declared winner of the competition to design the extension to the National Gallery, also heard the Prince suggest: 'Instead of designing an extension to the elegant façade of the National Gallery, which complements it and continues the concept of columns and domes, we may be presented with a kind of municipal fire station, complete

Deyan Sudjic

Above: The Lloyd's room. Built before the digital revolution, Richard Rogers' masterpiece was designed to be as adaptable as possible, with space for underwriters to expand into the upper levels reached by tiers of escalators. The bell was salvaged from Lloyd's previous building.

Above: Richard Rogers' design for the Lloyd's building (1986) was inspired by the Estonian American architect Louis Kahn's vision of architecture organized into served and servant spaces. At Lloyd's all the servant spaces are pulled out into the external towers, leaving an uncluttered open interior.

Above: China's construction boom in the years after 2000 pulled in many British architects. For Wilkinson Eyre, the Guangzhou twin towers project (completed 2009) gave the practice its first chance to build a skyscraper. The two towers overshadow Zaha Hadid's opera house, to the right-hand side of the image.

Above: Behind the sleek skin of the towers is an unconventional structure that carries the load on the edge of the building, rather than through a standard column grid.

with the sort of tower that contains the siren.' It would be, he famously said, 'a monstrous carbuncle on the face of a much-loved and elegant friend'.

The Prince wanted to find a public role as he waited to be king. Architecture was his chosen instrument, and exploding the status quo was his strategy. For several years after his outburst, it looked as if architecture might really be on the brink of an officially enforced neoclassical revival. The Prince succeeded in scoring a series of what were taken as victories. He had the National Gallery competition set aside. He stopped the building of what would have been Mies van der Rohe's only tower in Europe. And he prevented Richard Rogers from remodelling Paternoster Square, the flawed setting of St Paul's. He started his own architectural school, began a magazine to put his views on design across, and started work with the Luxembourg-born architect Léon Krier on the master-planning of a town in Dorset – Poundbury.

While he proved highly effective at publicity, the Prince had a harder time getting his own way. The National Gallery ended up with the neurotic Sainsbury Wing designed by Robert Venturi, which, while being Britain's only authentic example of American-style postmodernism, is not the most comfortable or the most confident-looking of designs. Mies van der Rohe's tower was axed. But the Prince was no happier with the eventual outcome – James Stirling's bloody-minded Number 1 Poultry – which the Prince described without affection as looking like a 1930s wireless.

The Prince, of course, had no power but exhortation and string-pulling. But initially royal disapproval was enough to stop most developers, architects and local authorities in their tracks. It was a game of chicken. Sooner or later would come the first realization that it was entirely possible to resist the Prince's will and find that the roof did not fall in. As it turned out, it happened in Edinburgh, when the Royal Museum wanted to create a new building in the heart of the city. Charles was recruited as a patron to help raise funds, but when he took against the winning entry in the competition to find a design, and made his disdain public, the Scottish establishment stood its ground and suggested it would find the money itself. Looking at the neo-Corbusian result (opened as the Museum of Scotland in 1998), it's hard to see what he was objecting to so vehemently. Since then, the massive cost overruns of Enric Miralles's parliament in Edinburgh have given Scotland a different architectural talking point.

The transformation of a skyline
In the 20 years that followed the carbuncle speech, things have moved in a direction exactly opposite to that hoped for by the Prince. It is inconceivable that Richard Rogers' plan for a striking 48-storey skyscraper directly opposite the Lloyd's building would have seen the light of day in 1984. At that time, it was taken for granted, and not just by the Prince of Wales, that skyscrapers were wrong for Britain's cities. But now, even though the credit crunch has lead to the mothballing of Rogers' plan for a wedge-shaped structure (so designed to keep its silhouette out of the protected views of St Paul's), the London skyline has been transformed beyond recognition. London's first directly elected mayor, Ken Livingstone, turned out to be an unexpected cheerleader for a Shanghai-style high-rise programme. When English Heritage attempted to block the first of what turned out to be a wave of high-rises, Livingstone described the organization as the Taliban, standing as obscurantist fanatics in the path of progress. Cesar Pelli's tower at Canary Wharf, which once stood in isolation, is now hemmed in by a dense thicket of newer buildings. Site clearance is complete for the

construction of Renzo Piano's by European standards ultra-tall tower at London Bridge.

In the City of London and the West End the buildings of the 1960s have been wiped out, as if by a selective neutron bomb, and the vocabulary of commercial architecture has been rewritten in glass. Norman Foster's office has been responsible for a remarkable percentage of it – from foreground projects such as the Swiss Re Tower (the 'Gherkin') and Wembley Stadium to bland background such as the office district around the new City Hall. The Thames meanwhile has been turned into a kind of culvert, with a continuous ribbon of apartment buildings on both sides looking balefully at each other, punctuated by Herzog & de Meuron's discreet transformation of Bankside Power Station into the most successful museum of modern art in the world. To the east, the Millennium Dome has against all expectations become a highly successful music venue, signalling the eastward shift of development, while the Olympic site takes shape with a pool designed by Zaha Hadid.

It took a while, but the spirit of this wave of development has spread out across Britain. The formerly industrial cities of Manchester, Liverpool, Leeds, Sheffield and Glasgow have discovered loft living, together with high-rise monuments to negative equity and buy-to-let schemes gone sour. In the process a few, notably Glasgow and Manchester, have managed to develop their distinctive architectural cultures in a contemporary way. In Glasgow, an active housing-association movement proved to be an enthusiastic promoter of contemporary Glasgow architects such as Elder & Cannon and Page \ Park, a process that reached its height in the shape of the Glasgow Green development built in 1999. A number of younger practices, including McKeown Alexander and Gareth Hoskins, followed in their footsteps.

Above: The new Wembley Stadium (2007), designed by Foster and Partners to replace a time-expired building, gave London a powerful new landmark, with its soaring elliptical arch visible from all over the city.

Opposite: Built on the site of the Baltic Exchange, badly damaged by an IRA bomb, St Mary Exe, or the Swiss Re tower as it is commonly known, was the first skyscraper to break with the conventional orthogonal geometry of the type. The shape reduced windload and makes better use of materials, while the twisting voids within the skin assist natural ventilation.

Above and left: The top of the Swiss Re tower employs a different structure from the lower floors of the building, and is used not for the chairman's office, as it might have been in some cultures, but as a shared café and meeting space for all the occupants of the building to enjoy views out over the city.

Manchester developed a brasher, more confident architectural language led by Stephenson Bell and Ian Simpson. The latter's 169-metre-high Beetham Tower, completed in 2006, is an extremely slender and impressive landmark on the city skyline, a mixed-use development that includes a hotel on its upper floors. Manchester's Civil Justice Centre, designed by Denton Corker Marshall from 2007, gave the city another impressive civic development.

The roots of change

It is certainly true that architecture in Britain had been at a low ebb at the end of the 1970s. The appeal of the concrete utopias of the recent past had waned. And the belief in modernism as a panacea had evaporated. Indeed, the late 1970s can be seen as a kind of collective nervous breakdown among architectural offices. New had come to mean worse.

At the same time, the Thatcherite revolution saw the state step back from house building, and the abolition of many of the public-sector architectural offices that were once such an important aspect of British architecture. At that time there was a sharp distinction between the kind of architecture practised by the small group of firms such as that led by Denys Lasdun (1914–2001) that were commissioned to design museums, galleries, theatres and universities, and the much larger group of so-called commercial architects, responsible for the speculative office buildings and shopping centres. It is a distinction that has now all but vanished.

By contrast with the lacklustre reality of building in the 1970s, the Architectural Association (AA) and a handful of other schools were fizzing with energy and speculation about what architecture might be like. This was the time when Zaha Hadid and Ron Arad were students at the AA, and when both Rem Koolhaas and Léon Krier – now apparently polar

Above: Ian Simpson has given Manchester a strong new architectural identity with a series of landmark projects, including the slender Beetham Tower (2006), one of Britain's tallest skyscrapers, which combines a hotel with residential apartments.

Right: Manchester's Civil Justice Centre (2007) is one of the city's most striking new architectural projects. Designed by Denton Corker Marshall, an architectural practice with roots in Australia, it is a building that is inviting, performs well in energy terms, and transforms the image of what a courthouse can be.

Left: Denton Corker Marshall's Manchester Civil Justice Centre stacks courtrooms one on top of the other, to one side of a soaring entrance hall that rises the height of the building, and immediately communicates to visitors that they are not in a routine office building but in a space with a civic function.

opposites, but in those days allies of a kind – were teaching there. The AA in particular acted as a kind of architectural establishment in exile. Its diploma shows were firework displays of imagination that sometimes had external examiners apoplectic with indignation that they were being asked to examine something that was not architecture at all. But it attracted students from around the world, and a generation of architects supplemented lean times by teaching there. It's where David Chipperfield studied, and where John Pawson spent a couple of years after he came back to Britain from a spell in Japan to learn how to be an architect.

Much of what has come to be associated with the postmillennial architectural explosion has its roots in the intellectual ferment at the AA 20 years earlier. Fuelled by easy credit for developers, and by lottery funding for cultural projects, a stream of striking new work appeared, from Nicholas Grimshaw's Buckminster Fuller–inspired domes at the Eden Project in Cornwall, to Norman Foster's complex shell structure for The Sage concert halls in Gateshead.

Roundheads and cavaliers

By the time of the credit crunch of 2008, British architectural practice was all but unrecognizable from that of two decades earlier, even if many of the same players were still at work. The most striking difference in architectural practice was its scale. In the 1980s a big architectural office numbered 50 people – even 25 was substantial; at one point in 2008 Foster and Partners had 1,200 people working for it. And even Zaha Hadid, who in the 1980s had caused a sensation when she won the competition for, but did not build, The Peak residential complex in Hong Kong, and who for another decade would be regarded as a theoretical architect rather than one interested in building, had 350 people working for her.

Closely connected with this scale shift – one that came even as digital drafting technology was transforming the nature of the design process – was the sheer volume of building, as architectural practice globalized on a scale hardly seen before. Just 20 per cent of Foster & Partners' work was in Britain, while London saw the establishment of several major American offices, including SOM, HOK and KPF. Overseas architects, from Herzog & de Meuron to Jean Nouvel, Rafael Viñoly and Daniel Liebeskind, were making major buildings in Britain.

The sterile conflict between tradition and high tech had become a quaint irrelevance. The argument now is very different from the situation when the Design Museum opened. The tension now is between those who revel in the possibilities of parametric modelling – the computer numeric–controlled techniques used to mill metal and cut cladding as if it was cloth by a tailor – and those who are again looking to find content and meeting in the social programmes of architecture.

Social housing had moved off the agenda, and the attempt to put it back on stage in the British Pavilion at the Venice Architecture Biennale in 2008 provoked a fierce clash between those who saw it as a dry return to the 1960s, and those who understood it as an attempt at modesty and social relevance. It presented only one side of a divide: between those who might be characterized as the roundheads – a strand in British architecture that can be traced back to the New Brutalist proponents Alison and Peter Smithson – and, on the other, the flamboyant work of Nigel Coates or Will Alsop, or the more poetic, expressive work of Zaha Hadid or Future Systems.

Though neither was represented in the exhibition, it is a tension that could be expressed in the gap between David Chipperfield (1953–) and Will Alsop (1947–). Alsop practises architecture as if he were a gravity-defying Dadaist performance artist. Let's turn Barnsley into a Tuscan hill town! Let's make Manchester's East Side into a lake by flooding the city! Let's build a stack of squashed doughnuts on Liverpool's Pier Head! Vibrant colours and eye-catching forms have won him many admirers, but many detractors, too. When it works, it's a strategy that is capable of conjuring miracles: his famous Stirling Prize–winning library in Peckham, south-east London, for example. When it fails, as in the brave but deluded construction of The Public, the arts centre in West Bromwich that was bankrupt before it opened its doors, it looks more like self-indulgence.

No two buildings could be more different in their assumptions than Alsop's extension to the Ontario College of Art & Design (OCAD) in Toronto and Chipperfield's strategy for bringing Berlin's long-derelict Neues Museum back to life. Alsop's addition hovers above the original school on stilts, like a Cubist flying saucer, patterned with random black-and-white splodges as if it were a Dalmatian puppy. The Neues Museum, by contrast, is a cool, eloquent and in the end richly rewarding assertion of the poetic power of architecture based on memory rather than novelty.

War damage and East German poverty meant that the Neues Museum stayed empty until Reunification prompted a rethinking of Berlin's overall cultural strategy. Rather than accept that the choice was between restoring the museum to its prewar condition or an exhibitionist pursuit of novelty, Chipperfield looked for an alternative that acknowledged the impact of historical events that have taken place in and around the museum. It is an approach that is both tactful and also capable of producing a powerful and deeply rewarding new work of architecture.

Opposite: Nicholas Grimshaw and Partners' Eden Project (2001) in Cornwall gave form to a visionary project to transform a derelict clay pit into a complex of greenhouses that have become one of the county's most successful tourist attractions. The interlocking domes with their hexagonal structure give a poetic twist to high-tech ideas.

Above and opposite: Will Alsop has pursued an independent course in British architecture, refusing to follow conventional orthodoxies about form or function. Working outside London in some of Britain's most deprived areas, he has tried to inject colour and a sense of distinctiveness. His projects have sometimes been realized, such as the housing development in New Islington, Manchester, and sometimes not yet built, as in the project in Walsall illustrated here.

Above and right: The reconstruction of central Manchester for the third time in a century has seen developer Urban Splash take a fresh approach, working with a number of more adventurous architectural practices, including FAT, established by Sean Griffiths, Charles Holland and Sam Jacob. The acronym stands for 'fashion, architecture and taste' and betrays an interest in the more populist tendencies of postmodernists such as Robert Venturi. Decorative brick and Dutch gables give presence to their development in what is now called New Islington.

Above and left: Selfridges in
Birmingham (2003) was commissioned from Future Systems, the
practice run by Jan Kaplicky and
Amanda Levete. The freeform
shape is finished in aluminium
discs. The glass bridge links it
with a neighbouring car park.

Above: Future Systems' first
major project to be realized was
the Lord's Media Centre (1999)
for cricket commentators, which
appears to float above the cricket
ground like a flying saucer.

Chipperfield – a 'European' British architect

Chipperfield was deeply affected by the shell-scarred halls of the museum. Caverns of exposed brick contrasted with glittering scraps of gilding, surviving frescoes and fragile nineteenth-century plaster. It was a powerful aesthetic experience that he was determined to retain in a reconstructed building. David Chipperfield's first substantial project was a shop for Japanese fashion designer Issey Miyake in London in 1984. It was an exercise in veined white marble, generously proportioned timber floorboards, and an intricate palette for the supporting cast of materials. A little rich for the Chipperfield of today, but a sophisticated exercise in place-making that, in its intentions and ambitions, is not so far from what he would be doing now. Even then he was ready to say that it was important not to do too much. All that a shop might need was a really beautiful floor.

The David Chipperfield of 2008 heads a substantial international practice, in which the Berlin office is in fact larger than its London parent. He is building or has built in China, America, Japan, Italy, Spain and Germany, but comparatively little in Britain. His response to the difficult climate of the 1980s was a refusal to compromise, either with the Prince of Wales and his acolytes or the cynical commercial developers of the period. There were a couple of bruising encounters with the militantly philistine nature of the British way of doing things. When Chipperfield designed an elegant house for the photographer Nick Knight in an otherwise undistinguished suburban street, the neighbours, unabashed by the militant banality of their own homes, did all that they could to prevent it from being built. Chipperfield had an equally hard time building his own offices in a mews in Camden, with the London evening paper gleefully egging on opponents of what was described as his 'aggressively

modernist and out of scale design'. In the process, Chipperfield realized that to have any chance of building, or indeed surviving, he would have to look beyond Britain to mainland Europe, where he could see himself as part of a group of architects who brought a seriousness and intellectual ambition to their work that went beyond stylistic tics or mannerisms. And so Chipperfield, who is in so many ways quintessentially English, has become the most European of British architects. It is a complex position in which to find himself, especially for an architect who believes in rooting his work in place, memory and material qualities. When you have joined the international flying circus, how do you resist its tendency toward the showy gesture and the quick fix?

Chipperfield's work could be seen as conservative in the best sense. He is looking for architecture that lasts, that resists the culture of spectacle. His design for a new headquarters for the BBC in Glasgow has a site on the edge of a derelict enclosed dock on the fringes of the city, surrounded by a howling void of anonymous and banal business parks and apartment towers. Chipperfield has described his task as trying to find a way to give some sense of permanence and place to an environment that looked, as he put it, as if it might blow away with the first gust of wind.

Given the restrictions of the budget, and the brutal simple-mindedness of a procurement procedure that saw the BBC outsourcing the project to a finance house, there were not too many options for Chipperfield. But he came up with a project that made the most of its interior. As in an Adolf Loos *Raumplan*, he took the fixed elements of the brief – the studios – and placed them on the floor of the building, like giant steps. He put the social spaces of the building on top of them in a cascading sequence of spaces that rises to the full height of the interior. In the process he made somewhere out of nowhere.

Opposite: The defining building of David Chipperfield's career is likely to be his resurrection of the long-derelict Neues Museum in Berlin, completed after ten years of work in 2009. Chipperfield has left visible the marks of wartime damage, introducing just a few new elements – such as the central staircase – to reflect the proportions of what has gone, but not its decorative detail.

Right: Chipperfield's strategy
for the Neues Museum interior
was to keep the remaining fragments
of the past, but not to imitate what
has been lost. The effect has a
painterly beauty that marks out
a new approach to architecture.

The challenge for his two early Japanese buildings had been almost the reverse – how to create a moment of stillness in the midst of the chaotic life of the suburban fringes of the contemporary Japanese city. He did it by creating a world within a world.

As Chipperfield's practice has grown and matured, he has stepped up to the challenge of exploring new types of brief and developing his own distinctive voice. There was a moment in the 1980s when he could be seen as part of the squad of architects associated with the Italian design and architecture magazine *Domus*, in the period when it was edited by Vittorio Lampugnani. But he has moved in several other fruitful directions. The most complex, and hardest to categorize, is the Berlin Neues Museum. This will undoubtedly stand as his first mature landmark, and perhaps also as the building in which he has taken the biggest conceptual risks, and where he has come up with solutions that are both traditional – in that they refer back to the strategies for dealing with the restoration of old buildings advocated by William Morris – and yet contemporary in their astringency. In its attitude to history, and its attempt to make something new out of it, the Neues Museum project is like nothing else that has been previously attempted.

Above and opposite: For many years Chipperfield worked almost exclusively outside Britain. That picture began to change with the completion of his design for the new BBC Scotland headquarters in Glasgow, where the restrained exterior conceals a spectacular interior intended to encourage casual meetings between staff as they move up the building on a series of terraces that are formed by the roofs of the studios below.

Hadid – passion at every scale

When in 2003 the Iraqi-born Zaha Hadid (1950–) was shortlisted for the European Union Prize for Contemporary Architecture Mies van der Rohe Award, the jury was split down the middle about her. Half of them were determined that she should win for her striking design of Strasbourg's tram interchange, a blend of artificial landscape and architectural objects. The rest seemed to have decided that she would be a 'safe' choice and wanted to look for somebody that they believed might somehow be more challenging. With bizarre speed, an architect who had been widely misunderstood as unbuildable had been transformed into the face of the architectural establishment. What was particularly odd was that Hadid appeared to have achieved this without actually building very much.

The early years of her career were marked by a remarkable series of projects that, despite the intensity and seriousness with which she approached them, remained unrealized. She maintained a studio in what had been one of the classrooms of a disused Victorian school in Clerkenwell. She built the fire station for the Vitra design complex in Weil am Rhein, an apartment building in Berlin, a bar in Japan. But it was her ideas and her sheer sense of conviction that made Hadid an architectural force of nature.

In the last five years, however, she has completed a series of major buildings that have established beyond doubt that she is an architect as profoundly interested in the material qualities of architecture as in its formal character. In particular, the Phaeno Science Centre in Wolfsburg, Germany, is an astonishing project that is at once an object and a piece of urbanism – a building that serves as a link between the industrial and the civic zones of Volkswagen's company town. Hadid is now delivering the promise of the remarkable series

Above: Zaha Hadid's Phaeno Science Centre (2005) in the German town of Wolfsburg, home of the Volkswagen car company, is part architecture, part landscape and part urbanism. It sits between Wolfburg's civic centre and the industrial zone, a powerful sculptural presence designed to attract visitors to its interactive displays.

Building in a Cold Climate_Architecture

Above: Hoisted up on moulded concrete legs, the Phaeno Science Centre's undercroft is used as an informal gathering place for Wolfsburg, as well as a route through the town centre. The legs are hollow, with some allowing access to the building above.

of images that defined her emergence as a major talent – her paintings for The Peak project in Hong Kong. She is working in Russia, America, Australia, the Middle East and China, and across Europe.

Hadid's work shows the same passionate intensity at every scale. At one end of the spectrum, her master plans in Istanbul and Singapore shape the terrain across kilometres, providing an infrastructure for decades to come. At the other, in the way that has been traditional for architects since the end of the nineteenth century, there are door handles and sets of cutlery. And in between there is a growing number of designs that cross the boundary between furniture and architectural space. Architecture and furniture are not the same. The issue of scale, if nothing else, divides them; so does the way that material works. But like her architecture, Hadid's design projects challenge us to understand space in a different way. She uses a whole range of starting points – mathematical and naturally occurring forms – to trigger her explorations of shape. She wants to eliminate the distinction between walls and floor, between roof and ground. She explores ways to animate space, to introduce the idea of movement and flow.

The only architect in Britain capable of matching Hadid's formal invention, and the fluid dynamism of her work, is the Czech-born Jan Kaplicky (1937–2009), founder of Future Systems. After working for both Richard Rogers and Norman Foster, his interest in a beautifully delineated kind of turbo-charged high tech declined. He began to build remarkable projects such as the Lord's Media Centre, bringing a huge aluminium disc to the cricket ground, and leaving it hovering in space over the stands, and the blue-and-silver Selfridges building in Birmingham that has become a logo for the city's renewal.

Above and top: For the German car maker BMW, Zaha Hadid's factory at Leipzig (2005) not only shows a commitment to its workforce, by offering attractive working conditions, but is also a reflection of the company's image in its use of a distinctive architecture.

Above: The car production line that is the factory's *raison d'être* remains visible throughout the building, swooping across the interior, and is a presence even in the office areas, removing the distinction between shop floor workers and management.

Above and left: Foreign Office Architects, established by Farshid Moussavi and Alejandro Zaera-Polo, came to prominence when they won the competition for the Yokohama Ocean Terminal. Their department store for John Lewis in Leicester (2008) takes its decorative skin from the local lacemaking tradition.

Beyond Foster and Rogers …

Architectural discourse is a conversation, conducted between cliques and allies using what are often private languages specifically designed to identify those who belong, and to exclude those who do not. But even though architectural sophisticates understand that they must use such vocabularies if they are to negotiate their way past the gatekeepers of criticism, in the end nothing matters more for an architect struggling to establish a reputation than the chance to build. This is the imperative that overcomes both ideology and theory.

The group that now has the leadership role among Britain's architects can still remember the fate of their predecessors. They were the people who taught them in the 1970s, condemned to a career of paper architecture and unbuilt competition wins, not by the nature of their work or even by the taste of those who commission buildings, but by the three-day week, the oil shock and the miners' strike. The generation that followed didn't want to go the same way and, given the boost of the huge wave of new building (only stopped in its tracks by the credit crunch of 2008), they have certainly managed to avoid that fate.

But until very recently their prospects for high visibility have still been obstructed by the big beasts ahead of them that so obstinately refuse to move over to let them pass, even as Britain's appetite for ambitious architecture has grown beyond all expectations. Norman Foster is still the most respected British architect internationally, producing such accomplished landmarks as the new Beijing airport and the Hearst Tower in New York. Richard Rogers is still the best politically connected architect in Britain. Nick Grimshaw, far from fading away as a high-tech period piece, has built a practice with real energy behind it. Terry Farrell is continuing to reinvent himself. And if the Alsops and the Chipperfields still aren't where they think they ought to be by now, where does this leave the generation coming after them?

Less discussed critically, but with a major impact on the face of Britain, is the careful, well-mannered work of successful large-scale practices such as Allies and Morrison, Wilkinson Eyre and Bennetts Associates that have made so much of the running. Other firms of note are the descendants of the high-tech impulse, notably Ian Ritchie and Stanton Williams. Behind them comes a new generation that at one end of the scale numbers Foreign Office Architects (FOA), Adjaye and Caruso St John, and at the other, the group that includes such smaller practices as de Rijke Morgan Marsh, FAT, Block, 6a that are jostling to establish themselves as leaders rather than followers.

Every generation tries to make its mark by making its predecessors look tired and out of touch. And FOA did that brilliantly. The two principals of FOA, Farshid Moussavi (1965–) and Alejandro Zaera-Polo (1963–), once suggested that:

The difference between our generation and the previous generation is that they were probably the first that had to deal head on with the internationalization of architecture. What did they do? The same thing that Mercedes or Coca-Cola did, develop a recognizable signature. Now we think this is no longer interesting. Nor do Nike and Coca-Cola think it is interesting.

Above and opposite: The Walsall Art Gallery (2000) designed by Caruso St John provides an elegant new home for the city's art collection, injecting a sophisticated sense of restraint into the commercial centre of Walsall.

Left and above: David Adjaye (1966–) began his career as an independent architect with a series of domestic projects for London-based architects, including the strikingly radical Elektra House (2000) in the East End, with its monolithic exterior and top-lit, light-suffused interior.

Building in a Cold Climate_Architecture

Above: Sackler Crossing (2006)
by John Pawson (1949–), in the
Royal Botanic Gardens, Kew, is
designed both to be a beautiful
addition to its landscape setting,
and also to provide a view of that
landscape to pedestrians moving
along its bronze handrail.

Breeding the Brand

Automotive
Andrew Nahum

In 1936, Paris-based millionaire playboy and amateur racing driver André Embiricos wanted a new car. As heir to a Greek shipping and banking dynasty, he could well afford the best – a bespoke sports saloon in the new aerodynamic style that the French coachbuilders did so well. His choice of designer was Georges Paulin (1902–42) at the Carrosserie Pourtout, builder of cars for plutocrats and even the French Prime Minister Georges Clemenceau. However, Embiricos did not want a French Delage, Delahaye, Hotchkiss, or even a Bugatti, but the excellent 4-litre Bentley produced by Rolls-Royce, known as 'the silent sports car'.

It was not unusual, in those days, for discerning clients to buy the 'chassis' for a car – in essence the whole mechanical package, from engine through to wheels – and take it to a coachbuilder for a special body. However, it now seems that Rolls-Royce also actively encouraged the deal, through their Paris agent, as a way of getting new design ideas for their Bentley marque, which was becoming slightly dated.

Three 'British' icons – the Bentley, Rolls-Royce and Mini

The Embiricos Bentley became rightly famous. Aerodynamically efficient and mechanically robust, it lapped the Brooklands circuit at 114 mph and was said to cruise at over 120 mph on the new continental autobahns – a phenomenal speed then. Even ten years later, in 1949, it came sixth in the Le Mans 24-hour race.

But the Franco-British hybrid was not simply an exotic one-off, for after World War II Rolls-Royce themselves used the body design as the basis for their own superfast tourer – the Bentley R-Type Continental. The development was a bold move in 1950, when the country was in the grip of post-war recession and when UK travellers could take only £25 out of the country. Times were tough – taxation and financial restrictions were so austere that Evelyn Waugh likened the regime imposed by Stafford Cripps, the Labour Chancellor of the Exchequer, to 'occupation by a foreign power'.

However, the launch in 1952 certainly vindicated the gamble. The UK trade magazine *Autocar* noted that it 'brings Bentley back to the forefront of the world's fastest cars. ... The acceleration from rest to 100 mph has not been approached by any other saloon car in [our] experience.' In fact, Rolls-Royce had created an extraordinary success that sold round the world to customers with names like Agnelli, Onassis and Rockefeller.

The undeniably mixed and transnational bloodline of this 'real British icon' is fascinating in the light of the recent, but equally tangled, re-creation of the recent Bentley Continental GT under the new ownership of the Volkswagen Audi Group. In 1998 the Rolls-Royce works at Crewe, which made both Rolls-Royces and Bentleys, was sold to the German company (though through some arcane commercial evolutions VW-Audi acquired only the right to build Bentleys, while their rivals, BMW, bought the Rolls-Royce car brand).

Central to plans to re-establish Bentley as one of the world's top marques was to be a re-creation of the Bentley Continental – a job that VW-Audi entrusted to one of its own design stars. Dirk van Braeckel, born in Belgium in 1958, had started work as a trainee designer at Ford in Cologne, then attended the celebrated automotive design course at the Royal College of Art in London, followed by several years in Audi's exterior design team before taking charge of design at the Czech Škoda company, which VW-Audi had bought.

Andrew Nahum

This page: In 1952 the Bentley R-type Continental was built in the aerodynamic language established before World War I by Parisian designer Georges Paulin. It spoke of a return to affluence after the grim post-war years.

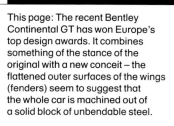

This page: The recent Bentley
Continental GT has won Europe's
top design awards. It combines
something of the stance of the
original with a new conceit – the
flattened outer surfaces of the wings
(fenders) seem to suggest that
the whole car is machined out of
a solid block of unbendable steel.

Nevertheless, the British association (or is it illusion?) was to be an important driver for the project. The cars were to be assembled at Crewe, with engines and mechanical parts shipped from Ingolstadt, Bavaria, just as once Rolls-Royce at Derby had sent the basis of the new Embiricos car to Paris. Equally importantly, a new Bentley design studio was established there, mining among other things the detailing of old Bentleys, and even layouts and typefaces from old handbooks and documents. The new Continental series, exemplified particularly by Continental GT, proved to be a hit. Some found it too 'retro', but it was nevertheless a highly considered and functional package, and sculpturally a strikingly well-resolved form.

If the new Bentley explored one, convoluted route to a perceived idea of Britishness, BMW tried another one with its own acquisition of the Rolls-Royce marque. BMW very discreetly took over a former high street bank building in Mayfair, as a kind of design 'skunk works', bringing back Marek Reichman (a Briton and Royal College of Art graduate, born in 1967) from their 'offshore' think tank Designworks in California, where he had been working on the Range Rover and 'the new Land Rover design DNA'. Installed near Marble Arch, Reichman (today Director of Design at Aston Martin) and a group of colleagues led the 'Rolls-Royce life', driving and riding in the current Rolls-Royce models and taking them to the kind of venues that were natural for Rolls-Royce users.

How much of their design work was reflected in the all-new Rolls-Royce Phantom, announced in 2002, is opaque. It seems likely that the Designworks studio in California must have had input, given the importance of the United States to luxury brands, and almost certainly the Designworks studio

in Munich had some too. The result, some say, is 'more Mafia than Queen Mother' (though the Queen Mother was generally driven in Daimlers – a royal tradition that went back to the 1920s). Nevertheless, BMW saved the name: under the old ownership, Rolls-Royce had been declining steadily and for years had not been able to access, and keep up with, the best automotive technology.

As a further twist, BMW then created an all-new factory to assemble the cars at Goodwood in Sussex, well known perhaps to Rolls-Royce owners fond of horse racing, but not much associated with industry until then. They even installed one of their top executives, Karl-Heinz Kalbfell, as CEO to set up the plant and to ensure that Goodwood Rolls-Royces were built to BMW quality standards. However, as with Audi's Bentley, the engines and mechanical parts were shipped in from the parent factories in Germany.

BMW was also responsible for the most successful reinterpretation of a British 'icon' of all time: the redesign and reinterpretation of the Mini, a job it started when it acquired Austin-Rover in 1994. Over the years the ailing UK car conglomerate had tried repeatedly to find something to replace the quirky and original Issigonis car. But just as Ruskin famously attributed the survival of Venice into modern times 'to the Goddess Poverty', so too Austin-Rover never could dedicate enough funding to develop an all-new replacement, and the Mini endured. Alec Issigonis (1906–88) himself had tried for a long time to get his 9X design accepted as the replacement – a design so wilfully austere and functional that it seemed he did not understand what had been so good about the original. But then, Issigonis was not in the least interested in form as a language of communication with

This page: BMW's acquisition of Rolls-Royce came just in time, for it had become increasingly clear that, as an independent, 'the best car in the world' could no longer afford the latest technologies.

Breeding the Brand_Automotive

Right: Living the Rolls-Royce life. The London-based design team drove the cars to 'Rolls-Royce' locations to internalize a sense of the marque and its associations.

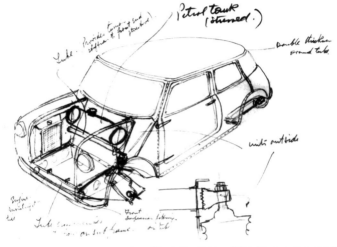

Top right: The winning Mini,
driven by Rauno Aaltonen, in
the 1967 Monte Carlo Rally.

Above: Alec Issigonis's powerful
freehand sketches were done
primarily to communicate his
intentions to his development team.

Above: Issigonis with the first Mini,
celebrating the building of more than
2.73 million cars.

Right: A contemporary publicity
shot linking the revolutionary car
with traditional English values.

Breeding the Brand_Automotive

the customer. What arrived, in his cars, was a synthesis of whatever engineering and aesthetic solutions seemed appropriate to him at the time – a blend of utilitarianism and his own naive, untaught, but often charming way with exterior design. Austin-Rover had various other ideas for replacements and in 1980 launched the Metro – in effect, an enhanced Mini. Although a useful product that stayed in production for 18 years (it became the Rover 100), the Metro had no emotional power left at the end of its life.

By the mid-1990s, Oliver Le Grice in the Austin-Rover design team at Gaydon was working on a completely new 'one volume' car, called the Spiritual, an original and beguiling design that even today looks timely, and to some extent anticipated the styling of the Mercedes A-Class and the Smart. The thinking was that a true successor to the Issigonis car should take space-efficiency to a new level.

BMW planners considered this concept ten years premature. Moreover, it did not quote the characteristics of the original Mini or reflect any of its 'emotion'. Indeed, what was seen as a problem to Austin-Rover – how to replace a too quirky and inconveniently long-lived original – was an opportunity to BMW, for they brought to the issue the car industry's most sophisticated understanding of the interplay between an evolving car form, model to model, and public appreciation and perception of a brand. One BMW product planner recalled:

We wanted to make a success of the Mini and [Rover] said 'Why? Forget it' – they were really not interested in this little jewel and it is a jewel – one which just needed to be polished up again. No one at Rover appeared to have a feeling of how valuable the Mini brand could be for them. There was no emotion there. ... Mini is the most emotional, and the most high-impact brand in the small sector. (Quoted in Graham Robson, *New Mini*, 2002)

Fascinatingly, it was a cosmopolitan American, Frank Stephenson (1959–), then working at BMW's Munich studio, and today heading up design at McLaren, who came up with a way forward. His sketch seemed to look into the soul of the Mini and showed BMW how to take it forward into this century. 'It's not an Issigonis package,' sniffed the purists when it came out and they tried the tiny back seats, but BMW had been smarter than they knew: they realized that, while the Mini had started out as an economy car, it had soon become a sporty one, too. In fact, specially tuned Mini Coopers won the Monte Carlo Rally three times between 1964 and 1967 (four times really – they were disqualified by French officials, after winning in 1966, on a contentious technicality concerning their lights).

Overall, the motor sport achievements were astonishing for a design that started life as a basic vehicle, and the Mini Coopers and other hot-rodded race or rally lookalikes that rocketed around the roads in the 1960s were not 'Issigonis packages' either – the owners had subverted that by dropping the steering wheel, pushing the seats back with brackets you could buy from Halfords and sticking long rubber stalks on the dash switches so that you could still reach them.

BMW understood all those associations, and in 2001 smartly made sure that they announced and launched MINI and MINI Cooper on the market simultaneously. What successful reinterpretations of historic designs have to take account of is that, though we think we know what a classic

This page: The Mini transcended mere engineering to become a movie character in its own right in *The Italian Job* (1969).

Above: 'It is a jewel – one that just needed to be polished up again.' BMW cleverly launched MINI with the hot Cooper variants at the same time.

Top and left: Every centimetre of the new MINI is considered in a knowing way that would have been alien to Issigonis. Details such as its intricate, specially composed headlights were known within BMW as 'jewellery icons'.

Above: The large speedometer quotes the more basic central dial of the original, while an offset rev counter (upper right on dash) recalls the after-market tuning goodies bought in the 1960s by 'boy racers'.

Mini, Rolls-Royce or Bentley is, it has to exist in an entirely new visual and semantic landscape where everything else is now different. Unless the car itself changes, its main connotation will be merely 'old'. At the same time, the new model must still work 'as its own car'. It's hard to do, but works brilliantly when it's right. The BMW MINI remains one of the great successes in relaunching and reconceiving a famous marque.

In spite of the undoubted success of these inter-nationalized Anglo-German hybrids, the association with BMW was finally unable to save Austin-Rover from a slow journey to extinction. Austin-Rover had been on government life support for years until it was bought by British Aerospace in 1988 for £150 million – a valuation that was attacked by EU officials as unrealistically low. Indeed, within a year BAe had recovered £126 million through the sale of assets. Sadly, BAe management relied largely on the association with Honda to produce new models and design development withered, although the neat MG F, engineered on a shoestring and designed by Gerry McGovern, showed that the group could originate interesting new cars.

That certainly was the belief of Berndt Pischetsrieder, Anglophile boss of BMW (and cousin of Alec Issigonis through his mother). Pischetsrieder had visited Issigonis and the Longbridge factory as a boy and was entranced by the cars and the then-famous English makes. In 1994 he announced the purchase of the Austin-Rover and the aim to rebuild Rover as a quality brand – a British BMW equivalent – but, in spite of substantial investment from BMW over several years, Austin-Rover failed to prosper, becoming known by opponents of Pischetsrieder inside BMW as 'the English

Patient'. The aesthetically successful Rover 75, positioned as a 'small Jaguar', and designed by Richard Woolley with his team, was voted 'Car of the Year' in 1999, though known in Munich as 'the Last Chance Saloon'. In fact, its sales figures failed to reverse the declining trend. The high value of sterling against the euro was one factor but, for whatever reason, Austin-Rover could not seem to achieve either the product quality or the operating economics required for survival.

BMW was by this time highly divided, with many deeply concerned for the company itself in the light of the costs of the English venture. This provoked the departure of Pischetsrieder and the sale of most of Austin-Rover (now as 'MG Rover') to the Phoenix Consortium. However, BMW left clutching a handful of British brand names, including Riley and Triumph (which was rumoured, before the recession, to be targeted for a revival). However, what BMW were most adamant about was that they should hold on to the Mini brand, the MINI revival project, and the former Morris plant at Cowley, Oxford, which was to build it. For MG Rover the sad final act was to be receivership and sale in 2005, to China where a 'Roewe' is still made.

Was there ever a British car?

So, is British car design simply about exploiting the name and image of famous, or once-famous, brands, whether successfully or unsuccessfully? One point is that the history and association of the brand count for very little if the product does not live up to the buyer's expectations. And anyway, what *is* the quality of 'Britishness'? In fact, the industry has always been transnational and 'national identity' in car design is a conundrum. After all, the first car in Britain was a French

Above: The MG F was a capable solution to the challenge of designing a mid-engined and affordable sports car. For a time it was Britain's best-selling sports car.

Top: The post-war 'Aunty' Rover spoke of stolid dependability, not modishness.

Top right: The 1989 Rover 820 SE, designed under the leadership of Roy Axe.

Above: 'Last Chance Saloon' – the 1999 Rover 75 was a nicely composed attempt at relaunching the brand as a 'small Jaguar', but was let down by quality and production issues.

Right: The baby Rover 216 benefited from excellent Honda mechanical parts.

Above: An Aston Martin Ulster in 1935. The prewar Aston Martin became the epitome of British sporting style, though it owed much to the Italian-born Bertelli brothers.

Panhard, imported in 1895, and for quite a while most cars in the UK were French. Of course, existing UK coach and carriage builders quickly adapted to the new trade of creating bodies for these new horseless carriages and their own tradition did impose a certain formality on UK designs. Even in the horse-drawn era, British vehicles had tended to be more neo-classical in feel than those on the Continent, and this carried through into the 'Georgian' characteristics exemplified particularly, by the longstanding radiator design of Rolls-Royce. Little Austin Sevens, Rovers, and even sporting MGs and Bentleys all had a more upright stance than cars from equivalent market sectors in neighbouring France, Germany and Italy.

Nevertheless, the great British marque of Aston Martin really only took off when it acquired the Italian-born Augustus Bertelli as a director in 1927. Bertelli had been brought from Italy as a child to Wales, but returned before World War I to his native country, where he worked at Fiat beside the great engineer and racing driver Felice Nazzaro. Back in England, he worked on aero engines before graduating after the war to the burgeoning sports car scene. His brother Enrico Bertelli also opened a body shop adjacent to the works in Feltham, where most of the cars were bodied. By the 1930s, Italian style (particularly the Alfa Romeo influence) was also creeping into British cars such as the Riley MPH and Adrian Squire's exclusive Squire sports cars.

The post-World War II period, however, produced a curious mixture of shapes, and it now seems surprising that people accepted such a huge range of forms and styles. Austin and Vauxhall looked to America (as did Ford at Dagenham of course), while performance cars such as Aston Martin (which made close connections with Zagato), and arguably Jaguar, were increasingly influenced by new sports car developments in Italy. Meanwhile, some companies such as Jowett, Lea Francis, Riley, Bristol and Lagonda persevered in trying to establish new home grown shapes for the post-war car, though all these attempts failed to spawn a new aesthetic, perhaps because the companies were simply too small.

Even where the UK motor industry was on a high, as with Austin and Morris (subsequently BMC) in the 1950s, the resident styling guru at Longbridge was Ricardo ('Dick') Burzi, an Argentine of Italian lineage, and the dominant style was a vague reinterpretation of American trends. Subsequently, Alec Issigonis became the dominant figure at BMC, assuming the role of chief engineer and exterior designer in one, and although he had studied automotive engineering (not design) in Battersea, he had been brought up as son of a Greek engineer father and a Bavarian mother in Smyrna – today Izmir in Turkey. However, during this period the most successful exterior designs for the company came from the Pininfarina studio in Turin – the A40, the A55 Austin Cambridge Mk II and the 1100.

All this shows that 'Britishness' as a design quality is less to do with a real and tangible design tradition than with the development of forms that we think are British – that we can be persuaded to locate, semantically, in the area that in our brains understands, or thinks it does, what 'a Jaguar' or 'a Mini' connotes. When a car is designed to touch base with a dimly perceived perception of what a marque used to be, topped up with creative retrospective advertising and the odd historical magazine article, are we being induced to undergo a sculptural equivalent, perhaps, of 'false memory syndrome'?

Right: An Aston Martin 'Le Mans' model on a sporting trial in 1933.

Far right: Morecambe Rally, 1952. The unusual Jowett Jupiter spoke of the rich variety and unresolved visual language that typified the post-World War II British motor industry.

Above: Aston Martin DB4 Zagato, 1961. The stylish post-war Aston Martins gained much from their associations with both the Touring and Zagato *carrozzerie* in Milan.

This page: 'Optimism is thinking
you can just about afford to run
an Aston Martin,' commented one
waggish journalist. The post-war
twin-cam engine inherited from the
Lagonda marque and designed by
W O Bentley (1888–1971) was
demanding and expensive to fix.

But to view Britain as a memory bank of old forms and as a launchpad from which they can be rejuvenated and exploited would be to seriously undervalue the modern, international-quality work that goes on in the country, and for which the 'classical' past is irrelevant. For example, Nissan opened a design studio in London in 2003, relocating from Munich to the newly developing Paddington Basin. To former Nissan designer Stephane Schwarz, London is almost like a 'Future Lab' – more multicultural than almost anywhere else, maybe more of a pressure cooker, trying experiments like the congestion charge, and with a fantastically vibrant cultural life, equivalent to say Paris or Barcelona, but less nationalistic. However, the design milieu of London was not swept up by Nissan in any programmatic way, as in the BMW/Rolls-Royce project, because, as Stephane Schwarz says, 'designers are like sponges'. David Godber, design manager at Nissan, echoes that London works as a base because '*our designers bring London to work with them* – they're inspired by its architecture, its clubs and bars, its music scene. ... London's design community – the latest trends in fashion, art and product design. So much of the city's energy feeds into the studio. London is at the centre of everything.'

The Nissan Qashqai, for example, billed as a new 'compact crossover that's 100 per cent urban-proof', reflects well the way much automotive design functions today in the UK, for the project was conceived as an urban car project: a 'European car, created for European buyers' that would take some of the values of 'multicultural London for its inspiration', reflecting the height and stance of increasingly popular SUVs but occupying a road footprint equivalent to a Ford Focus. Swiss-born Schwarz worked on it initially at

the Nissan studio in Japan but later in the Paddington studio, London. There are certainly no historical allusions, even to the preceding Nissan range, and the most distinctive motif is the crease along the belt line that rises, slightly mysteriously, behind the front wheel arch. Nissan call it a 'bone line' because, Stephane Schwarz says, the inspiration was the 'tensioned limbs of athletes'.

Men in sheds? Sports cars and micro-manufacturers

Throughout this period Britain has also maintained a reasonably healthy sports car and performance car capacity. Lotus had always pursued performance and handling, with no particular embedded aesthetic, and so the 1989 Elan designed by Peter Stevens (1945–) was an original take on what a two-seat sports car could be. The effective Lotus Elise, designed by Stevens' successor there, Julian Thompson, continued the tradition of creating pretty and effective small sports cars, while Stevens moved on to design the McLaren F1 road car – a design that owes nothing to nationalist allusions but sets out only to redefine what an extreme-performance road car can be if virtually no expense is spared. He subsequently renewed the MG TF, which became for a while the UK's best-selling sports car.

At Aston Martin, Marek Reichman has brought a new lightness and poise to a series of cars that in recent years had become bulky, and had relied on solutions from various external consultancies. Jaguar, too, has design successes with chief designers Geoff Lawson and today Ian Callum, although sadly its middle-price cars have never achieved a breakthrough into the 'BMW belt' in Europe or the executive car bracket in the States. Somehow, price, quality and

Above: The Nissan Qashqai exemplifies the use of London as 'Future Lab' for design development, but also reflects the transnational exchanges between their studios around the world on which car companies now rely.

Above left: Peter Stevens' 1989 Lotus Elan was a highly original attempt at giving the two-seat sports car a new form.

This page: 'More holes than car'?
In spite of the original architecture
for air management, Julian
Thompson's pretty Lotus Elise has
echoes of the earlier Ferrari Dino,
which had pioneered a new
aesthetic for mid-engined cars.

Above and opposite: Awesome technology – awesome price. McLaren F1 designer Gordon Murray deployed full-strength solutions from Grand Prix racing and, with former Lotus designer Peter Stevens, crafted Britain's most capable and original supercar.

depreciation calculations never stacked up against German executive car equivalents and Ford, which owned it, found the money only going the wrong way into its holdings in Jaguar and Land Rover. Once, Ford had needed Jaguar as 'a luxury brand with global pulling power', and Land Rover too, as 'a terrific global brand with a wonderful heritage'. In 2008 Ford sold both to the Tata company of India for £2.3 billion – about half what it had paid for the two marques in 1989.

But in spite of the uncertainties of the volume motor industry, the UK has also sustained a surprising number of specialist low-volume sports car makers. Lotus crossed the divide from kit car to become 'properly grown up' a long time ago, partly because its Formula One successes brought so much credibility. The smaller outfits, though, can produce extremely effective cars, partly because they can call on Britain's highly adept race car and competition car design community for chassis design, and the niche industry is also sustained by the UK's 'single vehicle type approval' legislation – a route that allows manufacturers to validate their vehicles as roadworthy without the very costly process of passing the full vehicle type approval necessary to sell in many markets.

Like Lotus, most of these small makers have tended to rely on the suitability of fibreglass (GRP) bodywork for small production runs owing to the low cost of tooling required and the ability it brings to change models rapidly. However, the design process for these small companies has been characterized by one designer from the mainstream car industry as 'men in sheds ... no flat surface plates – just a big block of foam in a shed, with the floor on the bonk'.

Many did find a way to short-circuit the expensive rendering and clay modelling of the mass producers, and do in fact model the car directly, full size, by carving industrial 'blue foam'. The shape is appraised, maybe modified, then sealed and finished with resins. This model itself then becomes the master for creating a set of female moulds in fibreglass, which in turn are used to create the body panels for production. 'We thought we were quick,' said one designer from an independent consultancy that pitched for design work to Blackpool-based TVR, 'but they did it in half the time.'

The shapes that result from this more 'vernacular' styling tradition are freer than any that would be passed for production by a volume car maker, and that, of course, is the point. TVR has survived for many years, trading on its ability to make cars that appealed to people who wanted muscular-looking, genuinely fast cars 'that could eat Porsches for breakfast', for under £50,000. The Sagaris, one of its most interesting designs in recent years, has been called 'a mixture of *Star Wars* prop, computer game graphic, deep-sea crustacean and Le Mans racer', but it also reflects experience gained with TVR's actual Le Mans project so is not entirely fantastical. Design was credited to Damian McTaggart, who subsequently moved to sports car maker Marcos, which sadly seems to have folded again, perhaps for the last time.

A relatively new entrant into the specialist sports car sector was Lee Noble, a longstanding competition car engineer who had worked on the McLaren F1 before founding his own company in Leicestershire in 2000. The Noble company claims to make real drivers' cars that don't allow excessive technology to intrude between the driver and the experience. They are 'analogue, not digital; light, incredibly fast, with brilliant handling. The world's best affordable super car.' To *Car Design News*, though, they are a wilfully missed

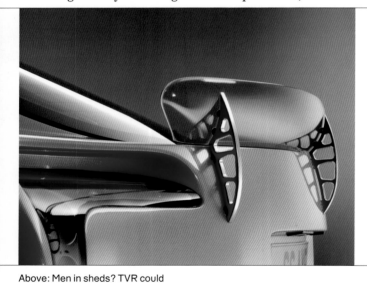

Above: Men in sheds? TVR could model cars full-size in foam and copy them using fibreglass female moulds to translate them into full-size cars with astonishing speed. The technique brings an immediacy and raw sculptural power that big company studio culture suppresses.

This page and overleaf: TVR Sagaris was not all fantasy; it used solutions deployed in TVR's 2004 Le Mans race attempt.

The freedom is the point. TVR's small production runs and its particular customer base allowed styling experiments (some called them excesses) that big makers would not dare try.

opportunity; 'the design is testimony to a misconception that is also archetypal of the British sports car industry; that an engineer can design a car as well as a designer.'

In an increasingly transnational world, monopolized by giant brands, it is nice to see that new entrants to this specialized form of auto engineering continually pop up in Britain. In Helston, Cornwall, Richard Oakes, a graduate of the Royal College of Art who has worked in the mainstream industry for Ford and Aston Martin, is making a beautifully designed and engineered high-performance three-wheeler called the Blackjack Zero. The car is light and designed to make the most of its Moto Guzzi V-twin motorbike engine, but, given Oakes' design background, it is not surprising that it is clothed in unusually svelte bodywork for a kit car.

Not far away, in Somerset, Simon Saunders builds the Ariel Atom ('No doors, no roof, no compromise'), a truly frantic small sports car with a completely original look that derives from an original 'exo-skeleton' design pioneered by Nic Smart, one of his former students in the automotive design course at Coventry University. The Atom exemplifies the design theory established by Colin Chapman of Lotus – 'simplificate, and add lightness'. It is not a fibreglass-bodied sports car, because really there is no body – mainly just four big alloy tubular beams that join the back to the front, race-bred suspension parts and brakes and a supercharged Honda engine. The Atom is highly considered, expertly engineered and brings circuit-racing technology to the road for a comparatively affordable £30,000, and is so light for its power that it out-accelerates supercars that cost half a million quid, at least up to 100 mph. Petrolhead TV presenter Jeremy Clarkson, on a track test, exclaimed, 'I have never, ever, driven anything that accelerates so fast ... for sheer excitement this thing is off the scale ... driving Nirvana.'

The longest-lived of the small sports car makers must be Morgan, which has been making cars at Malvern in Gloucestershire since 1910. The styling of the Morgan is not so much retro as reactionary, and their vintage-style two-seaters are clearly connected to the cars they built before World War II. However, in recent years they have modernized the offer, but only by going as far as the late 1930s and using the aerodynamic idiom that was coming in then with cars such as Jean Bugatti's Atlantic, with a design said to have been developed by Charles Morgan himself. It was quite a clever move because the marque seemed to defy modernization, though mainstream car designers feel it would have worked better if Morgan had used industry professionals. For his part, the present Charles Morgan, third in the line of the family owners, would probably argue that their input would have provided exactly the kind of homogeneity that Morgan buyers don't want.

Design for the global industry

For a period in the 1980s and 1990s, the UK developed a number of independent consultancies such as International Auto Design (IAD) of Worthing, which had been founded by John Shute, an experienced and savvy auto industry body engineer. Others included MGA Developments in Coventry (Geoff Matthews) and Canewdon Consultants in Essex, an 'Anglo-Swedish' practice established specifically to work with Volvo and Saab.

These new outfits offered the capability to design and engineer complete 'turnkey' packages for new cars that

Above left: Budget supercar? Noble was a new start-up in 1999 and has done well to survive in a tough world. Amazing capability for the money.

This page: The Ariel Atom fuses an original engineering solution for the sports car with a new aesthetic.

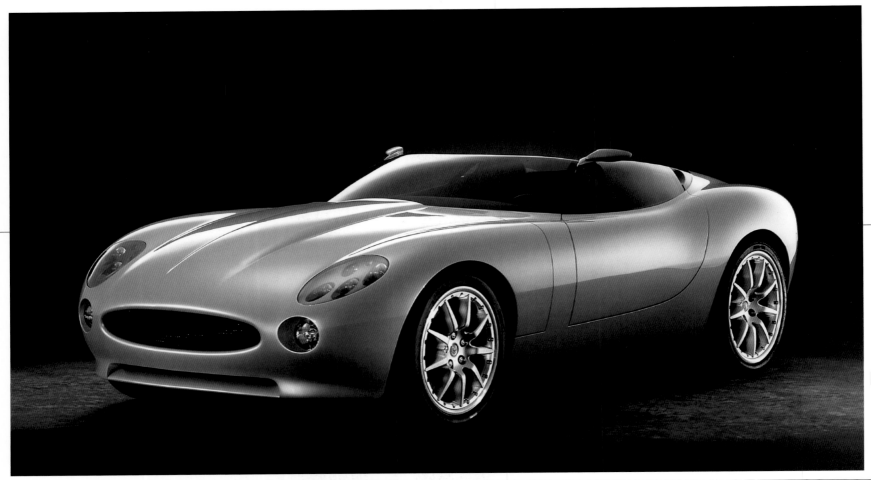

This page: The Jaguar F-type concept car deployed insightful and honest design in its attempt to survive as an onshore UK luxury manufacturer. It was not enough.

Breeding the Brand_Automotive

covered exterior and interior design aesthetics as well as the 'body engineering' or structure. The aspiration was to match the kind of service provided, pre-eminently by Giorgetto Giugiaro and Aldo Mantovani's Italdesign consultancy in Turin, which was unique, for a time, in offering aesthetic design integrated with body-engineering and production solutions. Much of the success of these consultancies was due to the great chance that occurred for them to pick up experienced clay modellers, draughtsmen and design engineers who had been shed by mainstream auto companies such as Austin-Rover in the Midlands.

Not surprisingly, perhaps, their productivity and engagement was far higher in these new firms than was apparent in the old car giants, and these new consultancies found clients from around the world. Established European and Japanese companies tended to require additional capacity for highly confidential body modelling or construction of complete prototypes, or perhaps competitive solutions against which they could benchmark the offerings from their own designers. However, new entrants into the industry, particularly from Korea and Malaysia, were less exacting and were often looking for comprehensive design solutions for complete new cars.

The most high-profile of these concerns, IAD, was brought down by the collapse of Korean car maker Daewoo, one of its key clients, though work seems also to have withered away for the others. One reason for this perhaps was the growing penetration of branding theory, as exemplified by BMW, which seemed to require a deep identification with company culture on the part of its own designers and studios – an internalized aesthetic instinct that could not easily be outsourced. The major companies, moreover, were making investments right around the world, putting their own offshore studios into 'cultural hotspots' that robbed these independents of their ability to offer competition and diversity.

However, one surprising new entrant into the field is the structural engineering firm Ove Arup, which in 1999 acquired the Warwick-based consultancy Design Research Associates (DRA), the result of a management buyout of the former Austin-Rover design studio in 1986 by its then boss, Roy Axe. Arups were looking for vehicle design capability as part of a holistic transport planning exercise they were undertaking for Florence.

The move was intended to capitalize on Arup's huge experience in the application of computational analysis and modelling to engineering. This went beyond computer-aided design (CAD) and was, they claimed, 'computer-aided engineering (CAE)' – a rhetoric that means, in effect, that the dynamic analysis of structures can be done with such confidence that prototypes are no longer necessary. This capability, Arups felt, closely matched the needs of the automotive industry – road behaviour, handling and even crash tests can be modelled and predicted with confidence.

Building and testing a prototype is costly. It also adds six or eight months to the time it takes to bring a car to market. Since an all-new car probably needs investment of around £500 million, any compression of the timescale saves large amounts of money. Increasingly, too, car companies are trying to escape the historic law of Fordism that ties costs to volume, and to develop large numbers of niche models – a pickup truck variant of the Ford Fiesta for Brazil, a 'jacked-up off-roader', or whatever you care to imagine.

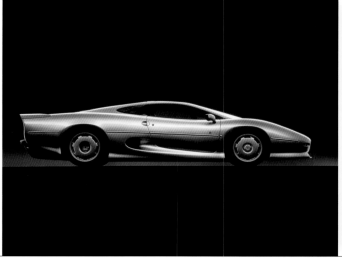 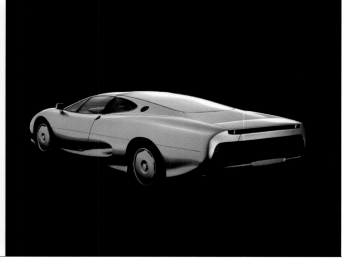

This page: The mid-engined V12 Jaguar XJ 220, produced in 1992, was the fastest production road car until the arrival of the McLaren F1. Controversially, it was presold by customer orders during development.

Above: Using the architecture of the late 1930s was a smart way to modernize (a little) a car that traded on rigid adherence to tradition. Mainstream designers may sniff, but the combination of retro and homemade aesthetics is what draws Morgan buyers.

The future of this type of integrated design service is an open question because, as with the older pattern, car companies can easily create these facilities in house if they wish. Already, it's been claimed that Fiat's new models have been engineered through to production in a similar way, and their confidence in validating the structures by virtual engineering is so great that the first cars actually subjected to real crash tests are the ones supplied for mandatory tests by government agencies.

The future of British automotive design

Any look at car design in Britain must take account of the excellent record here in design education. Coventry University has longstanding courses in automotive design at both undergraduate and postgraduate level, with former students spread throughout the global industry – for example, Steve Mattin from the Coventry course was responsible for the Mercedes A-Class and today is head of design at Volvo. In London, the all-postgraduate Royal College of Art instituted its automotive design course in 1968 and has had an extraordinary track record, with students taking influential jobs in leading car companies around the world. In fact, most design heads in the European car industry have spent time at the RCA, either before they entered the industry or when sent by their sponsoring companies to broaden their horizons. Certainly a peculiarly British take on design is not seen as a key selling point for these courses – much more to the point is the development of skill, maximum imagination, an understanding of evolving 'design narratives' (which do not need to be 'retro' at all), combined with a really informed view of evolving industry practice.

The context for vehicles has changed radically in recent years, but so have these educational departments. Moreover, few students arrive designing Ferraris these days – most have a keen appreciation of the debate around mobility, congestion and climate, and bring a wish to explore new lighter, smarter cars with a smaller environmental footprint.

The current recession promises to bring a huge shakeout for the world's car industry, and no one knows which groups will survive or what their product range will be in a few years' time. However, it is clear that mobility is both personally precious and economically essential. People will continue to demand personal transportation, whatever future cars look like, or whichever power source they run on. The UK will continue to be a 'mobility consumer' and therefore UK design will continue to be an indispensable element in selling credible products in the country. Some might challenge this, predicting that the future will bring a kind of 'cargo cult consumerism' in which we passively purchase cheap cars conceived and manufactured in China.

However, though price is always an argument, the truth is that for products to have any real significance and appeal they need to connect to local culture and they have to establish their own meaning and 'story' for us. Without that, the only emotional arguments for purchase are that the product should be cheap and last long enough. A proportion of the market will without doubt fall to that argument, but the wish for differentiation and for 'connection' to the brand will not go away. Much car manufacture has gone offshore (though a surprising amount does remain), but it seems inevitable that the UK will continue to play a global role in car design and in vehicle development.

This page: Morgan buyers don't want the homogeneity conferred by the mainstream car industry's design practices. The current Aero is said to have been schemed by Charles Morgan himself.

Form and Content

Graphics
Rick Poynor

There is a good case for arguing that British graphic design is as vigorous today as it has ever been, though it can also be seen as a field undergoing some fundamental changes. While it would be possible to debate at length whether designers still hit the creative highs seen at regular intervals since graphic design began to gain momentum in the 1960s, what cannot be disputed is the great variety of design approaches over the years and the practice's deep roots in British visual culture. This relatively new discipline is now made up of several generations, each layering its own distinctive contribution on the last.

Veteran designers who emerged in the 1960s and went on to shape the practice – figures such as Ken Garland, Derek Birdsall, David Gentleman, Richard Hollis and Michael Wolff – are still working, lecturing or writing about graphic design, and the late Alan Fletcher (1931–2006) must be added to this group. The outpouring of feeling when Fletcher died, shortly before a retrospective opened at the Design Museum, bore witness to his enduring influence on designers of all ages, and his monumental book, *The Art of Looking Sideways*, first published in 2001, is a perennial best-seller.

The same longevity is seen among some of the talented designers who followed these pioneers. Peter Saville (1955–), a leading figure in the graphic new wave of the early 1980s, has made a dramatic return to favour – he was subject of a Design Museum exhibition in 2003 – and is now one of Britain's best-known designers, familiar beyond the boundaries of the design world to a public that once knew little about graphic design. Designers who made their names in the early 1990s, such as Why Not Associates, Graphic Thought Facility (GTF) and Jonathan Barnbrook,

remain vital forces on the British graphic design scene, their work publicized and admired around the world.

Graphic anarchy

If this brief roll call of celebrated designers suggests a discipline set in its ways, quite the opposite is in fact the case. Graphic design, already turning into a young person's activity in the 1980s, has in the last 20 years become ever more relentlessly youthful, with a fixation on fashion, a constant quest for newness and a continuous turnover of styles. Studios making the biggest waves today were in all likelihood yet to enter the business just five years ago. Meanwhile, the smallest visual nuances can date so fast that the passing of just half a decade is enough to leave work looking locked in its moment, if not completely passé. 'British' graphic design is, at the same time, an increasingly cosmopolitan activity. Thousands of students come from overseas to study the subject in design schools regarded as being among the finest in the world – Central Saint Martins, the London College of Communication, the Royal College of Art, to name only three – and plenty decide to stay on when they graduate. Today, designers in some of the UK's most creatively adventurous studios hail from Belgium, Germany, Sweden, Denmark, Norway, Japan, the United States and many other countries.

The graphic design Britain produces can rightly be described as pluralistic, but it is a pluralism bound by certain limits. In some crucial respects, the contemporary scene is still in reaction against the upheavals that occurred in graphic design in the early 1990s, not just in Britain but globally. This was a period when the possibilities of the new computer technology prompted a re-evaluation of typographic

Rick Poynor

Form and Content_Graphics

Above: Alan Fletcher's *The Art of Looking Sideways* (2001), published by Phaidon, is a massive compendium of insights into verbal and visual expression.

Left: Anti-Blair poster (2003) by David Gentleman for the Stop the War Coalition, protesting at Britain's involvement in the 'war' against terrorism.

Above: Graphic Thought Facility's design for Alan Fletcher's exhibition at the Design Museum, which opened shortly after he died in 2006, re-created the eclectic ambience of his London studio with a life-sized photograph. Objects mounted on the wall recalled his methods as a collector and collagist.

Left: Photograph by Peter Saville from *It All Looks Like Art to Me Now* (2005), a slide projection shown at an exhibition of his work in Zurich. The pictures demonstrate how visual ideas from avant-garde art and design are now part of everyday British visual culture.

Above: Jonathan Barnbrook was invited by the organizers of the Art Grandeur Nature project to create a series of billboards for display in a park in Seine-Saint-Denis (2004). He was free to determine the content and his anti-capitalist slogans were translated into French.

ONCE WE BRANDED OUR SLAVES
NOW WE ARE SLAVES TO OUR BRANDS

standards, as designers took charge of the tools of typesetting, and their often controversial typographic experiments pushed conventions of legibility to breaking point. Some of the most notable British examples came from Why Not Associates and from Jonathan Barnbrook, who collaborated with Why Not on projects for the retailer Next before establishing himself as the most consistently inventive and idiosyncratic British graphic designer of his generation. (In 2007 Barnbrook also received a Design Museum exhibition.) Traces of this ornately embroidered, early-1990s digital aesthetic – strong traces in Barnbrook's case – can still be seen in their work today.

The increasingly distressed and grungy international anti-style reached its apogee with the American designer David Carson's work of 1992–9 for *Ray Gun* magazine). The closest British equivalent to this was the speeding lines, seismic layering and colliding letterforms of the design collective Tomato, formed in 1991, and Chris Ashworth's scratchy, fractured page layouts for the music magazine *Blah Blah Blah*, launched in Britain in 1996 by *Ray Gun*'s publisher. By this time, it seemed that every rule previously believed vital to govern the creation of 'good' graphic design had been thrown in the dustbin. Graphic design as a teachable, professionalized, systematic activity had come perilously close to implosion. When it came to form, there was nowhere left to go other than back.

Refuseniks and provocateurs

So, British graphic designers working in the late 1990s faced a problem. The deeply ingrained ambition of many visual communicators who came of age in this era was to invent new kinds of graphic form, and this remains an essential motivation for many even now. Yet the prospects for formal development, immediately after the anything-goes digital meltdown, seemed limited indeed.

For the more reflective designers, the excesses of form looked increasingly indulgent and fruitless. What was the point of inventing a new style as a vaguely intended form of resistance, or even simply as an assertion of difference, if its inevitable fate was to be co-opted by commerce as the latest trendy look and plastered over everything for as long as it remained fashionable? This had happened to Neville Brody (1957–) and other new-wave designers who put the accent on stylistic expression in the 1980s, and it happened again, less than a decade later, with experimental typography. Some of the typographic rebels even attempted to cash in this time around by commodifying their own styles in work for advertisers and corporate clients as they went along.

It was quite obvious to any designer who gave it some thought that graphic design had become part of the problem, especially where it merged with advertising. The disenchantment and retreat from primarily formal concerns was particularly apparent at postgraduate level. In the late 1990s at the Royal College of Art, it was common to encounter young designers who wanted no part in this process, preferring to direct a manner of thinking still defined (not always clearly) as 'graphic' into other kinds of endeavour: moving image, installations, performance and sound. Daniel Eatock (1975–), an MA student at the college from 1996 to 1998, was one of the most determined refuseniks. He even had his own slogan: 'Say YES to fun and function and NO to seductive imagery and colour.'

Right: Poster by John Warwicker of Tomato for 'Cowgirl' (1994), a single by Underworld, the electronic band founded by members of the Tomato collective. Tomato's designs often had an agitated, provisional air, as though they had been captured in a state of becoming something else.

Above: Spread by Chris Ashworth, Neil Fletcher and Amanda Sissons of Substance for the second issue of the music magazine *Blah Blah Blah* (1996), launched by Ray Gun Publishing. The energy of the 'Brit Pop' band Oasis, then at their height, is expressed by the grungy, distressed typography.

Left and above: *A Flock of Words* (2003), created by Why Not Associates in collaboration with the artist Gordon Young, is a 300m typographic pavement in Morecambe, made from granite, concrete, glass, steel, brass and bronze. The poems, song lyrics and traditional sayings all relate to birds.

Above: Graphic Thought Facility's
Digitopolis installation (2000) about
digital technology at the Science
Museum, London, employs vacuum
fluorescent displays, LCD
messaging and electro-luminescent
messaging. The studio is renowned
for research into unusual materials
that expand the possibilities of
environmental graphic design.

This kind of restraint had first appeared during the early 1990s' digital feeding frenzy, in the work of two notable mavericks, Paul Elliman (1961–), a design provocateur operating on the margins of the London scene, and Fuel, a three-man team of graphic hardliners, whose work gloried in a brutal directness completely at odds with the times. From Brody to Why Not Associates, would-be progressive designers had made a point of noisily rejecting the 1960s' and 1970s' preference for strong visual concepts, exemplified by the work of Alan Fletcher and his colleagues at Pentagram. Now the commanding graphic idea, in an updated, contemporary form, became the preferred course of action for a new group of designers.

Graphic Thought Facility – its very name a little manifesto – was the 1990s design team most visibly connected to the tradition of the so-called 'big idea'. An emblematic GTF poster, designed in 1996 for a British Council graphic design exhibition, 'Work from London', renders the city's landmarks (Battersea Power Station, Big Ben, Tower Bridge) as items found on the table in a workers' caff (a mug of tea, a bottle of sauce, matchboxes and fags) to form a wittily informal map, showing locations in the capital where designers featured in the exhibition were based. The simplified linear outlines invoke similar scenes by Patrick Caulfield painted during the Pop Art years.

By comparison even with GTF, more recent designers favour an uncompromisingly reticent form of design where the aim seems to be to beguile the viewer with the smallest amount of fuss. Younger designers such as Eatock, James Goggin, Frith Kerr and Amelia Noble (Kerr/Noble), Kirsty Carter and Emma Thomas (A Practice for Everyday Life)

and Sara De Bondt would never resort to making wildly expressive marks in an egotistical signature style. Their work tends to be spare, orderly and delicate, but given life by elegant touches of whimsy – especially in the use of quirky typefaces that sometimes recall the stranger alphabetic blooms of the 1990s – and moments of charmingly wry humour. Eatock, whose most visible commissions are his series of optical eye logos for the *Big Brother* reality TV show, specializes in eccentric, concept-driven exercises that exist somewhere between design, art and performance. For *The world's largest signed and numbered limited edition artwork*, also undertaken for Channel 4, Eatock and nine other people spent 14 days signing one million numbered copies of a red postcard printed with the work's title.

Modernism revisited

Closer to the commercial heart of the profession, designers were also struggling with the question of direction now that a style based on strangulated typographic 'deconstruction' had run its course. As far back as the mid-1980s, some designers had been reassessing the possibilities of post-war typographic modernism. Both Brody and Saville had produced starkly simple designs, based on plain sans-serif typefaces and lashings of pure white space, but it was the design team 8vo, publishers of the manifesto/magazine *Octavo* (1986–92), who demonstrated the most knowledgeable and determined commitment to the principles espoused by Swiss modernists from Max Bill to Wolfgang Weingart. In the course of the 1990s it became clear that 8vo had exerted an influence on later designers that went much deeper than the passing craze for digital doodling. The design firms Cartlidge Levene, North,

Above: *Proclamations for a Beautiful City* (2006) was a collaboration between A Practice for Everyday Life and Alain de Botton for the Architecture Foundation. The writer's thoughts on beauty and architecture, posted on The Yard gallery's facade, are treated like phrases from a manifesto.

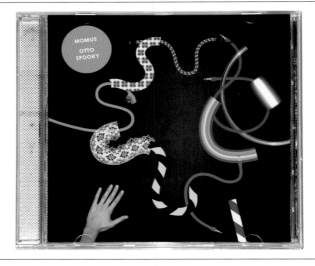

Above: CD graphics for the album *Otto Spooky* by Momus (2005), designed by James Goggin, who describes the cover image as a 'meandering path, stuck in an infinite loop and assembled in a bricolage construction of lyric references, cables, tubes and packing tape'.

Form and Content_Graphics

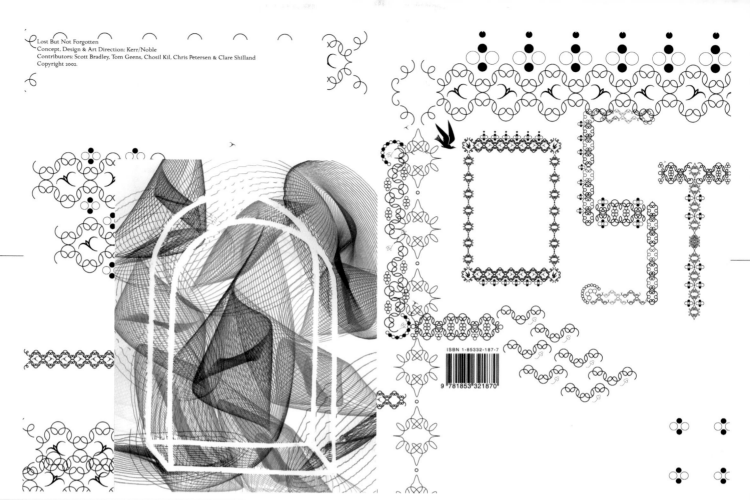

ISBN 1-85332-187-7

Laurie Britton Newell

Out of the Ordinary: Spectacular Craft

V&A Publications and the Crafts Council

Above and left: *Out of the Ordinary: Spectacular Craft* (2007), designed by Sara De Bondt for the Victoria & Albert Museum. The die-cut main title reveals the image below, while the uncovered spine, showing the stitched signatures, has the same feeling of a process exposed.

Top: Front and back cover of *Lost But Not Forgotten* (2002), edited, designed and self-published by Kerr/Noble. The typeface, specially created for the issue, was inspired by ornamental details seen in London's Highgate Cemetery: an informal, 21st-century update of tight-laced Victorian design.

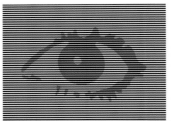 

This page: Daniel Eatock's ever-evolving identity based on an all-seeing eye for Channel 4's *Big Brother* has become a television landmark. In 2004 it was treated like land art as a series of marks in the British landscape, including a sand drawing on the beach in Carmarthenshire, Wales.

Above and right: MadeThought's bottle design and packaging for fashion designer Stella McCartney's In Two fragrance combines the use of graduated opaque glass to recall traditional ceramic bottles with angular contemporary forms. The aim was to endow the perfume with a fashionable image.

and Farrow Design – 8vo's most obvious successors – produced work that looked more European than British in its boyish passion for cleanly engineered visual structures built from typographic elements selected with precision and then locked into exactly the right position. What was most interesting about 8vo's work, though, was the way it picked up where Weingart left off, overlaying the functional frameworks of modernism with subjective devices that owed just as much to the postmodern influences that by then permeated international graphic design.

The latterday modernists who started emerging at the end of the 1990s tended not to concern themselves with these possibilities. Modernism's largely unstated though self-evident appeal as a less manifestly personal style was that it provided a readymade kit of parts that could be applied to almost any task – a CD cover, a mobile phone network, a bank – with the guarantee that, so long as its prescriptions were followed with consistency and taste, the results would look good. Another curious benefit of this 50-year-old style was that anything it touched would somehow look bang-up-to-date and even – contemporary gold dust – cool. Designers delving into the neo-modernist toolbox would, at a stroke, extricate themselves from the need to invent new kinds of form, devoting their efforts instead to subtle adjustments to the basic template to keep the familiar style looking fresh. Exponents included Spin (identity for the Whitechapel Art Gallery), SEA (brand identity for TV chef Jamie Oliver's Flavour Shaker), MadeThought (packaging for Stella McCartney's Stella In Two fragrances), and Bibliothèque (editorial design of the best-selling guide *How To Be a Graphic Designer, Without Losing Your Soul*). These designers also made

their allegiances fully explicit in various acts of homage. SEA organized an exhibition of posters by eminent Dutch modernist Wim Crouwel for their gallery. Spin, in collaboration with Mark Holt, founder of 8vo, put on a show of posters by Crouwel, Max Bill, Josef Müller-Brockmann, Karl Gerstner and other modernist heroes. Bibliothèque staged an exhibition, drawn from their own collection, of Otl Aicher's exemplary designs for the 1972 Munich Olympics at the impeccably modernist Vitsœ shelving company.

Although neo-modernism is now established as a vernacular so versatile and durable, so inoffensive and acceptable, that it seems unlikely to fall from favour any time soon, it is still possible to wrench it in unfamiliar directions. Kjell Ekhorn and Jon Forss, founders of Non-Format, succeeded in doing this with their designs for *Wire* new music magazine, from 2001 to 2005, where they combined a lean modernist grid, used to give the text a clear structure, with outbursts of intense emotional expression that harked back to the graphic excitement of the previous decade. They decorated and defaced headlines with plant-like tendrils, swirling out across the white voids around them and invading nearby pictures, or with wiry filaments that resembled the uncontrolled scribbles of a robot's damaged arm.

Craft, not style

Work like this, oscillating between tight typographic control and explosive graphic release, involves a high level of craft, and craft is today one priority on which most British graphic designers, whatever their stylistic predilections, are likely to agree. 'The idea of crafting something is important to us,' says Simon Earith of YES, a studio founded in 2004 by two former

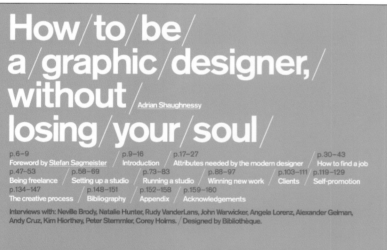

Left: The typographic confidence and inventive layouts of *How to Be a Graphic Designer, Without Losing Your Soul* (2005) are clearly signalled by Bibliothèque's cover design, which is unusually loaded with text, while communicating a positive message of pride in craft to its intended student readers.

Above: SEA Design's identity for TV chef and national food campaigner Jamie Oliver uses strong rounded forms to express his ebullient good humour and sense of purpose. It also connects the Oliver brand with the dominant neo-modernist currents of contemporary British design.

This page: In 2007, in an attempt to encourage debate about the design of the 2012 Olympics, Bibliothèque's founders exhibited their collection of 1972 Olympics designs by Otl Aicher at Vitsœ's London showroom. They regard the identity as 'one of the benchmarks of twentieth-century graphic design'.

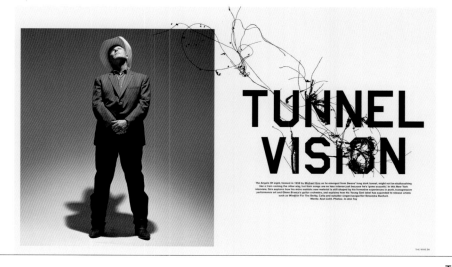

Above: Cover and spread from *Wire* (2003), showing a story about the American musician Michael Gira. Non-Format's layouts for the magazine, which is devoted to experimental music, unite strong photography – here by Jo Ann Toy – with expressive bursts of drawing.

Top: Spin's emphatically typographic identity for the Whitechapel Gallery was based on a modular system that could be applied to invitations, booklets, signage and exhibition posters (2003). Its lattice-like internal structure allowed it to float delicately within the images it branded.

art directors of Blue Source. 'It's craft that underpins our work,' notes Henrik Kubel, partner in A2/SW/HK. 'Tradition is great. Our work is not style – and it's not influenced by the latest filter.' A2/SW/HK's editorial designs, such as their book for the Victoria and Albert Museum's 'Cold War Modern' exhibition, are always based on typefaces they have designed specially for the project, a huge investment of extra time (they could, after all, simply use existing typefaces) that can only be described as a labour of love.

The renewed emphasis on craft, an article of faith among the neo-modernists shared by all the most highly regarded studios, is a perfectly logical answer to the graphic anarchy of the 1990s. Claims that it wasn't necessary to master the rules of design before presuming to break them, and that unchained individual intuition was all someone needed to create an original design, could lead only to the end of design as an organized activity if pursued to their natural conclusion. It was tantamount to saying that anyone could do it, and from a designer's point of view this was not a good message to spread at a time when ubiquitous personal computer power made do-it-yourself graphic design a possibility for anyone who cared to give it a try.

Craft was a way of reasserting the commercial and cultural necessity of graphic design as a professional activity best handled by experts. Moreover, digital tools meant that designs could now be tweaked and polished to levels of perfection unattainable when the task involved drawing inky lines on paper and sticking blocks of type to the artwork by hand. The danger is that craft can become an end in itself, a kind of fetish. Despite the high level of technical accomplishment that most of us take for granted now, contemporary graphic design can sometimes look over-processed, even sterile.

Music design – a dying art?

British graphic design has faced other kinds of pressure in the last decade. In the late 1970s and 1980s the field was energized and ultimately transformed by designers who chose to specialize in music graphics. An area once seen as peripheral by some seasoned designers because of its artistic freedom and lack of concern with proper 'problem solving' was now the source of much of the most inventive and original graphic design. The designers who emerged in the final days of the vinyl era, with its lavish 12-inch sleeves – Saville, Brody, Malcolm Garrett (1956–), Vaughan Oliver (1957–), Stylorouge, The Designers Republic – became emblematic of the new graphic Britain, and their designs, seen wherever the music was listened to, gained international recognition. Oliver's work for the 4AD independent record label in Wandsworth, south London received large exhibitions in Paris, Tokyo and Los Angeles, a level of attention given to few mainstream British designers, then or now.

Many of the young designers entering the field in the 1980s and early 1990s were introduced to the idea of a career in graphics by the record sleeves they had pored over as teenage music fans, and these experiences conditioned the assumptions they brought with them about the potential for self-expression through design. Designers such as Mark Farrow (1945–) (for the Pet Shop Boys), Tomato (Underworld), Tom Hingston (Massive Attack), Intro (Primal Scream) and Blue Source (Coldplay) continued this tradition, producing some of the most memorable British graphic design of the last

This page: Cover and spread of *Cold War Modern* (2008), which accompanied the Victoria and Albert Museum's exhibition about design in the post-war period. The industrial-looking display typeface designed for the book by A2/SW/HK suggests the mighty power blocs of a world divided on ideological lines.

20 years, even though the CD was now the primary means of distributing music, and only limited, if any, quantities of vinyl were produced. It was nevertheless still sometimes possible to break free from the straitjacket of the plastic jewel case and produce packaging that showed a commitment and care that was once standard with the 12-inch sleeve. Tom Hingston Studio's design for the double album *Abattoir Blues/The Lyre of Orpheus* (2004) by Nick Cave & the Bad Seeds is a beautifully crafted, cloth-covered slipcase holding two CDs, in pastel-coloured sleeves, and a lyric booklet printed on sturdy paper. The delicate hues, understated, almost classical typography and avoidance of graphic bombast create a deceptively sedate container – from this artist – for music that proves to possess as much raucous attack as Cave's audience has come to expect from him.

While the poster ceased to be a viable medium for regular graphic innovation in Britain as long ago as the 1960s, powerful music-related designs are occasionally still possible. In 2007 Village Green, another offshoot from Blue Source, designed a compellingly bizarre trio of posters for the Fabric nightclub in Smithfield, among them a photograph of a masked figure with a long, sinister, beak-like nose, a reference to the plague doctors who patrolled this part of London in the seventeenth century as the pestilence took its toll. The image mines a seam of dark cultural memory not usually accessible to the bright, smooth surfaces of neo-modernist design.

Music graphics made such a deep impression on the national design consciousness and were invested with so much feeling for so long that some find it hard to accept its day is over. It isn't quite. Good work is still being done, though it takes more digging than it once did to find it. Nevertheless,

big music labels care much less than they used to about the packaging of their artists, budgets are correspondingly smaller, and no one doubts that this is the age of the digital download, where the first image you will probably see, unless you insist on going to a shop, is a tiny little graphic on an mp3 player's minuscule display.

Book design – graphic experiment

If the album cover is in long-term decline, going the same way as the poster, then the book cover is one sector in which an uninhibited graphic sensibility continues to flourish, at least for now. Specialists in book-cover design don't always receive the acknowledgment they deserve, though the surface area they handle is larger than the more glamorous music designer's restricted canvas and book covers are displayed to make a greater impression in the shops. Yet some of the most resourceful designers still prefer to concentrate on this area, responding to the challenge of a highly competitive market with what is some of the most inventive graphic design seen in Britain today.

The most striking development has been the resurrection of Penguin – until recently a fallen champion of visual quality – as a publisher willing to try new design ideas that are more than equal to its former glories. The paperback covers designed from 2004 to 2008 by David Pearson and others for Penguin's Great Ideas series of short texts by the world's great thinkers are masterly interpretations of the styles of typography and layout current at the time the writing was first published. Yet, far from looking dated, or worse appearing to be no more than hackneyed pastiches, these images, luxuriously impressed into creamy paper, exude a

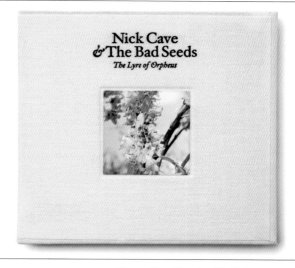

Right: Poster for Fabric nightclub in London (2007) by Tom Darracott of Village Green, one of a series based on characters concealed behind strange, handmade masks. Darracott wanted these figures 'to seem "believable" even though the masks they're wearing are entirely fantastical.'

Above: Tom Hingston Studio's slipcase for *Abattoir Blues/The Lyre of Orpheus* (2004) by Nick Cave & the Bad Seeds. Only by eschewing the plastic jewel case and devising alternative forms of CD container is it possible to match the presence of the old vinyl sleeve.

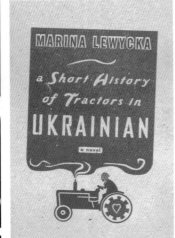

Above: Covers by Gray318 for the novels *Everything Is Illuminated* (2002) by Jonathan Safran Foer and *A Short History of Tractors in Ukrainian* (2005) by Marina Lewycka. Jonathan Gray's work shows the versatility of concept and style essential to successful book cover design.

Above and above left: Vince Frost and Matt Willey's design for the fifth issue of the literary magazine *Zembla* (2004) combines unexpectedly glamorous photography with playful layouts for articles such as an imaginary interview between novelist Geoff Dyer and the long-deceased philosopher Friedrich Nietzsche.

contemporary spirit of playful inquiry, reanimating authors such as Seneca, Montaigne and Kierkegaard for a new generation of readers.

Designers such as Jamie Keenan, John Gray (known as Gray318) and William Webb, in-house design director at Bloomsbury, show great versatility and range, moving deftly between graphic styles as each new project demands. Keenan's George Orwell covers for Penguin use overprinted circles of colour to mix new colours in the overlaps and generate a flexible, abstract, almost painterly series identity. Emblematic images drawn from the books, such as a cigarette for *Down and Out in Paris and London*, or a pig for *Animal Farm*, are also constructed from prismatic dots of colour. It was an audacious decision to present one of Britain's most influential twentieth-century writers in such a fresh and unusual way: the cover treatment, sidestepping any hint of Eng Lit worthiness, subtly asserts the writer's continuing relevance for contemporary readers.

Book covers permit a degree of expressiveness and even waywardness that more corporate areas of graphic design, often held in neo-modernism's tight grip, no longer allow. For American writer Jonathan Safran Foer's first novel, *Everything Is Illuminated* (2002), John Gray draws the author's name, title and cover blurb with strokes of white paint, filling the surface from edge to edge with informal, energetically dancing letterforms. This accurately conveys the exuberance of the writing, while underscoring the publisher's confidence in the book. Gray's cover for Marina Lewycka's best-selling novel *A Short History of Tractors in Ukrainian* (2005) responds to the unlikely title's droll visual cues with a title-piece that recalls the kind of deadpan farming motif seen on Soviet prints and

textiles of the revolutionary period. Combined with the title, this rough, simple image on tactile, brown paper proved irresistible to browsers.

Magazine and newspaper design

While the general standard of editorial design in Britain is higher than it has ever been, truly distinctive ventures – in the sense that *Nova* was distinctive in the 1960s or *The Face* in the 1980s – have occurred less often in commercial publishing in recent years. In publications aimed at wide audiences, marketing considerations tend to override visual concerns. Mass-market magazines make slick use of the formatting possibilities and production short cuts in programs such as QuarkXPress and Adobe InDesign, leading to intricate, much more highly worked pages than would once have been possible, but these developments entrench established editorial formulas rather than challenging them.

Departing from tried and tested conventions can be risky. The literary magazine *Zembla* (2003–5), one of the most original recent British magazines in its use of design, went bust after just eight issues, having failed to attract enough readers or sufficient advertising to sustain it. *Zembla*'s designers, Vince Frost and Matt Willey, proceeded from the assumption, shared by its publisher and its editor, that modern literary readers are as interested in how texts are presented as they are in the writing. Frost and Willey invented what was in effect a style magazine for bookworms. They poured text into unusual shapes, devised arrestingly visual opening spreads, scattered the pages with pictures, and put stylish photographs of highly educated film stars such as Rachel Weisz and Tilda Swinton, a contributing editor, on the cover.

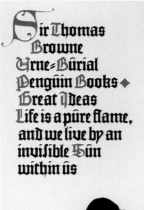

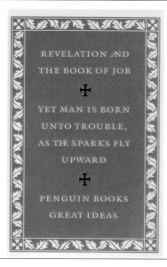

Above: Covers by David Pearson for the second series of Penguin's Great Ideas (2005): left to right, *Urne Burial* by Sir Thomas Browne, *Revelation and The Book of Job*, and *Fear and Trembling* by Søren Kierkegaard. Despite their typographic diversity, all clearly belong to the same collection.

Above: Cover by Jamie Keenan for Penguin's Orwell Centenary Edition of *Down and Out in Paris and London* (2003). The irregular placement of the Penguin logo within the black circle exemplifies the new freedom in the publisher's handling of its identity seen in recent years.

FENNESZ **BLACK SEA**

Hildur Gudnadóttir
Without Sinking

This page: Jon Wozencroft's design and photography establish a powerful atmospheric presence for his Touch label. Although he seeks to differentiate the musicians, a connecting narrative is evident in CD covers for *Black Sea* (2008) by Fennesz and *Without Sinking* (2009) by Hildur Gudnadóttir.

Form and Content_Graphics

If *Zembla* had succeeded, it would have been strong evidence that a new generation of readers that still keeps up with the latest Philip Roth really does now think in visual as well as verbal terms.

This idea of the visually engaged reader also helps to explain the impact of the most remarkable publishing project seen in Britain in recent times, the continuing evolution of the *Guardian*. The story began two decades ago, when the paper commissioned David Hillman, then a partner at Pentagram, to redesign it. In the landscape of British newspapers, the European panache of the *Guardian*'s new Helvetica look immediately established it as contemporary in a way that none of its broadsheet rivals could equal.

Over the next 15 years, Hillman, Simon Esterson and Mark Porter, appointed as design director, honed every aspect of the paper's design, underlining its commitment to an identity that was now regarded as a supremely effective brand, and maintaining the paper's lead over its competitors. A series of imaginative and beautifully designed special supplements on subjects such as surveillance and food consolidated the brand image.

In 2005 the paper's brilliantly managed move to a smaller page size, the Berliner format, and to full colour ushered in a new phase – despite the reservations of some former admirers, who were especially mortified by the loss of Hillman's classic masthead. If anything, Porter's redesign confirms that the *Guardian* has fully grasped the possibilities of using a consistent design approach across every aspect of its output, including its website, to make an attractive, informative, usable and entertaining news source that feels as boldly up-to-date as it is intelligent. The importance of design is never once forgotten, and no other British paper achieves such a carefully judged and nimble balance of content and form.

The 'designer as author'

The past two decades have also seen increasing numbers of projects initiated by designers who become in essence their own clients. There had always been a certain amount of British work of this kind, but it tended to happen piecemeal, on the side, and before the 1990s no one suggested that it might become a central activity, given equal weight with client work, let alone replace it. By the end of the 1980s some designers, particularly those involved in design education in the United States, were starting to talk about the 'designer as author', responsible for developing content, although the term took time to catch on in Britain, where pragmatically inclined designers are less disposed to theorize about their practice.

Jon Wozencroft (1958–), who studied graphic design at the London College of Printing, was a pioneering example of a designer committed to his own projects. His audiovisual magazine, *Touch*, started in 1982, consisted of a printed publication and a C90 audio cassette and, by the 1990s, had evolved into an independent record label, releasing albums by experimental musicians, with cover artwork by Wozencroft himself. The designs, based on his photographs of landscapes, counterpointed with delicate typography, become images for contemplation, infused with stillness and silence. The Touch catalogue, produced in addition to Wozencroft's collaborations with Neville Brody and his teaching activities at the Royal College of Art, now runs to dozens of releases.

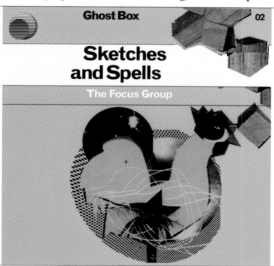
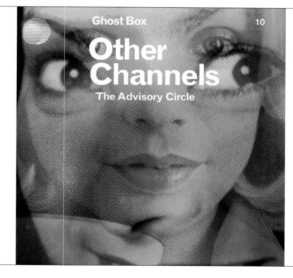

This page: Since its launch in 2004, Julian House's identity for his Ghost Box label has evolved, while maintaining a consistent visual theme, from the Penguin-esque structure and palette of *Sketches and Spells* (2004) to the surreal, full-bleed montage of *Other Channels* (2008).

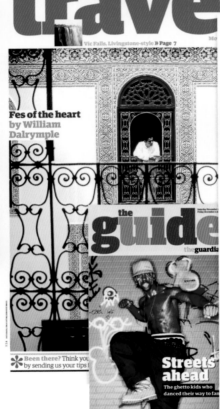

Form and Content_Graphics

This page and opposite: The 2005 redesign of the *Guardian* by Mark Porter, using the Guardian Egyptian typeface designed by Paul Barnes and Christian Schwarz. 'If everyone else is shouting louder and louder, the only way you can be heard is by talking in a normal tone of voice – or even whispering,' says Porter.

Irvine Welsh
Scotland's
murderous
heart

G2 Page 8

White alert - next summer's must-have colour,
G2 Page 12

Catherine Bennett
The men who
fuel the sex trade

G2 Page 7

The world's most
expensive mobile

Technology Page 6

£0.60

Thursday 20.10.05
Published
in London and
Manchester
guardian.co.uk

theguardian

'I am the president of Iraq.
I do not recognise this court'

Arguments and scuffling as defiant Saddam appears on mass murder charge

Jonathan Steele

Combative and truculent, Iraq's former dictator, Saddam Hussein, argued with the judge and scuffled with security guards yesterday as he went on trial for mass murder in a Baghdad courtroom that was as much a theatre as a forum for justice. Beamed across the Middle East on television, the trial marked the first criminal proceedings against an Arab leader in modern times.

Echoing the defiance he showed when first charged last year, Saddam refused to give his name when asked to confirm his identity. "I am the president of Iraq," he said. "You know me," he told Judge Rizgar Mohammed Amin, a Kurd. When the session opened, he stood and asked Amin: "Who are you? I want to know who you are."

Denouncing the American invasion and making it clear he was appealing to a world audience, he said: "I do not respond to this so-called court, with all due respect to its people, and I retain my constitutional right as the president of Iraq." Brushing off the judge's attempts to interrupt him, he declared: "Neither do I recognise the body that has designated and authorised you, nor the aggression, because all that has been built on a false basis." Later he objected to being referred to as "former" president.

Five black-robed judges sat in the specially-built courtroom in the marble building that once served as the National Command Headquarters of the Ba'ath party in what is now the fortified Green Zone. Only the presiding judge's face was seen on TV. His name had come out in the media earlier.

The broadcast was subject to a deliberate 30-minute delay to allow for control over what went out and give the authorities the chance to censor Saddam's comments. After the three-hour hearing the judge adjourned the trial until November 28, saying that around 30 or 40 witnesses

Guardian
journalist
abducted
in Baghdad

Ewen MacAskill

The Guardian's Iraq correspondent, Rory Carroll, was last night missing after being kidnapped by gunmen in Baghdad. Carroll, 33, an experienced foreign correspondent, had been conducting an interview in the city with a victim of Saddam Hussein's regime. He had been preparing an article for today's paper on the opening of the former dictator's trial yesterday.

Carroll, who was accompanied by two drivers and a translator, was confronted by the gunmen as he left the house where he had been carrying out the interview. He and one of the drivers were bundled into cars. The driver was released about 20 minutes later.

Carroll has been in Iraq since January. He volunteered for the assignment and his coverage has been critical of the US-led coalition. Before Iraq, he had been the pa-

Rory Carroll, 33,
the Guardian's
correspondent in
Baghdad, who was
abducted after
interviewing an
Iraqi family

per's correspondent in Africa, based in Johannesburg, since 2002. In the previous three years he had been based in Rome, where he covered the aftermath of the Kosovo war.

He was born in Dublin, attended university there and worked for various Irish papers before moving to London. He has an Irish passport. The Irish government was last night in contact with its embassies throughout the Middle East to try to secure help in finding him.

Alan Rusbridger, the Guardian's editor, said: "We're deeply concerned at Rory's disappearance. He is in Iraq as a professional journalist — and he's a very good, straight journalist whose only concern is to report fairly and truthfully about the country. We urge those holding him to

In 2004 a similar engagement with music – often found among graphic designers – led Julian House, a designer at Intro, to launch the Ghost Box independent label, with Jim Jupp, a composer. House records for the label as The Focus Group; Jupp as The Belbury Poly. Ghost Box's covers are based on a consistent grid and title style that immediately brings to mind Penguin book covers of the 1960s. Surreal, monochromatic fragments of photographs evoke memories of modernist montage and post-war science fiction, and a feeling that the uncanny can be found in the ordinary. 'Penguin belongs to a particular post-war consensus that we're drawn to, a particularly modernist culture for the common man sensibility,' says House.

Since the early 1990s, in the field of print, Fuel – started by Peter Miles, Damon Murray and Stephen Sorrell – has been the design team most consistently dedicated to its own projects. They began publishing their own magazine, also titled *Fuel*, while still MA students at the Royal College of Art, and this led to self-initiated books and short films, in which they combined words and images to produce sharp and sometimes gnomic visual commentaries on social themes. Since Miles left the team, Fuel has blossomed into a small independent publishing house, alongside its design work, producing volumes about Russian tattoos, street notices and folk artifacts, visual surveys devoted to record sleeves, old football programmes and arcane images from the Internet, and, in a new departure, a warped comic interpretation of the romantic novel genre by the artist Jake Chapman. Here, they function not as originators of content, but as editorial enablers for other authors, who share their interest in quirky popular culture and in harder, more disturbing subject matter, as in

the frequently obscene tattoo books or Alix Lambert's *Crime* (2008). Fuel's discreet visual signature, expressed in typography, paper choice and binding, sets the books apart from more ordinary publishers' fare. Browns, founded by Jonathan Ellery, is another example of a design company that has started its own imprint, Browns Editions, with books by photographers and two volumes by the acerbic British satirical illustrator Paul Davis.

Designers on design

These projects testify to a vigorous design scene that can sometimes extend far beyond the traditional model of graphic design as merely a service for communicating other people's messages. Designers tend to be the most highly motivated custodians of this design culture, with a deep interest in its history and development, and here too British designers have made a mark in the last two decades. Numerous designers have authored books about the subject, usually undertaking both the writing and the design. Notable examples include Robin Kinross's *Modern Typography: An Essay in Critical History* (revised in 2004), published by his own imprint, Hyphen Press; David Crow's *Visible Signs: An Introduction to Semiotics* (2003); and Lucienne Roberts' *Good: An Introduction to Ethics in Graphic Design* (2006).

Dot Dot Dot magazine was launched in 2000 by Stuart Bailey, a British designer educated in the Department of Typography and Graphic Communication at Reading University, and Peter Bilak, a Slovakian designer. The magazine has outgrown its beginnings as a journal focused primarily on visual communication (though it never remotely resembled a trade publication) to become one of the most

Above: The three volumes of *Russian Criminal Tattoo* (2003–8), edited, designed and published by Fuel, explore a history of graphic expression previously unknown outside the criminal subculture. Drawings and photographs document the sometimes shocking symbols and the text analyses their meaning.

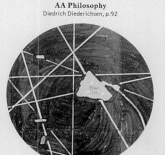

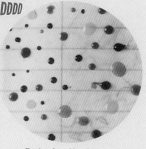

Equation for a Composite Design (3)
Stuart Bailey, p.76

AA Philosophy
Diedrich Diederichsen, p.92

Design for a New Disease
John Körmeling, p.48

...n human natur..
..eelings and songs, that
..wn out or shout down the st...
..aking of Orange Juice, The M...
..b, Dexy's Midnight Runners, A...
..een forgotten. The aesthetic ac...
..y rock, and queer culture-led j...
..tributed to this hardly spect...
..music. A few years later, T

DDDDDDD

( )

THOMAS BELLER'S

THE SLEEP-
OVER ARTIST

In the same way J.D. Salinger
carved out the niche of mail
...escence...Thomas Beller
...at mutable boy-to-

A Coming Of Age Reading Checklist
Brian McMullen, p.19

T...
VAR...
...

..pen some
Saturday in Ma,
reveal anything abo...
name Czech Dream (...
days before its 'opening...
that the new temple of con...
ed its customers in Prague
trict. [...]
    But no new hypermar'
one on the outskirts of Pra
Vít Klusák and Filip R
shooting a documenta
advantage of peo...
They alleged...

Manchester City Centre
Jim Medway (pullout)

Czech Dream Project
Antonín Kosík, p.71

88   *J.J. King: L*

...LLE'S CRI...
...er, and seeks the assis...
...uction:

What is certain is t
conform to proper ac...
tions. Perhaps the ac...
in his undertaking '
mental faculties. T'
betrayed a lifel...
not for a m...

'... I am anxious to have a shor
My name is Smith, Mr Robert Smit'
explosive clock.'
    'Charmed to meet you, Lord Ar
    'Don't look so alarmed, it is my dut'

said:

..hat the opposite is
..'s too fucking obviou'
..s and people

Dead Americans (excerpt)
J.J. King, p.82

...es with a pe...
...ex who performs such ...
...g you of personal birthdays, p.
foreign cities, and locating hard-t...
l member reportedly dispatched a c...
...ead Sea by motorcycle to return with...
s school project in London).

t color signifies exclusivity now? It's no...
f silver, nor the flash of gold, not even
...of platinum. The ultimate privele...
...city – total privacy and absolut...

Cloak & Dagger
Steve Rushton, p.86

Equation for a Composite Design (2)
Stuart Bailey, 60

(nothing)

..othing. This is the conclusion ...
..nothing' has been studied by ph...
..ly depending on the cultural ba...
..und in the work of Thomas Aq...
..was creatio ex nihilo. The en...
..he's Faust sets out on his '
..d my All.' Hegel writ
.. East, the ...

ocatief
xtra
dubbeldik
ulnummer
royaal

Black, American, Express
David Reinfurt, p.30

Journal of High-Principled Typography
Karel Martens, p.65

About Nothing, Really
Peter Biľak, p.107

ISBN 90-77620-02-8

Above: A remarkable amount of visual material once hidden in the archives of libraries and other institutions is now available online. *BibliOdyssey* (2007), published by Fuel, presents images and links from the blog of the anonymous 'PK', who trawls the Internet looking for visual wonders to share.

Right: Cover of *Dot Dot Dot* no. 8 (2004), edited, designed and published by Stuart Bailey and Peter Biľak. The typographically sober but always quirky and unpredictable publication occupies an editorial position somewhere between a conventional visual arts magazine and an academic journal.

original magazines of its moment. In London, Spin has initiated a series of broadsheets – entitled *Spin* – in which it has published lists of designers' favourite reading and an issue called 'Action Time Vision' devoted to design educator Russell Bestley's exhaustive PhD research into the punk record sleeve.

A similar publish-it-yourself energy can be found in the blogosphere, where some graphic designers have been quick to seize the opportunity to record their opinions on design for the benefit of colleagues. 'Thought for the Week', a blog by Michael Johnson of Johnson Banks, is one of the most consistently interesting, offering timely subjects and well-chosen visuals. 'Ace Jet 170' is less discursive, concentrating on graphic and typographic material chosen with an unerring eye. Reading it regularly is like being welcomed into the designer's studio and given the opportunity to delve into private treasures hidden in the plan chests and tucked away on the shelves. Since 2007 the field has even had its own radio show, *Graphic Design on the Radio*, on London-based community radio station Resonance FM, in which presenter (and designer) Adrian Shaughnessy has interviewed Neville Brody, Jonathan Barnbrook and other designers, offering them the chance to play their favourite music between bursts of conversation.

The future: democratization and branding

There is some irony in the fact that these developments have occurred at a time when the future of graphic design is by no means certain. It may be that these more inward-looking expressions and celebrations of what graphic designers can do represent a diversion of energy as old outlets are blocked.

Right: Personal blogs allow designers to open the drawers of their private design collections and show them off to colleagues online. In this post from 2007, 'Ace Jet 170' – 'Found type, print and stuff' – presents the first instalment of his collection of Pelican non-fiction titles.

Found type, print and stuff

ABOUT

SEARCH

[search]

MY OTHER PLACES

My Twitterings

Mr V's Book (extracts from)

Mr B's Book (in brief)

My flickr

My del.icio.us

ELSEWHERE

New DIN Microsite

PUFF

Fuck You, Penguin
Via Dan Germain

Typo Tour of London

As if by magic: The four minute book

Spend your way out of the shit

How To Keep Awake While Reading

Polaroid lives!
Via Swiss Miss

Everyone's new favourite font family just got bigger

Pierre Mendell on Design Boom

CATEGORIES

Books

Chickens

Collage

Designers

Events

Fletcher Week

Found Type Friday

Helvetica Week

Lost in (the loft) Space

Lyddle End 2050

Maps

Music

Online Trickery

Pelican Books

Penguin Books

Penguin Poets

Penrose

Photography

Plot Watch

Postal

Print

Television

Things

Tickets

Travel

Type

Uncommon Knowledge

RECENT POSTS

Fulltron

The Return of Descriptive Geometry with 3D Figures

Safety

Duck Fight Season

« Uncommon Knowledge: 005 | Main | MICA ID »

All My Pelicans: Part 1

Every now and then I mention my loft-based Pelican collection and make an empty promise to get them online. Well here they are, or at least nearly half of them. You may have seen some of them before but I'm trying to get them all together and present them in a consistent way (on a knackered old box).

Stand out covers include Jock Kinnier's startlingly contemporary design for *Sex in Society*, the brilliant David Gentleman's cover for *Aspects of the Novel* and Herbert Spencer's cunning solution for *A Short History of Religion*.

03 April 2007 in Pelican Books | Permalink

Q▾ (Find)

Older | Home | Newer

20.06.07
All change

It's official. The age of the static brand is coming to an end. Organisations, companies, institutions, even charities are realizing that having identity schemes that 'flex' and adapt to circumstances are more appropriate in the multi-channel, multi-lingual world that brands now inhabit.

Over-controlled brands are starting to look stiff and old-fashioned, but not all clients (and certainly not all design companies) have yet woken up to this latest shift.

It's not as though we didn't have any warning. As long ago as the 70s, this fantastic scheme for Boston's WGBH TV was developed, where the channel's numeral keeps modulating for different stings.

The germ of this identity was developed in the USA when MTV launched with many adaptations of their channel bumpers and was developed again in the UK with the schemes for Channel 4 and BBC2. More recently TV Asahi in Japan has taken some of these ideas even further.

Thought for the week is a regular posting-place for the visual and verbal observations of London design consultancy johnson banks.

Follow this link if you want to see some recent work.

If you want to comment or suggest something yourself please contact thought@johnsonbanks.co.uk

Feeds: (RSS 2.0 or Atom)

Latest thoughts
29.04.09
Time Flies

28.04.09
It's great. But did it work?

24.04.09
From the archive: Paper Advisory Service Posters

21.04.09
Let them eat Teacake

20.04.09
OAB's at St Brides

Thoughts by month

2009
May
April
March
February
January

2008
December
November
October
September
August
July
June
May
April
March
February
January

2007
December
November
October
September
August
July
June
May
April
March
February
January

2006
December
November
October
September
August
July
June
May
April
March
February

Best thoughts so far...

about crowdsourcing design
about hanging on to obsolete software
about branding's future
about blogging
about brand Obama
about designer monographs
about turning into Monocle man
about found alphabets
about moodboards
about guitars and graphics
about how designers can never agree
about how to do a Pecha Kucha
about how long a logo lasts
about explaining design to children
about the economics of design
about the questions we often get asked
about working for La Villette
about eighties design
about making clients value design a little more
about the copyright of ideas
about going green
about hidden design
about D&AD's annual covers
about Indian billboards
about logo design
about sketchbooks
about subway maps
about Mr B's book
about accidental design
about the early days of design companies
about designing ethically
about flexible identities
about Olympic logos
about Save the Children
about student portfolios
about design education
about the future of graphic design
about the end of a style
about the crossover of design and advertising
about design awards
about reading lists for designers
about Alan Fletcher
about Japan
about rounded typefaces

Q▾ (Find)

27.02.09
End of February Timepieces

Here are some more of the time pieces readers have sent in this month.

Matt Hallock sent us the image above saying 'it's how much gas $20 purchases for a 10 gallon car'.

Ben Archer in New Zealand sent us this flywheel: 'I've had the attached image for longer than I recall. A photographer friend gave me a watch with a revealed movement. I put it on my trusty flatbed scanner. The movement of the flywheel on the left generated the interference patterns as the scanner head passed underneath it'.

Thought for the week is a regular posting-place for the visual and verbal observations of London design consultancy johnson banks.

Follow this link if you want to see some recent work.

If you want to comment or suggest something yourself please contact thought@johnsonbanks.co.uk

Feeds: (RSS 2.0 or Atom)

Latest thoughts
02.04.09
So Very Fooled?

01.04.09
So Very Different

31.03.09
Cats and their designers

29.03.09
What made you want to be a graphic designer?

24.03.09
How not to launch a new logo

Thoughts by month

2009
April
March
February
January

2008
December
November

Best thoughts so far...

about branding's future
about blogging
about brand Obama
about designer monographs
about turning into Monocle man
about found alphabets
about moodboards
about guitars and graphics
about how designers can never agree
about how to do a Pecha Kucha
about how long a logo lasts
about explaining design to children
about the economics of design
about the questions we often get asked
about working for La Villette
about eighties design
about making clients value design a little more
about the copyright of ideas
about going green
about hidden design
about D&AD's annual covers
about Indian billboards
about logo design
about sketchbooks
about subway maps
about Mr B's book
about accidental design

This page: Screens from Michael Johnson's 'Thought for the Week' blog. In a post from 2007 (above right), he considers the ways that logos such as the BBC2 television ident can now be interpreted in different styles yet still preserve the essential elements of their identity.

As many designers sensed would happen, the arrival of desktop technology changed not only the nature of practice and production, but the nature of their relationship with clients. Graphic design and typography were no longer arcane endeavours to which only specialists – designers – had access. The fact that everyone uses essentially the same digital tools in business and at home – choosing preferred typefaces from drop-down menus, laying out documents and presentations, modifying digital photos, customizing social networking profiles – has demystified design.

Organizations and businesses have a better understanding of what it involves and are more likely to express or impose their views. In the early days of graphic design, designers had considerably more freedom to do exactly what they liked, assuring their clients that it was in their best interests. Today design-aware, cost-conscious, efficiency-minded clients are much less likely to accept the 'trust me, I'm a designer' argument. They want firmer guarantees that the design is going to do exactly what they want it to do.

At the same time, the idea of branding has emerged as the central concern of visual communication. It is now so familiar that it has become an everyday term, which certainly wasn't the case 20 years ago. According to Wally Olins (who writes on this subject later in this book), a brand is simply the personality of a product, organization or service. Olins, co-founder of Wolff Olins in the 1960s, has in recent years rebranded himself and now, as chairman of Saffron Brand Consultants, he brings the same missionary zeal to branding in his books *On Brand* (2003) and *The Brand Handbook* (2008) that he once brought to corporate identity.

Any design company hoping to succeed in today's marketplace must come to terms with the new language of branding and its imperatives.

Branding has been so successful that it has spread rapidly beyond the commercial world, where brands have always existed, into Britain's visual arts community, once immune from such market-conscious considerations. National galleries now regard themselves not simply as collections housed in impressive buildings that require logos to put on letterheads and the spines of catalogues, but as valuable brands that need to attract the public in great numbers by expressing the essence of their 'personality' in a consistent manner through every visual communication they send into the world. The Tate Gallery's new identity, introduced when Tate Modern opened in 2000 at the former Bankside Power Station, had to encompass four institutions: the old Tate Gallery (now Tate Britain), Tate Liverpool and Tate St Ives, as well as the new site. Wolff Olins' blurred Tate logo felt unusually contemporary for a national gallery, and its application in varying degrees of optical focus showed that an art organization with a competitive global presence could make visual flexibility key to its image – this, again, suggested an attractively contemporary attitude.

Yet the idea of strong arts branding also had its critics among designers. Surely what mattered most, some argued, was the identity of the art that a gallery happened to be showing at the time. The Barbican Art Gallery's brand identity by North (2004) revealed the drawback. The heavy, slanting typography, based on the Futura typeface, dominated everything, swamping the visual character of the art. Why should the idea of an institution take precedence over the

This page: The Tate brand developed by Wolff Olins (2000) was intended to challenge visitors to look again at the institution. The logos move in and out of focus, 'suggesting the dynamic nature of Tate – always changing but always recognizable,' say the designers.

Form and Content_Graphics

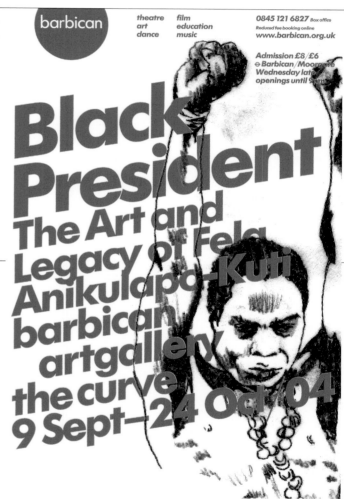

This page: North's typographic identity for the Barbican Art Gallery (2004) applied to exhibition posters for British artist Helen Chadwick, African musician Fela Kuti and American architect Daniel Libeskind. While the subject matter and visual content are highly varied, the branding remains the same.

cultural work that it exists to show? And, anyway, wasn't this work supposed to provide viewers with a form of experience quite separate from the commercial and branding concerns that pervade everyday life?

The Olympic logo – the end of an era?

The ultimate measure of the power of branding and its potential to command attention came in 2007, with the launch of the London 2012 Olympic and Paralympic Games symbol. This is without question the biggest, most contentious graphic design story of the last 20 years. According to the designers, Wolff Olins, and London's Organizing Committee, the angular, deliberately dissonant fragments, representing the numbers 2012, are supposed to convey London's qualities as an edgy, modern city. They say the brand is intended for everyone, regardless of age, culture and language, and that it will inspire a global audience of four billion people.

The immediate response was almost universal criticism. Members of the public ridiculed the £400,000 symbol as 'bad Stone Age art', as a couple engaged in a sex act, and as something that looks like it was designed in the 1980s (which it does). Stephen Bayley, the first director of the Design Museum, branded the brand 'a puerile mess, an artistic flop and a commercial scandal'. An online petition attempted to get it scrapped and mischievous publications piled in by inviting readers to come up with a better design of their own. Some found the symbol's attempts to appeal to young people by referring to graffiti tags (or signatures) in its shape to be strained and patronizing – this was the work of a big, calculating branding agency, after all, not the spontaneous expression of a street artist.

The symbol's problem is that to view it in its flat, static state is to see it in its most ungainly and least engaging form. It is designed to be flexible, to change outline and colour, to be filled in with images and pattern, to move around in animations. Wolff Olins insists that we can expect to see it evolve, and maybe, when it comes alive in use, it will start to win people over. While the public's dismay and scorn wasn't what the designers and organizers hoped for, it certainly showed that people want to be involved, because it would be pointless to disown something so virulently if you didn't want to feel a sense of ownership in the first place. People clearly expect to identify with significant symbols because of what they stand for and design does have the potential to express emotional meaning.

We will have to wait until 2012 to find out whether the branding works, or whether it is as monstrously misguided as some claim. Either way, especially when compared with the aesthetic and functional triumph of the 1972 Olympics design system, it suggests the end of an era. There is nothing remotely precious about the 2012 symbol, which owes far more to popular culture than it does to the austere modernism that some designers find so hard to relinquish. The pressing question for British graphic design is whether it can adapt to changes that pose deep challenges to its traditions and standards without losing itself on the way.

Form and Content_Graphics

Right and opposite: The jagged
outlines of the Olympic 2012 logo,
designed by Wolff Olins in 2007,
form a graphic container that can
be filled up with different kinds
of imagery and pattern, from
photographs of sporting activity
to easily identifiable fragments
of the national flag.

Demand the Impossible

Fashion
Susannah Frankel

In 1976, the fashion designer Vivienne Westwood (1941–), the punk legend Jordan and the singer Chrissie Hynde were photographed at Westwood and her then partner Malcolm McLaren's notorious King's Road boutique, SEX. In this now iconic image, all the participants are wearing the type of rubber clothing, inspired by fetish and pornography, for which the store was famous. Westwood herself, however though wearing black PVC trousers and a pair of platform-soled boots is otherwise dressed in nothing more subversive than a crisp white masculine shirt.

This apparently classic garment might seem unremarkable by comparison, were it not for the fact that it is printed with the famous French Situationist slogan 'Be reasonable: demand the impossible' – five words (originally anonymous graffiti on a Parisian wall) that could, in fact, not unreasonably be used to encapsulate not only Westwood's own trajectory but indeed that of the contemporary British fashion industry as a whole.

Certainly it is unimaginable that anyone hailing from the rather more cushioned European designer fashion system might have conceived such an aggressively sloganeering garment, or for that matter one with such clearly denoted intellectual pretensions. The young Yves Saint Laurent (1936–2008), for example, spent his early years tortured by internal demons, certainly, but never had to fight to ensure his craft was afforded the respect it was due. He was originally inspired, he often said, simply by his mother's great beauty. A renowned socialite of privileged background, she cast a spell on her young son, who used to watch in wonderment as she prepared to go out in the evening. Jean-Paul Gaultier (1952–), meanwhile, enfant terrible or no, first identified his affinity with fashion while knitting clothing for his teddy bears. This time it was his grandmother who showed him the

way. In Italy, meanwhile, even Gianni Versace (1946–97), famously of humble southern Italian stock, learned everything he needed to know from his mother, a dressmaker, and from the sophisticated northern cities of his home country, where fashion was – and is – a revered part of everyday life.

In Britain, fashion is not embraced in so wholehearted a manner. Instead, this essentially Protestant nation has for centuries frowned upon the frivolity of self-adornment, viewing it as nothing more than a flagrant demonstration of vanity. Fashion that is conceptual by nature is more mistrusted still: a dress is a dress, the thinking goes, a no-nonsense garment designed to cover women's bodies in an attractive – but preferably not too attractive – way. To this day, the British are deeply suspicious of the French tendency to spend a significant proportion of their salary on clothing – witness the rise and rise of Primark and its ilk. The Italian aesthetic is similarly frowned upon, often judged as over-embellished or just plain vulgar.

The story of British fashion, then, and of the youth culture with which it is inextricably linked, is that of the triumph of creativity, provocation and also audacity in the face of adversity. Britain, with its uniform-obsessed society and repressive class system, has been responsible for many of the most grand-scale sartorial gestures of modern times. Grand-scale, to a greater or lesser extent, because they are reactionary – flying in the face of a proudly anachronistic adherence to hierarchy, rejecting dress codes that have more often been prescribed than a product of self-expression, and finally, reacting to the fact that – let's be honest – fashion is still not something it's seemly to take very seriously.

Conversely, and stretching right back to the post-war period, the young and creative have consistently

Susannah Frankel

Top left: Queen Elizabeth II wears a gown designed by Norman Hartnell for her coronation in 1953. The history of British fashion decrees that tradition should be both embraced and subverted. Aspiration is key, as is the ability of the young to appropriate conservative dress codes – and the pomp and circumstance of the British monarchy in particular.

Left: As well as ceremonial dress, the countrified looks of the British aristocracy have provided inspiration for everyone from Vivienne Westwood to Burberry's Christopher Bailey. The Duke and Duchess of Windsor, here photographed at Ednam Lodge, Sunningdale, in 1946, epitomized this style perfectly.

Above: The high priestess of punk and grande dame of British fashion Vivienne Westwood is photographed in 1976 at her notorious King's Road boutique, SEX. She is wearing a masculine white shirt emblazoned with the French Situationist slogan 'Be reasonable: demand the impossible'. This could be a mantra for British fashion as a whole. Also in the picture are Steve Jones, Alan Jones, Jordan, and Chrissie Hynde, a shop assistant at the time.

Above: Beatlemania swept the world both musically and sartorially. The sharp-dressing glossy-haired bright young things influenced the wardrobes of an entire generation. Here they are photographed backstage at the BBC Old Paris Cinema, London, in 1963.

Above: The symbiotic relationship between British music and fashion is highly significant: the radical nature of both creative industries has provided valuable cross-fertilization since the mid-twentieth century. Here Mick Jagger and Bianca Pérez-Mora Macías are photographed just after their wedding in Saint-Tropez, France, on 12 May 1971, wearing white tailored trouser suits by the tailor Tommy Nutter.

Top right: It is not only British fashion designers who have set the standards for youth culture internationally in the modern age. Fashion photographers and models, too, have consistently broken the bourgeois mould and pushed their respective professions forward. In this instance, David Bailey sets up a shot of his then partner Jean Shrimpton, c.1963.

demonstrated that fashion is not only a vital force via which to express individuality, but also a medium that allows young people to aspire to greater things and to appropriate the sartorial vocabulary of their more conservative elders. And they have done so extremely effectively. After all, whether their treatment of it is ironic, heartfelt or both, this is a language they have grown up with and understand, whatever their background may be. Any sentimental rags-to-riches style pigeonholing aside, (and the media in particular find such fairytale fodder almost impossible to resist), the determination and spirit involved in establishing oneself as a big name in fashion in Britain are very real indeed.

Here is Alexander McQueen speaking on the subject at the end of the last millennium, and long before he had become the major international fashion force he is today:

I was literally three years old when I started drawing. I did it all my life, through primary school, secondary school, all my life. I always, always wanted to be a designer. I read books on fashion from the age of 12. I followed designers' careers. I knew Giorgio Armani was a window-dresser, Emanuel Ungaro was a tailor. People just ignored me. That was fine. I was doing it for myself. But I always knew I would be something in fashion. I didn't know how big, but I always knew I'd be something. I don't think you can become a good designer, or a great designer. To me, you just are one. I think to know about colour, proportion, shape, cut, balance is part of a gene. Yeah, there has been this big thing about the East End yob made good but, you know, the press started that, not me. The press started that, and I played on it. It's the Michael Caine syndrome, Pygmalion. But at the end of the day, you're a good designer or not and it doesn't matter where you come from. The East End boy who worked on Savile Row. The East End boy who worked wherever ... whatever ...

Above: With their slicked-back hair and prohibitively expensive tailored jackets, the Teddy Boys transformed the art of dressing to impress into an act of defiance – the peacock male at his most unabashed.

Skinheads and Daisy Dolls

The genesis of modern British fashion has its roots in the street culture of the 1950s. The war time 'Utility' rationing scheme, with specially designed furniture and clothing that made the most economical use possible of scarce raw materials, planted the seed of the idea that the immovable class system the nation was founded upon might finally be breaking down. This not only provided practical benefits, in as much as the lower classes were offered just the same product as those with means, but also raised design consciousness more broadly. By the end of the 1950s employment for all, decreased production costs and increased exports led to a consumer boom. At the same time, youth culture was establishing itself in Britain. Whereas before the war men and women dressed like children until their late teens and then adopted the wardrobe attire of their parents, by the late 1950s they had their own distinctive style.

'The single most important fact about teenagers of this time [the late 1950s] is that, after the war, Britain experienced its highest birth rate since 1880,' writes Catherine McDermott in *Street Style: British Design in the 1980s*. 'By 1959 there were 4,000,000 single persons aged between 13 and 25. For the first time teenagers emerged as a power in the market. They enjoyed a special status, more money than before and the freedom to enjoy it without the usual constraints of age, family or career obligations.'

The potent visual imagery that these teenagers conceived has influenced British fashion from that time forward. And the main protagonists were remarkable for the fact that they were, almost without exception, working class. They had found jobs and had their own disposable income while their middle-class peers were still at school and only

Above: Young Mods in Britain, c.1964. Until the late 1950s, young people on the cusp of adulthood had emulated the styles of their elders. From the late 1950s onwards, however, tribes of young women and men in particular established diverse and highly coded looks that couldn't have been further from that of their parents', as this image of booted and suited young Mods goes to show.

Opposite: Teenagers gathering on the beach at Brighton in 1965. The potent visual imagery conceived by British teenagers in the latter part of the 1950s and throughout the 1960s influenced fashion – and fashion for young people in particular – the world over. While internationally fashion had largely been a middle- and upper-class concern, in Britain at this point the main protagonists were remarkable for the fact that they were almost without exception working class.

Top: The language of punk decreed that anybody could make a statement through the way that they dressed, whatever their sex, age, body size or class. Standing out in a crowd was the point.

Above: Paradoxically, the punk movement had more in common with ceremonial dress than with the prevailing bland fashions of the time. By now, punks were as iconic a marker of the London landscape as Her Majesty the Queen herself.

Above: The British photographer Nick Knight famously spent much of his early career documenting skinhead dress and culture – a sub-section of British society that was largely ignored and even reviled but with an enormously elevated sense of fashion and label awareness.

dreaming of better things to come. The Teddy Boys, with their expensive Edwardian-style tailored jackets, drainpipe trousers, DayGlo socks and beetle-crusher shoes, turned the combing of one's coiffed hair in public into an act of defiance – this was the peacock male and his unabashed vanity made his more straitlaced upper-class counterparts quake in their Oxfords. They were only the first in a long line of increasingly elaborate and 'dressed-up' street subcultures, soon to be joined by Vespa-riding Mods and the much maligned and somewhat misconstrued skinheads.

The British photographer Nick Knight famously spent his early career documenting the latter. 'Thirty years ago, when I worked on *Skinheads*, they were largely culturally ignored in much the same way as so-called chavs are today,' he argues. 'But actually their sense of fashion was enormously elevated, really strict and coded. They would only buy into certain labels and even then they were very specifically aware, for example, of the date of a certain Ben Sherman shirt as signified by nothing more obvious than where the buttons were placed.' The skinheads are particularly interesting given that the aggressively masculine, no-frills precision of their look was clearly a reaction against the more obviously dandified – and indeed openly nostalgic – styles sold on Carnaby Street at that time. 'But they were just as passionate and devoted,' Knight explains.

If you had the wrong pair of shoes or the wrong pair of socks you just didn't cut it and today the so-called chavs have an equally rigorous dress code. You don't really get that in Europe apart from, to a certain degree, with the immigrant populations in the suburbs of major cities. That way of expressing who you are through the way you dress is steeped in British street culture and that sort of very precise awareness of what you should and shouldn't wear.

If the Teddy Boys looked, in fact, to America for inspirations, and Mods to Italy, Mary Quant (1934–), the single most influential British women's wear designer of the 1960s, was interested in historical clothing that was closer to home, taking the staples of Edwardian dress – and specifically Edwardian children's dress – and reinventing it in surprising fabrics – PVC in particular – to reflect the optimistic spirit of the day. Quant, who opened Bazaar on London's King's Road with her husband, Archie McNair, in 1955, played a large part in the democratization of British fashion. The only requirement necessary to go shopping – and to be seen shopping – at Bazaar was youth. Quant's was also among the original fully fledged British brands, complete with not only clothing but also cosmetics and even a flaxen-haired, gingham dress–wearing Daisy Doll, Swinging London's far cooler and more emancipated alternative to America's Barbie. There was, for a start, no Ken on this miniature mannequin's agenda.

If Quant was a great British success story in her own right, it is also with this designer that the time-honoured view that British fashion is a cottage industry, as compared to its European and American counterparts, established itself. And so, uncertainty over the originality of her most famous creation – the miniskirt – continues to cause ripples today. The British claim it as their own, but the French have always insisted that it was the futuristic fashion designer André Courrèges (1923–) who introduced it to the world, not at street level, but on the ultra-exclusive haute couture catwalk. In a similar vein, Ossie Clark (1942–96) designed trouser suits for women in the mid-1960s, but Saint Laurent is widely credited with having established it as an international – not to mention highly lucrative – women's wear staple even though he didn't show it for the first time until 1968. By the mid-1970s, of course, Clark, while wildly

Top: Model Jackie Bowyer swings on a lamp post wearing a black matching oilskin coat, hat and boots by Mary Quant, the most successful women's wear designer working in London throughout the 1960s.

Above left: Women the world over flocked to Mary Quant's too-cool-for-school boutique Bazaar, located in the King's Road in Chelsea, to buy her consistently blithe and optimistic designs that so perfectly captured the spirit of the age.

Above: The Mary Quant Collection , autumn and winter 1967. Quant's signature was to take the staples of Edwardian children's wear and to re-create them in colours and fabrics – PVC in particular – that were not readily associated with that era.

Above: When this picture of Ossie Clark and his then business partner Alice Pollock was taken in the designer's studio in 1968, Swinging London had reached its peak and Clark was, in his own words, as famous as 'egg foo yong'.

famous on home turf, was already struggling to make ends meet. He certainly had the raw talent required to succeed, and his snake-hipped, miraculously tailored suiting and equally ingenious dresses crafted in black crepe or blithely printed chiffon were beloved by the beautiful people the world over, but the support structure that overseas designers had long had at their disposal was missing.

There was a naivety to British fashion design of that period that hampered its global position – then as now. 'I mean the truth of the matter was it was so haphazard,' Celia Birtwell (1941–), Clark's former wife and creative collaborator, has said: 'It was so innocent and so sweet. I mean Alice Pollock [founder of the Quorum boutique and Clark's business partner] was the one who said, "Oh we'll have a show at the Albert Hall". I mean, can you imagine. It was only a quarter full. You thought to yourself, you can't do that, you haven't got the marketing or the structure, but she did.' It is the stuff of fashion legend that, while Clark enjoyed a brief and highly colourful decade of fame, he spent the rest of his life trying to set up again. Ultimately he failed, 'We never thought about copyrights and owning your name or anything like that,' Birtwell has since said. 'We never thought about it. We just did it because we loved it.'

The fate of the Ossie Clark label – it has since been relaunched, though without the support of his immediate family – is by no means exceptional. The iconic Biba brand set up by the Polish-born designer Barbara Hulanicki (1936–) suffered a similar blow when its business partners sold out a majority stake to the investment company British Land, a sell-out that eventually led to Hulanicki's departure. Doing something simply because one wants to – 'because we loved it', if you will – and without taking into account the business considerations that necessarily go hand-in-hand with a craft

form that, however elevated, is also a consumer concern, has for some time now been identified as British fashion's weakness, even as it may also be its ultimate strength.

Westwood – grande dame of British fashion

Nevertheless, by the 1980s British fashion was all set to undergo its second boom-and-bust incarnation – now with its own showcase, the London Designer Collections set up by Annette Worsley-Taylor in 1975. The talent was brilliantly diverse, encompassing among others Bodymap, Rifat Ozbek (1953–), Katharine Hamnett (1947–), Jasper Conran (1959–), Betty Jackson (1949–) and, perhaps most significantly, the aforementioned Westwood and John Galliano.

If ever there was an exception that proves the rule where British fashion is concerned, it must surely be Vivienne Westwood, a designer whose creative power has endured for more than 30 years, who today owns her own globally recognized and extremely successful label, and who is the godmother of every contemporary British designer from John Galliano to Gareth Pugh (1971–).

Westwood was born Vivienne Isabel Swire in Glossop, Derbyshire, in 1941; her mother was a cotton weaver and her father a shoemaker. In the book that accompanied the Victoria and Albert Museum retrospective of the designer's work in 2004, Westwood describes her first memory of fashion thus: 'We lived in a row of cottages between villages and this woman was walking from Tintwhistle past our house down to Hollingsworth. I remember my mum saying: "She's got [Christian Dior's] New Look on, come and a have look." She thought it was horrible, with this long coat down to her ankles.' Her daughter thought otherwise and emulated Dior's style when she customized her school uniform. 'It was a new thing, putting that on was such a symbol of sexuality.'

22 CONDUIT STREET LONDON W1

Above: A 1970s magazine advertisment for Biba. Biba – set up by Polish-born Barbara Hulanicki – was perhaps Britain's first fully fledged lifestyle brand, in its heyday boasting its own advertising campaigns and everything from cosmetics to home furnishings and textiles, as well as some of the world's most fashionable clothes.

This page: By the 1980s, British fashion was all set to undergo its second boom-and-bust incarnation with its own showcase – the London Designer Collections – and talent as brilliantly diverse as Rifat Ozbek, Katharine Hamnett, Jasper Conran, Betty Jackson and Bodymap.

Bodymap in particular made its mark by staging striking, elaborately conceptual presentations that made the traditional catwalk seem about as interesting as waiting for a bus.

Above: In 1993 model Naomi Campbell famously fell off a pair of Vivienne Westwood's elevated rocking horse shoes in front of the entire fashion fraternity, responding the way only a model of her professional stature might – by collapsing still further with laughter.

Above: Sara Stockbridge, long-time Westwood muse, models the designer's signature corseted top, a prime post-punk example of her penchant for exaggerating the female form. Stockbridge's doll-with-attitude looks epitomized Westwood's take on femininity at this time.

By the late 1950s the Swire family had moved to north-west London, where at 16, having left school, their eldest child enrolled at the Harrow School of Art. She left after just one term – 'because I didn't really know how a working-class girl like me could possibly make a living in the art world' – retrained as a schoolteacher and met her first husband, Derek Westwood. The marriage lasted three years and produced a son, Ben. Westwood taught and ran a jewellery stall at Portobello Road at weekends. At around the same time, she was introduced to Malcolm McLaren – then known as Malcolm Edwards – and became pregnant with her second son, Joseph. She carried on teaching until, in 1971, McLaren decided to open a shop and Westwood knew she could fill it. She once said, 'I wanted to read and I was intending to go to university, but I started to help Malcolm,' she says. And the rest is history.

Since that time Westwood has given the world not only the uniform of punk, but also Pirates (1981), which triggered the New Romantic movement; Savages (1982), western fashion's first foray into asymmetric layering; and Buffalo Girls (also 1982), inspired by Latin American Indian dress and featuring layered skirts and petticoats, bowler hats worn with head scarves and, most significantly, bras worn over blouses. Madonna's now legendary conical bra, created by Jean-Paul Gaultier and worn throughout her Blonde Ambition tour nearly ten years later, would never have happened if it hadn't been for Westwood. The undisputed grande dame of British fashion is indebted to French eighteenth-century painting – she reinvented both the crinoline, in her hands worn short and sweet, and the corset. The staples of upper-class British traditional dress – from hunting jackets to Harris tweed and from the exuberant tartans beloved of Queen Victoria to the British crown itself – have also always been a source of inspiration.

While Westwood now shows her Red Label second line in London, her Gold Label main line is shown in Paris and her men's wear in Milan, safe in the knowledge that they will attract more prestigious international buyers and critics in both these cities. Her production is mainly in Italy. 'For years, I struggled to manufacture in England,' she has said:

But the breakthrough came for me when I finally started to produce in Italy because before that I could never really overcome the problem of production in high enough quantities. The gap between cottage industry, which is where I started and where a lot of other people started in England, and the kind of people who produce for Marks & Spencer [the last of the high-street chains to produce in Britain, although it too has recently begun working with overseas suppliers] is an unbridgeable chasm. There isn't the infrastructure or the mentality to help anybody mass-manufacture from a creative point in England.

Today Westwood is a national institution, a woman who not only continues to produce critically acclaimed collections but also communicates her political views through her work. She is on the board of the human rights organization Liberty and travels the world promoting her own manifesto to young people, which aims, in its author's own words, 'to encourage intellectuals in the fight against propaganda'. 'There are three constituents to propaganda,' Westwood argues, 'nationalism, organized lying and non-stop distraction. We need a different ethic.' Westwood believes that it is through our appreciation and understanding of culture – and that includes fashion – that we develop our powers of discrimination. Imagination is more important than reason and our insatiable thirst for the new – the modern – in particular is stultifying. 'The idea of keeping up with the times is just ridiculous. If you're always

Above: Vivienne Westwood's own exits are among the most anticipated of the fashion season. Here she comes out at the end of her spring/summer 2007 Gold Label Paris collection against a specially commissioned backdrop graffitied with political slogans – flame-haired and dressed, unusually, from head to toe in black.

Left: With autumn/winter 1995's
Vive la Cocotte, a collection inspired
by Ninon de l'Enclos, Westwood
combines and reworks the ideas that
have defined her collections of this
era. The designer is, at this point,
using influences from both French
and English fashion tradition equally.

Above: The dialogue between French and British fashion continues with this corseted dress from the same collection that plays off an exaggeration of the sexy French secretary style with a more irreverent and iconoclastic London-based look.

Above: Westwood's spring/summer 1996 collection culminated in a final sequence of ball gowns in painterly colours that have gone on to become one of her best-loved signatures. Britain's most famous fashion designer has by now come a long way from her early days as pioneer of the uniform of punk.

chasing after the latest thing you don't see anything at all. Great art is timeless. Either it is great, or it isn't. It doesn't matter when it was done.' True, her views have attracted as many detractors as they have supporters – despite her maturity, Westwood remains a powerful agent provocateur. How can a fashion designer, making a living on exorbitantly priced clothes, have the audacity to promote an anti-consumerist message, the former inevitably argue. More importantly, those unamused by her considerable charm are quick to point out that Westwood is a fashion designer first and foremost. She should stick to that, they argue, and leave the politics to the more high-minded among us.

Westwood is taken increasingly seriously, however, both on and off the catwalk, which in itself represents quite a breakthrough. 'And isn't Vivienne just in the perfect position to say those things,' Andreas Kronthaler, her current husband and creative partner, has said. 'The message is about consuming and not thinking, about not choosing and about how people can do whatever they want with you and you just go along with it and swallow everything. It's Vivienne Westwood the rebel coming through.'

And Vivienne Westwood the rebel is the woman who made it possible for the aforementioned Galliano and later McQueen – both iconoclastic in the extreme – not to mention just about any other young British fashion designer one might care to mention, to make their own, equally grand design statements in the years and even decades that followed her initial rise to fame.

British fashion and the art school

Westwood is unusual on every level, not least because, unlike the vast majority of her profession in Britain, her one term at college hardly qualifies her as having benefited from an art school education. McLaren, though, her original partner, was art school-educated. Ossie Clark, in his time, went to the Royal College of Art, where he met not only Birtwell but also the artists David Hockney and Mo McDermott, all of whom were not only extremely supportive but also collaborated with the designer on one level or another throughout his career. Galliano is Saint Martins trained and so too are Hussein Chalayan (1970–), Alexander McQueen (1969–), Gareth Pugh … the list goes on. Whereas overseas graduate and postgraduate fashion schools tend to be given over to fashion alone and therefore any coursework is technically and commercially focused, in Britain the foremost colleges are predominantly part of a larger, fine-art educational institution, meaning that designers mix with more purely creative souls than do their international counterparts.

'Of course, the art school system has been pretty decimated over the past ten years,' says Louise Wilson, MA fashion course director at Central Saint Martins since 1992:

Even so nobody else in the world benefits from the fact that their fashion schools are within art colleges, which means that there is a very productive fusion of ideas. It gives people a sense of freedom and, of course, these always were very rebellious places. Furthermore, the grant system meant that an art teacher might notice you and direct you towards fashion college. Would John Galliano have come to Saint Martins without a grant? I think that would have been unlikely. Once you were at fashion college, you made your own clothes – you couldn't afford to buy any. You could dress any way you chose; in fact the more bizarre the outfit the more you were respected. By making things for yourself, by taking those risks, you were creating your own fantasy. People like Galliano, McQueen, Gareth Pugh all started out making clothes for themselves and for their friends to go out in.

Above: For her autumn/winter 2006 collection Westwood sent out T-shirts printed with the words 'I AM EXPENSIV', a reaction, she claimed at the time, against rampant and indiscriminate consumerism at the cost of individuality and creativity.

Opposite: Sara Stockbridge, photographed by Nick Knight, wearing the Harris tweed crown from the designer's autumn/winter 1987 collection featuring myriad appropriations of British royal dress.

The Gibraltar-born John Galliano has described his initial schooling in Britain as at best confusing and at worst punishing. 'I don't think people in England understood where I was coming from,' he says of his early days in south London:

and I certainly didn't understand where they were coming from. It was quite a shock, coming from that sort of family, that sort of colour. My mother brought it with her on the plane though, you know, the religious aspect and all that was still with us when we were at home. The people I went to school with were very different from me. They were Church of England, I was Roman Catholic. That's a big difference ...

It was only once he'd moved on to the City and East London College to study for O and A levels, and from there to Saint Martins, that he found his feet, meeting 'people who were a bit more like me' as well as discovering the direction his professional life would take. 'I worked very hard at Saint Martins, I was really into what I was doing. I was always in the library, sketching endlessly.' It is the stuff of fashion folklore that his degree collection, shown in 1984, was bought in its entirety by Joan Burstein, proprietor of the designer fashion mecca Browns, and duly installed in her shop window. If anything characterizes the British fashion industry it is surely the fact that a mere student is able to receive this level of exposure. Over a decade later, Chalayan also had his final collection showcased by Browns. Today the Central Saint Martins MA course benefits from its own annual slot on the official London Fashion Week schedule. It remains the place to see and be seen by talent scouts looking not only for the next big thing but also for designers to staff the creative teams of many of the world's most high-profile brands.

'I think perhaps that in Britain a student feels there is something to aim for,' says Wilson:

In France and Italy it is much more difficult to break through. We don't have that top-heavy barrier of Armani, say, in Italy, or Louis Vuitton, Givenchy or whoever in France, names which, to a greater or lesser extent, control the collections because of their money and power. You can be an important person at London Fashion Week even if you are straight out of college and you wouldn't have a hope in hell of doing that anywhere else. If Ossie Clark had said he was showing in the Albert Hall and the Albert Hall was in Paris, Yves Saint Laurent would have said: 'That's my idea. I'm going to show there', and that would have been that.

Only adding to the unprecedented publicity afforded to Britain's young designers was the emergence of style magazines – in the 1980s *i-D*, *The Face* and *Blitz* were the first wave; *Dazed & Confused*, founded by Katie Grand, then at Saint Martins, with Rankin Waddell and Jefferson Hack, followed in the 1990s. 'You cannot overestimate the importance of those publications,' Wilson says:

You could never have had *i-D* in France; there would have been no fashionable street culture to document at that point, they didn't have clubs like Blitz and Taboo. And if the magazine started off running photographs of people they found on the street because they looked fashionable, that developed and it became a vehicle via which young designers, designers, who could never have afforded to pay for an advertising campaign, could promote their work.

Highs and lows

Achieving such a high profile at such an early stage in your career can be a double-edged sword, as any designer who rose to fame in the 1980s will be quick to testify. 'It was such an exciting time,' says Betty Jackson, who showed at the London

This page: In his 1993 spring/summer collection the Gibraltar-born, London-educated designer John Galliano paraded anglophile tendencies with a jacket crafted out of the Union Jack. The narrowness of the tailoring and fluidity of the ethnic-inspired chiffon skirt are both representative of his style at this point, here modelled by a young Kate Moss.

Designer Collections in the early 1980s alongside an equally fêted group of contemporaries. 'It must have been around 1983. We were overrun with Americans in particular, literally screaming for the stuff we were designing because nobody else had the sort of independent image we had. They were just dropping money. You wouldn't believe it. We had queues outside the showroom.'

Bodymap – the label created by Middlesex College of Art students Stevie Stewart and David Holah – staged shows that were as close to pure theatrical performance as fashion had ever come. Boasting deliberately opaque titles to match – 1984's Cat in the Hat Takes a Ramble with Techno Fish was one – these set the stage for contemporary designers including Galliano, Chalayan and McQueen, all of whom have gone on to turn the blockbuster fashion presentation into something of an art form. While many designers from this period enjoyed a cult following, a few of them at least became household names. Who could forget, to cite just one particularly potent example, Katharine Hamnett's formal introduction to the then British Prime Minister, Margaret Thatcher, at a Downing Street reception, when she paraded the words '58% DON'T WANT PERSHING' across her oversized white T-shirt?

Inevitably, however, recession hit, and unsurprisingly it was the young independent labels that felt the economic downturn most acutely. 'It was a meteoric rise and a bit scary because we really didn't know what we were doing at all,' according to Jackson. 'We were working from tiny premises and trying desperately to get things made without understanding the international level we were playing on. We were silly about delivery dates, about quality. And then, overnight, it all just stopped.' Jackson was one of the lucky ones though, able to revive her career a decade later. Others were less fortunate.

Even Galliano, by now one of international fashion's brightest stars, was not immune to the fact that being well known and celebrated by no means guaranteed commercial success.

Born to a Gibraltarian father and a Spanish mother, Galliano moved in the mid 1960s to Streatham, south London, where his father worked as a plumber. The designer's aforementioned degree collection, Les Incroyables, was inspired by an internship dressing a production of Büchner's *Danton's Death* at the National Theatre. There were jackets worn upside down and inside out and romantic organdy shirts, all finished with the type of idiosyncratic and determinedly whimsical accessories – smashed spectacles worn tangled in hair, for example – that still characterize his work. 'I was just so into that collection,' Galliano has since said:

It completely overtook me. I still love it. I love the romance, you know, charging through cobbled streets in all that amazing organdy. There are a lot of things in that collection that still haunt me. Afterwards, of course, I realized that something had gone down. Everything happened so quickly. Mrs Burstein cleared the Browns window that same afternoon, I think. Then she invited me to come down to the boutique to meet the customers and sell the collection. Diana Ross walked in. Everything was just flying off the rails.

Not content with merely launching the designer, Burstein also forwarded Galliano money to go out and buy fabric to make more and supply increased demands. 'I went to Notting Hill Gate and bought some furnishing fabrics. Luckily my parents were away, so it was all right to turn their sitting room into a mini-factory.'

Even the man who will doubtless go down in British fashion history as the biggest next big thing of them all quickly became aware of the pitfalls of a reputation that far outweighs

Above: Paul Smith's Covent Garden store was part homage to the Savile Row tradition and part cabinet of curiosities, where the modern male could travel to buy everything from his signature tailoring to floral print boxer shorts to Filofax diaries.

Above: At a Downing Street reception, a young Katharine Hamnett's is formally introduced to the then British Prime Minister, Margaret Thatcher, dressed in an oversized white T-shirt printed with the words '58% DON'T WANT PERSHING'.

Above: Paul Smith, Britain's most successful independent designer, is photographed in the early days looking suitably dapper in his own 'tailored with a twist' designs.

Above: The supermodels of their day are captured en masse in John Galliano's unashamedly romantic spring/summer 1995 collection, which featured many of his signatures – from Belle Epoque-inspired tailoring to bias-cut slip dresses. The predominance of dusty English-country-garden colours is also very much part of this designer's handwriting.

any business infrastructure. 'It put an enormous amount of pressure on me. You had to do all your growing up in public. You made a fool of yourself in front of people you still have to work with today. So what? I'm human.' In the ten years that followed Galliano's graduation, two backers withdrew their support and there were several seasons when he couldn't afford to show at all. In the early 1990s, disillusioned by the difficulties of running a fashion business in the UK, the designer moved to Paris, where both Katharine Hamnett and Paul Smith (1946–) were also showing by that point. There, almost penniless, Galliano slept on friends' floors, cobbling together a first collection by calling in favours – only to find that, despite critical acclaim, he was just as impoverished by the time the next one came around.

Help came in the form of the American *Vogue* editor-in-chief Anna Wintour (1949–) who, in an unprecedented relationship between editor and designer, took Galliano under her wing. The next time it looked like he was heading for financial difficulty, Wintour used her considerable influence to find him a backer (investment bank PaineWebber International) and even a venue (the crumbling Parisian mansion of the socialite Sao Schlumberger). Still it was a scramble. There were only 17 outfits, put together at the last minute and entirely in black – several bolts of black lining fabric were all that John Galliano could afford. But what outfits! The show was a monumental success and John Galliano's reputation as one of the late twentieth century's great designers was sealed.

British designers go global

The buying spree that characterized international fashion in the mid-1990s changed the face of fashion irrevocably both in Britain and abroad. LVMH (Moët Hennessy Louis Vuitton)

Above: The fashion fantasy at its most lovely is the story here, as exemplified by a strapless overblown striped gown from Galliano's spring/summer 1994 collection. Not content with a conservative runway presentation, Galliano gives each of his models only one outfit and requires that she act her part with gusto.

Above: John Galliano celebrates the 60th anniversary of Christian Dior with perhaps the most extravagant fashion show in history, staged at the Orangerie in Versailles in autumn 2007 and featuring every big-name model past and present. The designs themselves were inspired by great painters from Fragonard to Picasso and from Velázquez to Cocteau.

Above: Galliano's spring/summer 2003 collection was inspired by the halcyon dress-to-impress days of the nightclub Taboo – the designer was there and wore the T-shirt – and culminated in some of the most over-sized designs the catwalk has yet seen. Big, brave and Wagnerian in their audacity, they were among his most remarkable creations to date.

and later the Gucci Group turned their attention to acquiring many of the world's best-known designer labels. These were often tired and in need of regeneration however, and where better to look for the young talent necessary to breathe life back into them than Britain? And so in 1996 Galliano found himself heading up LVMH-owned Givenchy. A year later McQueen, having shown only eight collections – and highly controversial ones at that – took over at the house best known for having Audrey Hepburn as its muse. Galliano, for his part, moved across to what is perhaps still France's most famous brand, the star of the LVMH stable, Christian Dior.

The conglomerate's visionary CEO, Bernard Arnault (1949–), was the man responsible for employing both designers and was well aware that the French fashion establishment's feathers would be more than a little ruffled as a result. McQueen's arrival at Givenchy in particular caused a stir. Here was a designer best known for having pioneered the bumster trouser, cut so low that the crease in models' bottoms was on display for all to see. His work was – and is – aggressively sexual and darkly romantic, almost to the point of the macabre, and consistently challenged preconceptions about cut and proportion. His shows were some of the most visually extreme and emotionally charged ever seen. In light of this, a cynic might argue that his perceived unsuitability was at least part of the attraction. Whichever way one chooses to look at it, both designers were considered upstarts at the time – and working-class, British upstarts to boot – and the column inches that this generated, even before their work for Givenchy and Dior made the catwalks, were considerable.

By the turn of the millennium it was all change again. McQueen resigned from Givenchy and set up his own label in partnership with the Gucci Group, by then owned by PPR (Pinault-Printemps-La Redoute). The American superstar

Right: The set of Alexander McQueen's spring/summer 2001 collection was a larger than life-size padded cell. The designer has always said that provoking an emotional response from his audience is of prime importance, and this was no exception. The unsettling nature of the mise en scène provided a direct contrast to the sheer beauty and romance of the clothes.

Above: One of McQueen's most
photographed London shows,
his autumn/winter 1998 collection,
Joan, culminated in the catwalk
bursting into flames. For previous
collections the designer had required
models to walk on water and through
showering rain, and even to skate
on snow and ice.

designer Tom Ford (1961–) was responsible for orchestrating the deal. Just months later, Stella McCartney (1971–) followed suit. 'People may still always talk about British fashion in terms of cottage industry,' says Louise Wilson, 'but the question I always ask myself is what new super-brands has Italy or France spawned? Not many. We could happily say, as British people, hang on, McQueen's got a label – it doesn't matter whether he's backed by a British company or not. Galliano's got a label and he's head of Dior. Stella's got a label ... and that's just in the past decade.'

Nor does it stop there. Paul Smith is a designer superstar both on home turf and abroad. His classic tailoring 'with a twist', and irreverent appropriation of every British staple from football to flowers into men's wear, is the secret of such success. Likewise, 'doing a Burberry' has become the holy grail of any British heritage label with its finger on the pulse. Since Royal College of Art graduate Christopher Bailey took over at that label in 2001 he has reversed the brand's fortunes to spectacular effect, ensuring not only that its history as the purveyor of British outerwear *par excellence* is upheld, but also transforming it into a trendsetting global fashion force to be reckoned with.

At the cutting edge

Hussein Chalayan is a designer whose uncompromisingly conceptual approach might have made him appear an unlikely prospect as a global concern. This is a creative talent who has in the past created some of the most thought-provoking installations imaginable, inspired by sources as diverse as Islamic dress and aerodynamics. His clothes are remarkable for the fact that they are resolutely modern, referring in the end only to themselves. After brief periods working for TSE Cashmere in New York and launching a women's wear

Above: The raw energy of McQueen's early work is remarkable, and throughout this period an unabashed sexuality characterized his designs. Photographed here is the now famous 'bumster' trouser from the Highland Rape autumn/winter 1995 collection, the garment that made his name. Cut so low that models' buttocks were displayed from behind, it influenced an entire generation of women to wear their jeans on their hip bones or beneath them.

Above: Up until this point Alexander McQueen had rarely been photographed. This uncompromisingly confrontational image, on the cover of the April 1998 issue of *The Face*, was his first high-profile portrait.

Top: This image from Dante, in McQueen's autumn/winter 1996 collection, shown in a consecrated church in Spitalfields, encapsulates the often dark nature of the designer's sensibilities.

This page: For the finale of his autumn/winter 2006 collection, McQueen created a ghostly image of Kate Moss that floated above the audience. The technique was a modern-day interpretation of the Victorian optical effect known as 'Pepper's ghost'.

Above: McQueen's autumn/ winter 2008 collection was inspired by punk princesses, toy soldiers, mid-twentieth-century British haute couture and, in particular, the wardrobe of the young Queen Elizabeth I. For the first time in his career the designer paired outfits with paper-flat slippers with elongated toes.

Above right: The final exit from Sarabande, McQueen's spring/ summer 2007 collection, was a gown made entirely out of freshly cut, frozen garden flowers. The fact that blooms fell from its skirts as the model wearing it walked only added to the romance of the proceedings.

collection for the British brand Asprey, Chalayan set up his own label, which now benefits from an international backer – the German sportswear giant, Puma. In 2008 Chalayan said of his appointment as creative director of that company: 'I became a designer to try and create a new language for clothes and another way to look at the body, culture, the environment, politics and so forth. Although our business has grown steadily, it has remained relatively small. This partnership will hopefully mean that my work will reach more people, both through designing for Puma and the expansion of my own business.'

Coming up in the wings, meanwhile, is Gareth Pugh who (in peculiarly British style) had dressed both Marilyn Manson and Kylie Minogue, not to mention appearing in every international glossy from *W* magazine to *Dazed & Confused*, before he had sold even a single stitch of clothing. His most famous creation to date is nothing more obviously commercial than a poodle suit, the head of which was famously created out of condoms. In the summer of 2008 the designer was awarded the prestigious ANDAM International Fashion Award, following in the footsteps of the Belgian designer Martin Margiela (1957–) and the Dutch-based Viktor & Rolf. His collections are now produced with the support of the West Coast US designer Rick Owens (1962–) and shown in Paris, testimony to the truly international nature of the world of fashion today. In truth, even labelling a designer as British now appears somewhat parochial.

Pugh was born in Sunderland: his father is a policeman; his mother worked in a call centre for the Littlewoods Catalogue for 15 years. Art school-educated, he opted for a fashion degree at Central Saint Martins, but the Slade School of Art would have been his second choice. He shot to fame

Above: Hussein Chalayan suspended one of his earliest designs from a helium-filled balloon. For his autumn/winter 2003 collection, and by this time showing in Paris, he revisited the theme – an exploration of weightlessness emphasized by the fact that the model was now also seated on a trampoline.

Demand the Impossible_Fashion

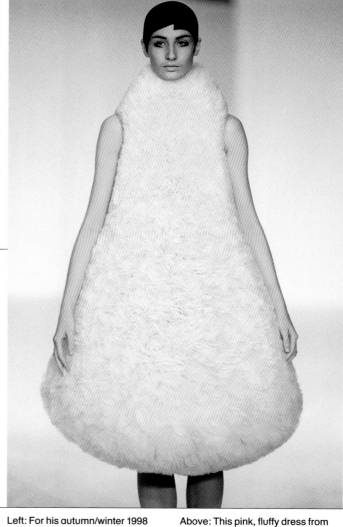

Above: Chalayan's London shows, and this one from spring/summer 2001 in particular, were more reminiscent of art installations than the traditional catwalk presentation. The architectural quality of everything from the clothing itself to the models' hair demonstrates a thoughtfulness and rigour that is unprecedented.

Left: For his autumn/winter 1998 collection, Chalayan encased models' heads in black and required that they walk around a set punctuated with mirrors. The effect was an austere – even monastic – procession that seems as modern now as when it was first shown.

Above: This pink, fluffy dress from the designer's spring/summer 2000 collection, reminiscent of nothing more than a stick of candyfloss, shows the flip side of Chalayan's sensibility, which may be playful and even humorous.

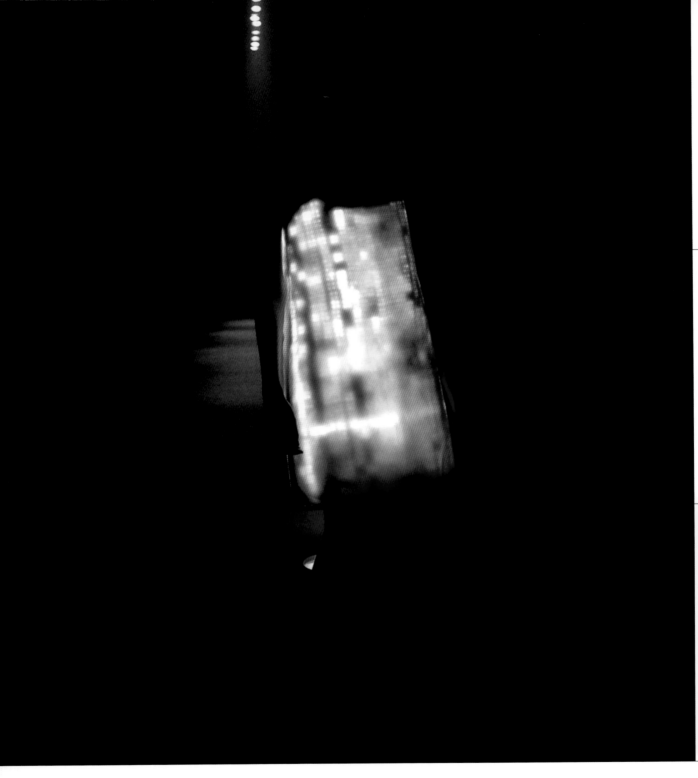

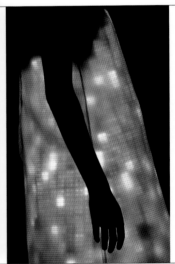

This page: As interested in technological advancement as he is in pure clothing design, for his autumn/winter 2007 collection Chalayan looked at climate change and mortality through an exploration of light. Pictured here is a shift dress embedded with an LED display.

This page: Mechanical clothing was also a preoccupation throughout Chalayan's autumn/winter 2007 collection. The coat in this picture came complete with a hood that rose up as if by magic to cover the face of the model wearing it.

immediately after graduating and set up a studio in a squat in south London appropriated by the art collective !WOWWOW! 'When you leave college you expect something to be handed to you, but it wasn't like that. It was like a decision that you make – do I get a job, or stick it out and see what comes? There was this squat in Peckham with a group of people living there. I always lived round the corner in my flat because I had housing benefit but my studio was there.' The turning point in his career came, he has said, when the diminutive Ms Minogue's stylist, William Baker, turned up with a bag of black fabric and asked Pugh to transform it into a showpiece:

It was like a tiny paper bag but the fabric inside cost £1,500. And there was this rampant dog which was just like ripping things up. Thankfully, it got hold of one of my T-shirts but not that bag. I started Kylie in a squat and finished it in the living room of the landlord of this pub who kindly let me use his house because we'd been kicked out. It all ended and started there.

'I think Gareth Pugh is interesting because people don't quite understand what he's doing,' Jefferson Hack, publisher of *Dazed & Confused* has said. The magazine championed Pugh's degree collection on its cover only months after he graduated from Central Saint Martins in 2003:

When I first saw Gareth's work, I knew that I loved it and I obviously felt confident in his ability, otherwise I wouldn't have put it on the front of the magazine so early on. I presumed, though, that he would probably end up showing once a year, maybe in a gallery, and produce a limited edition of ten pieces, say, that might sell for £50,000 each. Now, though, it's becoming clearer and clearer how important a designer he is and what his place in fashion might be.

Above: Gareth Pugh's debut Paris collection, shown in spring/summer 2009, was white from the front and black from behind, giving the impression of a woman coming out of the darkness. The designer's preoccupation with extreme volume is clearly at play here.

Demand the Impossible_Fashion

Right: The Elizabethan ruff has long featured in Pugh's work, but the overriding mood is futuristic as opposed to nostalgic. The craft that goes into creating such pieces becomes increasingly elaborate as the designer's career develops.

This page: Pugh's work is often more readily associated with sculpture than designer fashion, as this bizarrely beautiful coat (left) goes to show in his autumn/winter 2008 collection. Even on more familiar fashion territory, shoulders are hugely exaggerated, as is the fullness of skirts (above).

As a photographer who has consistently championed the work of young British design talent for more than 30 years, Nick Knight – who was picture editor of *i-D* in 1990, shoots for everyone from *Dazed & Confused* to *Vogue* and funds his own pioneering fashion website – understands the nature of this particular beast better than most. The early designs of Westwood, Galliano, McQueen, Chalayan and now Pugh have all passed through his hands, and he continues to support all these designers and more. 'Why does Britain produce such fantastical fashion?' he wonders:

I do think it's partly to do with our culture and how regimented it was post-war, about school uniforms and the class division and those sorts of things, all of which produce a desire to be different. There is a real sense of formal dress in England and therefore there is also a sense of being able to break that formality. The strict coding in Britain over the past 40 or 50 years has produced a desire to rebel, to create a vision of the universe that is different to anything we recognize.

I think that people succeed here partly because of their talent and partly because of their motivation to change the situation they are in. In Britain there is a culture of supporting and being interested in that sort of emerging creative talent. We recognize it and it is a vision of the world that we export very well.

Above: The infamous black rabbit that Pugh sent out for his autumn/winter 2006 collection was in fact a poodle – a comment, the designer once said, on the primped and preened nature of fashion. True to London style, the head was lovingly created out of nothing more *haute* than inky-black condoms.

After the Object

Interaction
Simon Waterfall

This book celebrates the twentieth anniversary of the opening of the Design Museum. Twenty years in digital design is almost its entire lifespan. It moves so fast and with such a voracious appetite for the new, for the 'next', that digital life should really be measured in dog years. That's seven years for every calendar one. This makes the Design Museum 140, my industry on its fourth or fifth generation, and me, in digital terms at least, a very old man indeed.

In the beginning…

At the tender age of six or seven I played with my very first computer in my grandfather's workshop. It was called a Commodore PET – a Personal Electronic Transactor – and even in those days it seemed a pretty cumbersome and ugly-looking device, a tool to be used in calculations, perhaps, but principally to show off to others, like a new flashy sports car. Like the car, the early personal computer was a stand-alone device – its own island that stood or failed on the information you put into its tank and the skill of its driver. They were all home-built or at least had to be home-customized for them to truly work.

The industry's giants we know today, like or loathe them, all have their origins in this era. Back then, though, it wasn't a commercial industry or even a competitive one. It was a matter of a few handfuls of people scattered around the globe who gradually, as they tinkered and fettled away, saw the 'tools' they were building become truly versatile. They were the very first people who saw in the computer a multipurpose machine and took the first tentative steps towards the virtual currency – information. These were the first few hesitant years in what would become an era of epic change.

I can remember the late nights and incalculable hours I spent typing in line after line of code from the computer magazines I had on special order from the States, only to have to wait a whole long month for the bugs to be posted in the next issue. Bugs, mice, viruses, processors … the language hadn't even been invented to describe the technology and it had to beg, borrow or steal adjectives and nouns from anything close enough for comparison. This became the norm in an industry which in 20 or so years has gone from a shed – literally, in the case of William Hewlett (1912–2001) and David Packard (1912–96) – to putting a battery and brain in everything and anything, including the kitchen sink.

The underground pioneers

Some people talk about those early days as the era of the amateur, but this implies that there was such a thing in the field as a professional! In fact, there were no schools or universities you could attend, no qualifications to obtain, no interweb superhighway you could quiz… There wasn't even a TV channel where this kind of stuff got mentioned or talked about. It was totally underground. Only a very few had access to anything that could do more than bleep and display ASCII characters on a dim green screen.

Nevertheless, these amateurs still had the urge to make it better. The Silicon Valley hobbyist computer club Homebrew, whose members included Bill Gates (1955–), Steve Jobs (1955–) and Steve Wozniak (1950–) among others, were just some of the kids who got the creative bug, who wanted to self-improve and make this inanimate box work better. In fact, the first computer that 'Woz' and Jobs shipped in July 1976 had to be built by the owners in just that – a natty wooden box.

Simon Waterfall

My first PET (left) – Commodore's Personal Electronic Transactor, 1977. A solid tin box that was so cold in winter that your fingers stuck to it. It was kept in my grandfather's workshop. His brother had Apple's 1990 Macintosh Classic (right). Mac v PC wars Day Zero.

After the Object_Interaction

It sold for $500, which, with the one-third mark-up, made it $666. Not the most auspicious start. They made 200 units which – although the 30 chips were already set into its 'motherboard' – still had to be built into a box with power supply and display. Many argue that the Altair 8800 was senior, but the Apple was the first with a keyboard, not just switches.

Bill Gates, meanwhile, built the software that ran on many of the boxes. Back then, people didn't grasp the monumental change taking place – that 'design' could encompass not just a physical object but a virtual code. Gates' famous letter to the Homebrew club defended the work of the hobbyist coder and his or her right to intellectual property – without that work, Gates pointed out, the box would be just that, a box. People were still coming to terms with this whole field, and how delicate its beginnings were – Mr Gates, after all, was just 21!

The restrictions of early computers didn't dampen the creative passions and imagination of the users. The computer industry developed through the sweat of like-minded mavericks, each pouring their time and energy into their individual passions. Tiny steps forward coalesced into new breakthroughs, making a bonanza of competing platforms that split allegiances in classrooms around the globe. I like to think that the war between Britain's own computer industry and the United States' in the early 1980s could have gone either way. Clive Sinclair's ZX Spectrum and the BBC Micro Model B jostled for supremacy with America's Commodore 64 and Amiga, among a raft of others. This excessive choice and lack of a single platform led to the early downfall of personal computers in the home, and for a while they were usurped by the standardization offered by games consoles and the overly adventurous claims of the games titles that my company and others were producing.

Mortal Kombat, Ghostbusters, Lemmings, Advanced Dungeons & Dragons, Attack of the Mutant Camels ...! These may have run on a tiny amount of memory and the sound was at best tinny, but they still pushed both the audience and the designers into a new realm, a different place that hadn't previously existed. You really had to have imagination to convince yourself that this random block of purple pixels really was an attacking llama that you could spit with 360 degrees of control to vanquish similar blocks of malformed pixels ... People think video games in particular dumb down 'kidz'; in my view it's completely the opposite, then and now. The whole immersive experience needs total concentration and total belief – the children and adults enmeshed in this world are as focused as athletes and snipers at 2,000 metres!

I don't want to dwell on this period but it's worth celebrating the people who made those first games. People who had the challenge of having tiny amounts of computer memory but who were rewarded with an audience with big imaginations. Who had to hand-build computers from parts and knew that, if *they* didn't populate the world with their own creativity, then it would remain forever empty. Who had a following that would be happy with almost anything because it was the new, the now. These were the same people who, almost ten years on, helped form the Internet.

The Wild, Wild Web
The Internet was born on the 25 December 1990. According to that font of all knowledge, Wikipedia, on that day Tim Berners-Lee (1955–), with help from Robert Cailliau, a young student at CERN, implemented the first successful

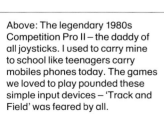

Above: The legendary 1980s Competition Pro II – the daddy of all joysticks. I used to carry mine to school like teenagers carry mobiles phones today. The games we loved to play pounded these simple input devices – 'Track and Field' was feared by all.

Above: 'Look at me, darling, I'm a tennis player.' 'Look at me sweetheart, I am an athlete. Look at me, I have a gun.' What is this moustachioed suit-wearing lothario doing? At least the TV is still in a wooden box.

communications between an HTTP client and server, via the 'Inter Net'. Now that's great but … 25 December … *Christmas Day*, come on! Unless Wikipedia is lying to me, then what Sir Tim was doing was crystallizing the Internet's philosophy and culture in one key stroke. This would be the place for people with no internal time clock, no social skills and very little sunlight in their lives. Massive Fail. But, thankfully, it didn't really turn out like that.

OK, so the Internet was born, and it was … well, nothing. Really, nothing. I can remember having one of the earliest email accounts and not knowing anyone to send anything to. I was kind of lonely. It really was the wild, wild West, and students, scientists and engineers were the only people populating it. They grasped at the blank empty space and wondered how they could make it work. The first sites I can remember were based on hypercards, whose basic principle works exactly like livetext links in every website you still use today. There were no graphics, no sound, no movement; it was like watching Ceefax, only with less information and a lot less purpose.

I have a mass of memories here. Content was traded and stockpiled; games stolen and jealously guarded. As there was no net, you met with your fellow dealers face to face in shady corners. It was all illegal but, as no one – yet – thought much about digital crimes, there was an exhilarating sense of freewheeling anarchy. The games moved you out of your world and into science fiction – you killed zombies, you raced cars, you traded goods in space, you kicked ass… It was a time when one or two families bought a computer to help with the homework or the family accounts, and it ended up with one kid in the village ruling the universe.

The Web was also a place that attracted and bred anarchists, conspirators and free-thinkers. The tools were so easily available and security so lax that many radicals exploited the ignorant. Whether you *could* do it was sometimes more important than whether you *should*. A site that used to strike fear into the hearts of one and all was www.jodi.com, where the experiments often bubbled over the edge of the keyboard and instigated crashes, screen-freezing and occasional hard-drive failure. It lives on today but with most of its back-door hacking fangs removed. Digital communications may have grown up, but their roots are still very much counterculture.

I asked members of my studio for their first memories of computers, how they first stumbled across this world and when the Internet hit them. Dogg remembers the time when *Tomorrow's World* broadcast a ZX Spectrum program that you could tape off the speaker in a quiet room so that you could then load the game on your computer. Tape it off the TV … awesome! The net was the door opening onto a vast playground of knowledge, and suddenly you were no longer alone. For many, I think, it was the first time they had acknowledged and communicated with others outside their own group of friends. It was a whole new dynamic, not taught at school or by your peers: communication with people you couldn't see, didn't know and with whom you had nothing in common except a passion to *be* there – virtually.

Fundamentally, I think, it was an era that was owned and grown by two extremes of the population, the very bright and the very, very young. They influenced each other, and a lot of the time you had a hard job separating who was who. It was a brave new world that inspired fresh-faced youth to become programmers, scientists and, of course, digital designers.

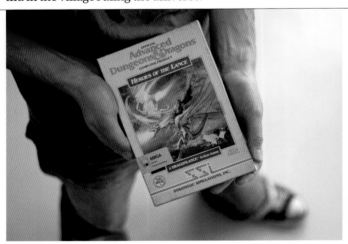

Above: Dungeons & Dragons for US Gold was one of my company's first products, released for the Amiga in 1988. My partner and I were 16 and still at school; we had to skip double geography lessons to have meetings with clients while still in our school uniforms.

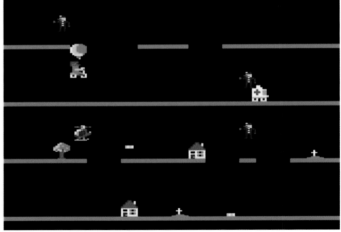

Above: Dare Devil Dennis, 1984, when BMX bandits had a lot-o'-fun. Platform games don't get much more simple and fun than this. There were not only sound effects, but a fully scripted soundtrack that stayed in your brain for a week.

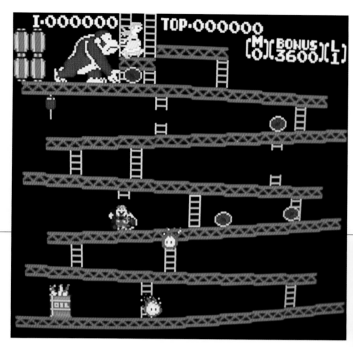

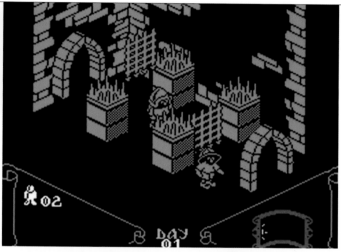

This page: Games developed at a frightening pace, and each new release was a first. Platform games ranged from Donkey Kong (above), to the first isometric game Knight Lore (middle) to the final work of art that was Syndicate (below), with its squad-based role-play games.

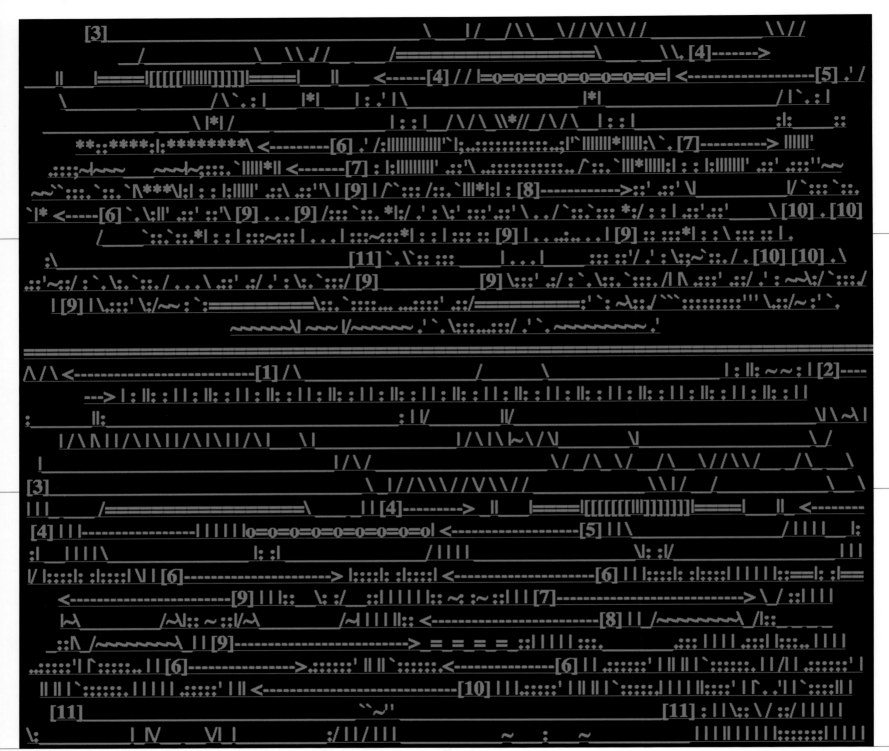

Above and opposite: One of the first websites to strike fear into viewers: www.jodi.org. Rumours whispered that it could wipe your hard drive, corrupt your files and cancel your student loan. It is still alive today with a rather more grown-up attitude, but it is still genius. It is as fresh and obscure as it ever was, with art-based thought processes as information graphics. Enter at your own risk.

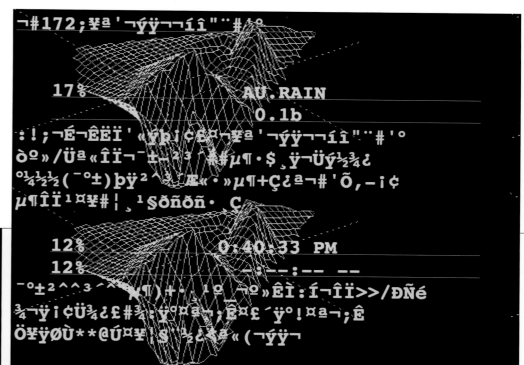

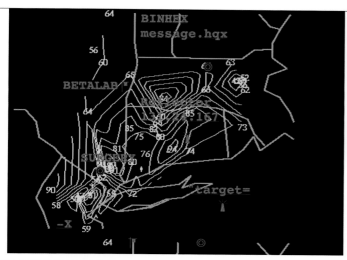

Three champions of the Web:
Dopplr (top) is one of the useful
Tools of the web, gone are the time
when 'content is King', these days
'Community is Kinger' and that is
what Dopplr represents for me; it is
a travel site that I log my trips in to
and my friends around the world
can meet me, help me or generally
shout abuse at me. I love airmiles.
TED videos (above) inspire me to
be better and it is great that we can
forget the BMW films case study and
talk about their sponsorship here.
Finally Google (right) – our collective
spare brain.

After the Object_Interaction

Design for the virtual space, however, was problematic. The studios had basic tools at their disposal, designed to help create and visualize real objects for product design, graphic layup or publishing, but the restrictions on designing in the virtual space were so intense that they put off most mainstream designers and so they abandoned it again to the hobbyist. This is a recurring theme.

Intelligent design

The Web started to make an impact in the wider world in the very early 1990s. There was certainly content about, but no one knew how to find it unless it was by word of mouth. The rise of the search engines – the pioneering Yahoo, AltaVista and Lycos – changed all of this. Although things have moved forward in the field hugely, even today the people at Google today call themselves 'Google Dumb'. I worked on a project for Google last year, and the day I turned up they had just bought eleven new buildings on their site in Palo Alto, California. Eleven! I asked why they had bought eleven – 'There weren't twelve for sale! We're gonna fill them with Google Smart.'

When you come to think about it, the typical Web search *is* pretty stupid. When you do a search online, using *any* of the search engines, they all go away and race through all available tagged data and will find anything you requested *blindly*, with any commonly searched or linked sites coming up first. (The system that rates this blind investigation has enabled people to 'Googlewhack' or hack the system and push up a specific result.) It's crazy – it's as if everybody in the world who uses the Internet is just one single person. Whoever they are. Whatever their differences. Whatever their needs.

This page: Vimeo is changing the face of video distribution and may also be the death of the TV remote control. It is one of the few websites that I do not encourage viewing in my studio as it is easy to lose an hour … or three.

After the Object_Interaction

Burble London, 2007. A massive structure composed of 1,000 helium balloons each containing LEDs and microcontrollers that create spectacular patterns of light across the surface of the structure. The public can control this rippling 'Burble' that sways in the evening sky, in response to movements of the long articulated interactive handle bar at the base of the structure. Part installation, part performance, the Burble enables people to contribute at an urban scale to a structure that occupies their city.

Imagine you're in your kitchen and you've just run out of rice. You type into your home laptop 'Uncle Ben' and Google takes 0.26 seconds to find 1,060,000 results, 0.15 seconds to find 1,300,000 images and 0.15 seconds to find 544 news stories. There's Uncle Ben the actor; thousands of pictures of everyone's Uncle Ben; a horse and a dog called Uncle Ben (because there's always a horse and a dog in every search); Uncle Ben from the *Spider-Man* comic book, and the cockney rhyming slang 'Lend me an Uncle Ben, will ya?' Somewhere there's also the 500g bag of long-grain brown rice you really wanted.

Then imagine a not-too-distant future where you do exactly the same. Now *smart* Google will start by having a chat with your own home computer...

Google search box: 'Uncle Ben'
Google: Hold on. Now where's Simon?
Home Computer: He's in the kitchen.
G: What's he been doing?
HC: Drinking a gin and tonic and cooking. He's just put an empty 500g bag of Uncle Ben's long-grain brown rice into the recycling bin.
G: Aha! Right ... when did he last throw a bag out?
HC: Errr ... two months ago.
G: Right, he uses a bag every two months?
HC: Yes, looks that way... Six in the year.
G: OK, when's his next Ocado delivery?
HC: This Thursday at 7:20 p.m.
G: OK, I'll ask Ocado if they'll do a deal on Uncle Ben's long-grain rice... Hold on... Yes, bonzer, they'll do 10 per cent off if he puts it into his two-month basket. Does he want any tomatoes with that? They go real well.

0.25 seconds 1 result: Uncle Ben's long-grain rice: would you like an offer?

This is smart Google, when you add *yourself* to a search. If you add anything to a search it only gets better. Add your shoe size when buying shoes and you'll get only results that fit. Add the bookmarks that already exist in your own browser and you'll get the best guess results you already like. Add someone else's bookmarks if they *really* know music, instead of phoning them and asking, and their knowledge will simplify things and extrapolate a better result for you.

This new idea of social slipstreaming will be very important in the future, for a huge and simple reason. In the UK in 2008, the average time spent on the Internet was 18.5 hours per week! That's all of *Lord of the Rings* the movie back to back TWICE every week. Of that 18.5 hours, 90 per cent of it starts with a search, not just a Google or Yahoo search, but a real search for a skirt from Topshop, or a bank balance, or tickets for a gig. They are all things you know you want and the Web will deliver them. So with such a high percentage of stuff you already know being searched for, how do you see anything new? By removing all that clutter, those adverts you never click on, those popups that annoy you, how do you find anything new? Where is the serendipity? You could *go* to a place that just lists the new things that are about such as Cool hunting.com or Crack unit, but because you have asked for the new, you haven't really been advertised to, you again have searched and found. I find all this very confusing in a landscape that hates advertising but exists only to share things.

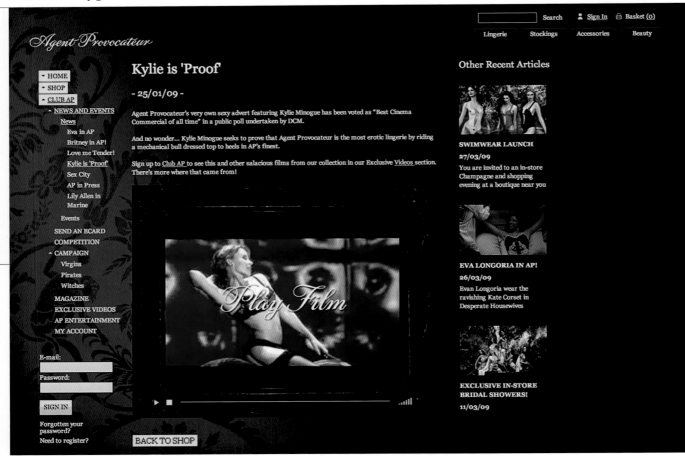

Left: The Web would not be the same without ... Kylie. Her 2001 advertisement campaign *Proof* for Agent Provocateur where she is seen riding a bull became the biggest sensation that year, and was voted best cinema commercial ever.

flickr

Search

Photos   Groups   People

[family   ]   **SEARCH**   Advanced Search
Search by Camera

⦿ Full text   ○ Tags only

☑ We found **9,716,816 results** matching family.

View: Most relevant • Most recent • Most interesting   Show: Details • Thumbnails   Slideshow ▾

The Damm Family in Their Car, Los Angeles, CA, USA, 1987, By Mary Ellen Mark by Thomas Hawk

💬 31 comments   ⭐ 70 faves   ▢ 1 note

Tagged with auto, family, bw, car ...
Taken on May 25, 2007, uploaded May 25, 2007

 See more of Thomas Hawk's photos, or visit his profile.

Family by Extra Medium

💬 60 comments   ⭐ 46 faves   ▢ 6 notes

Tagged with ocean, california, family, reflection ...
Taken on November 1, 2008, uploaded November 6, 2008

See Extra Medium's photos or profile.

...family home... by :petra:

💬 22 comments   ⭐ 24 faves   ▢ 7 notes

Tagged with house, art, brasil, painting ...
Taken on July 4, 2007, uploaded July 7, 2007

 See more of :petra:'s photos, or visit her

Above: Everyone's family album – flickr. We gave everybody a camera and then we made them curators; the ability to inspire and share became ubiquitous. It did not make everybody David Bailey but it made a lot of people aware of the beauty of photography.

197

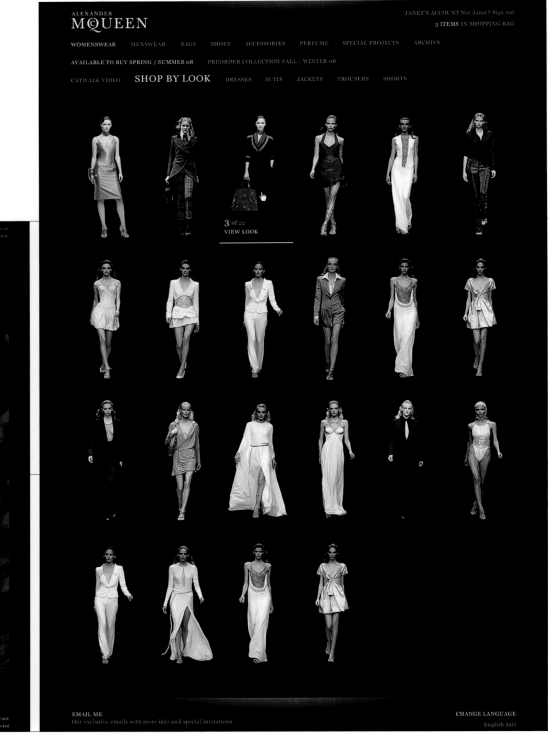

This page and opposite:
Alexander McQueen's website,
which Poke has worked on for the
past six years. What started as a
love affair between fashion and
navigation has now developed
within the Gucci group into a full
e-commerce platform.

After the Object_Interaction

WOMENSWEAR . MENSWEAR . BAGS . SHOES . ACCESSORIES . PERFUME . SPECIAL PROJECTS . ARCHIVE

AVAILABLE TO BUY SPRING / SUMMER 08 . PREORDER COLLECTION FALL / WINTER 08

CATWALK VIDEO . **SHOP BY LOOK** . DRESSES . SUITS . JACKETS . TROUSERS . SHORTS

Look **3** of 22

PREVIOUS . ALL LOOKS . NEXT

MORE VIEWS

ACCESSORIES

PRINT DETAILS
SEND TO A FRIEND

**To get this full look, buy
the items listed below.**

RED & BLACK SUMMER
SCARFE
£65.00
VIEW DETAILS ▶

RED & BLACK SUMMER
KNIT TOP
£425.00
VIEW DETAILS ▶

BLACK COTTEN TROUSERS
£375.00
VIEW DETAILS ▶

RED LIPSTICK NOVAK BAG
£880.00
VIEW DETAILS ▶

BLACK LEATHER HEELS
£650.00
VIEW DETAILS ▶

EMAIL ME
Our exclusive emails with more info and special invitations

STORE LOCATOR . SIZE GUIDE & WASHCARE . RETURNS POLICY

ABOUT MCQUEEN . CONTACT US . TERMS & CONDITIONS

© ALEXANDER MCQUEEN 2007 ALL RIGHTS RESERVED

CHANGE LANGUAGE

English Intl

Français

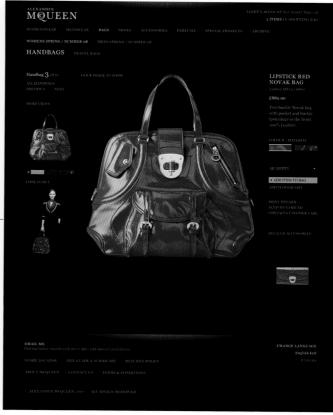

ALEXANDER
MCQUEEN

JANET'S ACCOUNT Not Janet? Sign out

3 ITEMS IN SHOPPING BAG

WOMENSWEAR MENSWEAR BAGS SHOES ACCESSORIES PERFUME SPECIAL PROJECTS ARCHIVE

WOMENS SPRING / SUMMER 08 MENS SPRING / SUMMER 08

HANDBAGS TRAVEL BAGS

Handbag **3** of 12 CLICK IMAGE TO ZOOM

ALL HANDBAGS
PREVIOUS NEXT

MORE VIEWS

LOOK TO BUY

**LIPSTICK RED
NOVAK BAG**

£880.00

Two buckle Novak bag
with pocket and buckle
fastenings to the front.
100% Leather.

COLOUR / MATERIAL

QUANTITY

▶ ADD ITEM TO BAG
ADD TO WISH LIST

PRINT DETAILS
SEND TO A FRIEND
CONTACT CUSTOMER CARE

RELATED ACCESSORIES

EMAIL ME
Our exclusive emails with more info and special invitations

STORE LOCATOR SIZE GUIDE & WASHCARE RETURNS POLICY

ABOUT MCQUEEN CONTACT US TERMS & CONDITIONS

© ALEXANDER MCQUEEN 2007 ALL RIGHTS RESERVED

CHANGE LANGUAGE

English Intl

Français

ALEXANDER
MCQUEEN

JANET'S ACCOUNT Not Janet? Sign out

3 ITEMS IN SHOPPING BAG

WOMENSWEAR MENSWEAR BAGS SHOES ACCESSORIES PERFUME SPECIAL PROJECTS ARCHIVE

WOMENS SPRING / SUMMER 08 MENS SPRING / SUMMER 08

CATWALK VIDEO SHOP BY LOOK DRESSES SUITS JACKETS TROUSERS SHORTS **KNIT TOPS**

Knit tops **5** of 16 CLICK IMAGE TO ZOOM

ALL KNIT TOPS
PREVIOUS NEXT

MORE VIEWS

LOOK TO BUY

**RED & BLACK
KNIT TOP**

£425.00

Cropped cashmere
button summer knit
cardigan. 100%
Cashmere.

COLOUR / MATERIAL

SIZE - EURO

SIZE GUIDE

QUANTITY

▶ ADD ITEM TO BAG
ADD TO WISH LIST

PRINT DETAILS
SEND TO A FRIEND
CONTACT CUSTOMER CARE

RELATED ACCESSORIES

EMAIL ME
Our exclusive emails with more info and special invitations

STORE LOCATOR SIZE GUIDE & WASHCARE RETURNS POLICY

ABOUT MCQUEEN CONTACT US TERMS & CONDITIONS

© ALEXANDER MCQUEEN 2007 ALL RIGHTS RESERVED

CHANGE LANGUAGE

English Intl

Français

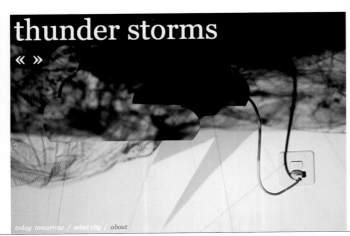

thunder storms

« »

today tomorrow / select city / about

snow

« »

today tomorrow / select city / about

london
wed 1 apr 2009
15°c
partly cloudy

today tomorrow / select city / about

Talking to a mass audience

I was chatting down The Owl and Pussycat with a mate of mine from a large advertising agency and asked him what he was doing at the moment, what his dream job was. He staggered me by saying 'posters' – in fact, more specifically cross-track posters on the London Underground! I always thought it would be cinema and TV ads, but he explained that, because TV has become so granular (after all, you can now watch whole channels dedicated to American cop reruns or redecorating your semi), the audience on these channels is so specific that you can't truly advertise to them. Cross-track posters, by contrast – or so my friend told me – are seen by everyone, with no demographic other than they're sick to death of commuting and could do with a new shirt. It really is talking to the mass audience. Marketing on the Internet has a similarly universal but somewhat haphazard demographic.

In the early days of the Web, brands struggled to find a reason to be online. Even now, the *why* is still a massive reason to fill out before you start any digital project, because it will place the user, the consumer, at the heart of the brief, not the marketing manager. Back then, though, when all brands could do was to stake out a claim online and guard their brand identity in the wilds of cyberspace, the only thing you could get from a brand was the interaction with it. The user journey was part of this. *How* you discovered information was as important as any content you found – if the navigation was slow and turgid, the brand was slow and turgid. The order in which you placed information, sometimes the *same* information, was important. 'Dog bites man' is natural; 'man bites dog' is a Tarantino movie. Same content in a different order can give a whole different story. And that's all designers,

then, really had to play with. You couldn't get a beer online, you couldn't drive that new VW Beetle, so you were left with designing the residual feeling the brand wanted to own.

Today e-commerce adds purpose to the Web question of why. The brand no longer needs to speak in riddles and offer souvenirs of itself; it can be the magazine for the new, the storefront for the magpies, assistant to the indecisive, and deliver on the promise of consumerism. Today, designing *beyond* the object involves not only the industrial designers, the packaging designers, the advertisers, the stores, but also the back-end server farm, the delivery company and the care they take to wrap it. Even the returns policy – how easy it is to send back that late-night Friday purchase – is *as* important as the money the brand spends on advertising.

Today's digital consumer is not a demographic sector – it's far bigger than that. The size of the Web is staggering. One single corner of the Web, MySpace, is currently running at more than 190 million users – that makes it, population-wise, the ninth biggest country in the world, bigger than Brazil. It's vast, and like a country it has its own rules and culture, its own internal police, and just about every creed, colour and age. Its only common religion is to show off or share. To change my metaphor, it's like a teenager's bedroom, with all the flat-pack IKEA furniture as the 2D building blocks on the Web, and the Athena posters of my years the brands' flyers posted on the 'wall'. And just like that teenager, the people on MySpace are constantly rearranging their furniture and friends according to the latest micro trend.

It's ridiculous to still find brands that think that, just because they're on MySpace, people will see them – it's like sending a postcard to Brazil and thinking everyone there will

london
thu 2 apr 2009
8°c
haze

today tomorrow / select city / about

rainy

« »

today tomorrow / select city / about

This page and opposite: The British obsession with weather is beautifully illustrated here in physical form. I love the partly cloudy skies with the light bulb. It is so good to see graphic design moving into new areas, even an area as well trodden as British weather. Find your own city at www.kurtli.com/weather.

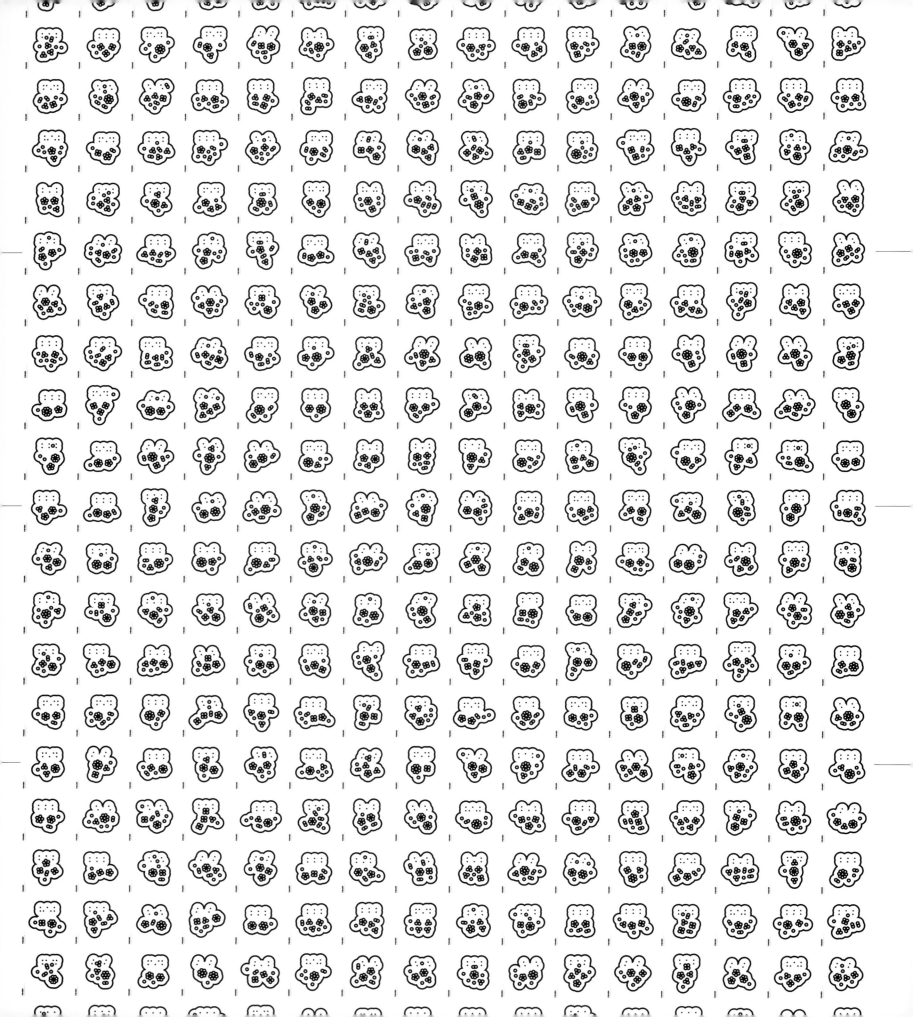

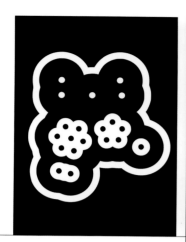

This page and opposite: Fid.Gen, created and designed by Karsten Schmidt, is an open source, generative design tool for creating fiducial markers to be used in computer vision-based interactive projects/installations, based on the popular open-source package reacTIVision (reactable.org). The tool fills a niche by enabling reacTIVision to be used in scenarios where hundreds or thousands of objects (or people) need to be identified.

The novel layout process of the markers is interactive and physics driven and realized through a simulation of a complex network of springs, which automatically arrange themselves into the most optimum constellation to form unique markers. Often the generated markers are reminiscent of cute abstract characters, so adding a more human touch to a primarily technical mechanism.

get to know about your holiday. Only by becoming involved with a culture, by interacting on a micro level, can you truly understand its people and win them over one by one. Brands have to tread very carefully – the Internet is geared to the active individual, not to some amorphous, passive 'masses', and that individual can wield enormous power. After all, it takes only one person to start a fire online. In the old days they said: 'Never pick a fight with a person who buys ink by the barrel.' Well, nowadays everyone has an inexhaustible supply of 'ink' and the power to connect to millions of people who may share their concerns. This can be a dangerous thing for brands that may have been more than just a little lackadaisical about their customer support.

The power to name and shame companies that either mistake their advertising for interesting content or 'misplace' the truth of some of their claims has forced them to learn – and learn fast – about the simple fact that if there's a lie out there the Web will find it. If your product claims to be everything to all people, but keeps all the dirt in the fine print, then that's the information that will be published and commented upon. The Web does not work with an asterisk*. If there is anything that excludes or curtails the advertised promise, then that's all the Web will talk about.

The amount of advertising and press needed to correct this type of slip-up has meant that the word 'truth' has been mentioned in boardrooms for the first time in decades. Because you can't whitewash the digital world any more, you have to clean your dirty linen in public. An example that had the potential to become nuclear happened to the computer giant Dell, which, late in 2006, had an overheating problem with a small number of their machines. When I say 'overheating' I mean catching fire – allegedly. Now Dell being based in one of the most litigious societies on the planet, they decided not to deny it but open themselves up to the whole world and started www.direct2dell.com, a blog about themselves and the problems and criticism they faced. They held up their hands and talked in a way that was human and understanding, and by doing so enabled the company to ride out the storm. Go and read it now – http://direct2dell.com. It has evolved a bit but it still talks in the first person – 'I did this ... I am changing that' and so on – and it puts you and your problems at the heart of Dell. Brilliant.

It is this type of thing that gives the Web its fluidity, so that it ebbs and flows like the sea. Digital design, then, is never – and never can be – 'finished' and, for this reason, it's like no other profession represented in the Design Museum. It is semi-disposable. How many other chapters in this book can say, 'the more we throw out, the better our world gets'? In digital, it's a never-ending feast of redefine and redesign.

An age of innocence

The democracy of the Web is often a very difficult proposition to sell to a client – the rules about what you can and cannot do may not be written down but are very much in evidence when you choose to look. Take, for example, YouTube, where glossy professional TV advertisements collide with people's own homemade film clips. Now the advertising industry has been around since the 1850s, it spends billions of pounds creating short film-based advertisements, and is the master of small messaging and promotion. YouTube is the digital repository for film and, since its inception back in 2006,

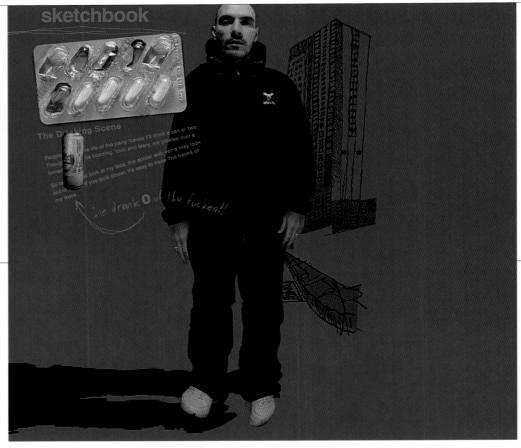

This page: The team behind www.martin-h.com and www.wefail.com, in their own words: 'WEFAIL have cried too many times over graphic design, but they won't be fooled again.' The experimentation that we all try and keep in our work is taken as a religion. We love this site.

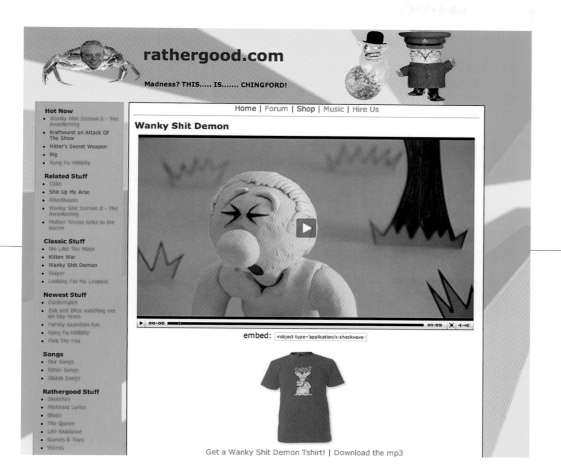

ratherbood.com

Madness? THIS..... IS....... CHINGFORD!

Home | Forum | **Shop** | Music | Hire Us

Wanky Shit Demon

embed: `<object type="application/x-shockwave-`

Get a Wanky Shit Demon Tshirt! | Download the mp3

Hot Now
- Wanky Shit Demon 2 - The Awardening
- Kraftwurst on Attack Of The Show
- Hitler's Secret Weapon
- Big
- Kung Fu Hillbilly

Related Stuff
- Cake
- Shit Up My Arse
- Ghosthouse
- Wanky Shit Demon 2 - The Awardening
- Mother Teresa talks to the Queen

Classic Stuff
- We Like The Moon
- Kitten War
- Wanky Shit Demon
- Slayer
- Looking For My Leopard

Newest Stuff
- Cuckenspiel
- Zak and Bliss watching me on Sky News
- Family Guardian fun
- Kung Fu Hillbilly
- Fink The Fox

Songs
- Our Songs
- Other Songs
- Jibjab Songs

Rathergood Stuff
- Sketches
- Misheard Lyrics
- Blogs
- The Queen
- Life Guidance
- Games & Toys
- Videos

IT'S NICE THAT

About
Submit
Publication
Issue 1
Features
Art of Football
Original Format
NSW Presents....
YCN Live
Categories
Advertising (33)
Animation (66)
Architecture (12)
Art (139)
Books (26)
Events (64)
Exhibitions (87)
Fashion (23)
Film (121)
Graphic Design (534)
Illustration (599)
Interactive (7)
It's Nice That (35)
It's Not Us (329)
Miscellaneous (70)
Music (116)
Photography (280)
Product Design (112)
Publications (32)
Sculpture (21)
Set Design (2)
Web (80)
Writing (9)
Archive
April 2009
March 2009
February 2009
January 2009
December 2008
November 2008
October 2008
September 2008
August 2008
July 2008
June 2008
May 2008
April 2008
March 2008
February 2008
January 2008
December 2007
November 2007
October 2007
September 2007

Interactive

TOMMASO LANZA
Interactive

Italian Tommaso Lanza is currently studying Design Interactions at the Royal College of Art in London.

Pictured is 'Industrial Fragility', the project tells a story of loneliness and neglectfulness. "Some of the most familiar and iconic items are either so ubiquitous that we stopped paying any sort of attention or silently disappearing from our lives because of technological obsolescence. Mundane and obsolete household objects are given new importance by slight modifications of their established nature, creating a new loving and fragile tension between us and them."

www.tommasolanza.com

Posted by Will / Mar 31, 2009

UNITED VISUAL ARTISTS
Interactive

Not sure if it's a recent update on the UVA site but always worth a look. Pictured is their responsive light installation consisting of 600 custom-designed mirrored LED tubes hanging above the entire Covent Garden market space.

www.uva.co.uk

Posted by Will / Mar 02, 2009

Above: What would the Web do without kittens? Singing kittens, in Viking helmets, in a gay bar? Joel Vietch is the mad magician ninja that is www.rathergood.com. He is directly responsible for 60 per cent of the madness that the Web has taken as its fuel. Here is his Wanky Shit Demon.

Right: www.ItsNiceThat.com Originating from my home town, Brighton, the graphic work from these contemporary designers bring a smile to any studio daily. More than inspiration, it is a guide to the creative landscape. They change the site regularly, but the work featured on it is consistently brilliant.

This page and opposite: Having given up my Playstation for slippers and a cigar, I was compelled to relate to the kids and feature the biggest game of the decade… Welcome to Little Big Planet. A BAFTA award-winning game that deserves to be bigger than Hollywood.

After the Object_Interaction

the community has watched more than 20,305 *years* of back-to-back video. Now the top 100 videos on YouTube voted for by this community do not move that often, and are a barometer of the most interesting films in the digital world. How many of this top 100 do you think are paid for, bought brand commercials, the ones the advertising companies make? *Four*! Just four – it's staggering to think that only four videos have made it into the list. I've been the president of the UK's Design and Art Direction Awards and judged years' and years' worth of paid advertising, and I know there's amazing work out there, so it's puzzling that it doesn't make it big in YouTube.

The reason is that the digital world is still, in a way, going through it own age of innocence. The Internet is a land built by those long-haired crazy pioneers the hobbyists, and it's still a land of the hobbyist. People don't want their best efforts to be compared with Ridley Scott's latest epic; they don't want their latest postings on Flickr to hang next to the professionals' masterpieces in a portrait gallery. They just want to play, and not be judged. It's not that they hate the professional; it's just they haven't found the professionalism within themselves yet.

Remember when your parents got their first colour camera cheap enough for them to be flagrant with the film? *Their* parents never had one, and so it was the age of exploration. They snapped away at anything, and I bet every family, at one point in their history, has hundreds of images of truncated sunburned bodies, with missing heads and feet... They took so many because it was exciting and new; they played with the technology, and only after a decade or so did they begin to have an inkling of the real techniques of photography, though they would never presume to call themselves 'photographers'. It's just like that today, though on a much grander scale. The mass digital audience have been given a plethora of creative tools and now they're playing ... and discovering just how hard it is to be a real photographer, a real filmmaker, a real journalist, and so on.

This creatively tooled-up audience are as engaged and as energetic as our forebears with that first camera, and it won't take ten years – remember, this is the digital world – before they start to realize that there are professionals out there and that there are new levels that they may themselves be driven to rise to. But what all of them will develop is a massive understanding and respect of *all* the different aspects of design and communication.

From science to emotion

Truth be told, 99 per cent of the Internet today is still *curated* work – people finding stuff, showing us new things, sharing their finds with an audience that may or not be there. Only 1 per cent of the digital world is *created* – made new by someone, designed by someone. It is this 1 per cent that is the currency of the Web, made by people who *contribute* rather than just *consume*.

I don't think there's been a better time in history to be a designer, to strive to create, and never a better time to bring that creation easily and truthfully to a mass audience who will appreciate it. Digital design has moved beyond the object, beyond the technology of its platform. It is not only inspired by 'how can we do it', but also focused by 'why should we do it'. The move is away from science and into emotions. Digital design is behaviour over brand.

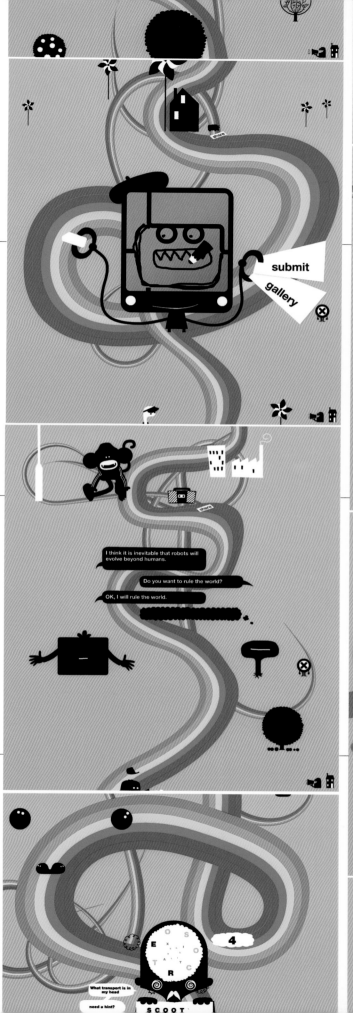
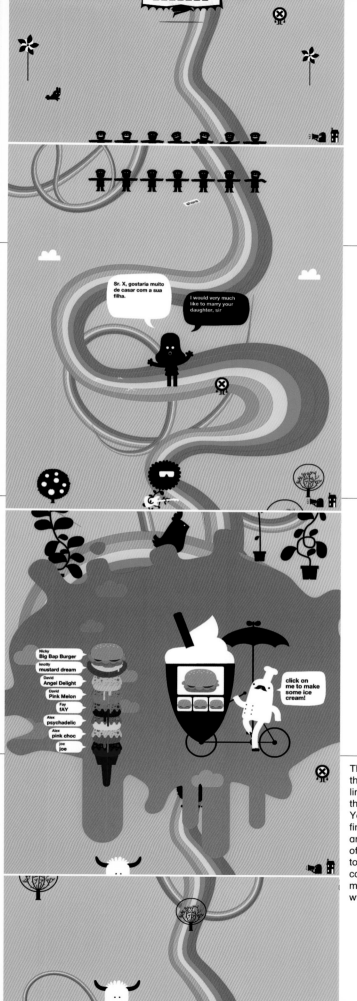

This page and opposite: 'Good things should never end' was the line that inspired Poke's work on the Orange Unlimited website. You can scroll all day and never find the bottom – it's full of games, animations and LOVE. All aspects of an advertising idea do not have to be identical, as long as their core thought is visualized in the most appropriate way. www.orangeunlimited.com

This page and opposite:
For Cobra Beer Poke made this
iPhone application, iBanter. I always
forget jokes in the pub, and used to
save them as texts from my mates.
Now it is easy, with new video jokes
sent every Friday from Britain's rising
comedians – as easy as the beer
on a Friday night.

After the Object_Interaction

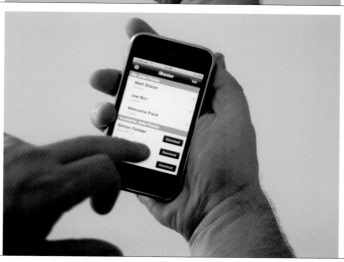
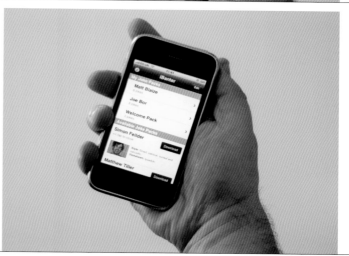

Making Marks

Identity
Wally Olins

Identity is now called branding, and it's ubiquitous. Everything from the nation to museums and from mobile phones to football clubs is branded, and everyone knows what branding is – or thinks they do.

Branding has always been part of the human condition. You don't need to be an anthropologist to see how visible manifestations of belonging have always been an intrinsic part of the identity of any group of human beings. From tribal markings to esoteric clothing, personal, religious, cultural, political and military affiliations have always been defined visually.

It's hardly a surprise, therefore, that as industrial corporations emerged and grew in size they adopted marks of identity. The identity of the industrial corporation first became visible during the railway age in the mid-nineteenth century. In Britain especially, staff uniforms, the livery of rolling stock and engines, and the architecture of the great termini were all visually distinctive and representative of the differing aspirations, styles and cultures of each of the major railway companies.

Perhaps the high-water mark of this first phase of visual identity in industry was reached in the early years of the twentieth century, when the architect Peter Behrens (1868–1940) – with the assistance of the young Walter Gropius (1883–1969) and other distinguished architects and designers of the Deutscher Werkbund ('German Work Federation') – developed the first modern corporate identity for the German industrial giant AEG. The programme embraced everything from buildings and products to advertising and graphics, including a distinctive logo. This ambitious programme was curtailed only by the outbreak of World War I in 1914.

Identity lost

Then, somehow, corporate identity lost its way – in industry at least. In the earlier half of the twentieth century, design as a significant manifestation of the identity of corporations (with one or two distinguished but isolated exceptions) more or less disappeared. The idea that the totality of the visual impact of the organization – its products, environments and graphic communication – could be coordinated and controlled became unfamiliar. Of course, companies had their logos, symbols or trademarks – created mostly by individual graphic artists working as jobbing designers on a one-off basis – but the concept of identity as a discrete and coordinated discipline sank into disuse – except in the European political world where it burgeoned. Paradoxically, the totalitarian regimes of the 1920s and 1930s, whether fascist, Nazi or communist, all used powerful, highly coordinated triumphalist symbolism to underline their monstrous ideologies, at a time when in industry identity languished.

Throughout the 1920s and 1930s only a very few business organizations commissioned what were mostly called 'house styles'. The great identity programmes of the period – such as those undertaken by London Transport in the UK, Olivetti in Italy or the Container Corporation in the United States – were inspired by corporate leaders who had either a social conscience or an aesthetic sensitivity, or occasionally even both. The industrial patrons of the earlier part of the twentieth century thought like the Medici in Renaissance Florence: they wanted to celebrate their own personal triumphs. Unlike the Medici, however, they also wanted to improve the working lives of their employees and to create a more agreeable and harmonious world.

Wally Olins

This page: During the early twentieth century Peter Behrens helped forge the first corporate identity – for German industrial giant AEG. This encompassed everything from the publicity – including this Jugendstil-inflected advertisement for light bulbs (1907–8; left) – to whole buildings, notably the rigorously geometric Turbine Hall (1910; right) in Berlin.

Right: The Italian typewriter manufacturer Olivetti was an early pioneer of corporate identity, and one of the first companies to feature women in their advertisements in a persuasive bid to make their products more visually appealing.

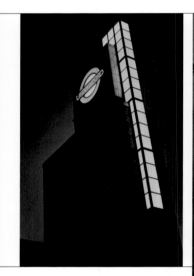

Above left: The illuminated tower
of Boston Manor Underground
station (1934), designed by Charles
Holden. During the early twentieth
century, London's previously
fragmented underground railway
system underwent a process of
integration the public interface of
which was a corporate-wide styling
that embraced architecture, graphics
and typography. (Photograph taken
in 1935.)

Above right: Travellers outside
an Underground station in the late
1930s. The Underground map was
a key ingredient in the development
of a unified London Transport
identity. The map shown here is
a version of the geographically
based Underground map first
introduced in 1908. In the 1930s
this was gradually superseded by
Harry Beck's iconic diagrammatic
Tube map, which was styled like
an electrical circuit.

The important identity programmes of the earlier part of the twentieth century frequently revolved about an idea that has recently re-emerged in a big way: corporate social responsibility (although of course it wasn't called that then). However, none of these programmes was effectively coordinated. Frank Pick (1878–1941), head of London Transport, worked together with the architect Charles Holden (1875–1960) and his team on the design of the city's Underground stations, but they had no direct relationship with either the graphic designers who worked on the posters and advertising (notably Edward McKnight Kauffer), or the industrial designers who worked on the Underground trains, buses and bus stops. Everything was ad hoc.

Nor was there a natural partner with whom the commissioning organization could work. There were virtually no design consultancies that could manage or coordinate an entire visual programme. The individual graphic artists (as they called themselves) who led the field thought of themselves as fastidious professionals who combined art with industry; indeed, a leading design magazine of the day was actually called *Art and Industry*. Graphic artists were often represented by agents, such as the Clement Dane Studio, notable for its work with London Transport in the post-war period. An agency solicited work for individual graphic artists, represented them and concluded financial transactions (usually in guineas) on their behalf, much as writers' agents do today.

There were of course a few design consultancies, notably the Design Research Unit, led by the architect Sir Misha Black (1910–77) and the graphic designer Milner Grey (1899–1997). Established between the world wars, the Design Research Unit at least attempted to grapple with larger jobs. There were one or two other companies in the field that also purported to carry out major design programmes, including one led by Richard Lonsdale-Hands (1913–69), but it is fair to say that these achieved little of real significance.

Most designers or graphic artists worked alone. Many had considerable reputations. Hans Schleger (1898–1970; better known under his nom de plume, Zero) and Frederic Henri Kay Henrion (1914–90) were both émigrés from Nazi Germany and brought with them a status rarely enjoyed by British designers at this time. Another young German expatriate, Walter Landor (1913–95), was in Britain for a few years before starting what became a highly successful career in San Francisco. There were also a number of well-known British designers, such as Abram Games (1914–96) and Ashley Havinden (1903–73), the latter, unusually, a creative director of an advertising agency, Crawford's. Many of these designers were essentially jobbing graphic artists. They received a commission, fulfilled it, and then went on to another job.

It was the advertising agency that regarded itself as the natural long-term communications partner for the client. The domination of the advertising agency was overwhelming. Virtually all major corporations regarded the advertising agency as their only serious link with design and the graphic arts – that is, insofar as they wanted one. They may have used individual graphic artists from time to time, but usually only to support the agency effort.

Because advertising agencies made their money out of billings in the media, they were not interested in much else to do with their clients' visual output – certainly not with products or the interiors of offices, shops and other corporate

Above right: A group of London Transport bus drivers and conductors, c.1935, wearing two distinct styles of uniform, the drivers distinguished by their long overcoats. The conductor on the left has an old-style PSV badge on his lapel, whereas the driver and conductor on the right have the new style of badge.

Far right: A line of London Transport buses standing in Upton Park bus garage, 1933.

WESTMINSTER
FROM THE THAMES

SEE THE MODEL OF THE NEW BUILDING

EARLS
COURT

IN THE TICKET HALL AT
CHARING CROSS STATION
NOVEMBER 9TH–26TH OPEN 10–10
★ SUNDAYS 12–8

SPECIAL AREAS EXHIBITION
★ JANUARY 30TH TO FEBRUARY 15TH

EVERY CITIZEN SHOULD SEE THIS

EXHIBITION ARRANGED BY THE COMMISSIONER FOR

SPECIAL AREAS ENGLAND & WALES
WITH THE HELP OF
THE MINISTRY OF LABOUR IN THE
TICKET HALL AT
CHARING CROSS STATION

This page and opposite: Under the auspices of London Transport director Frank Pick, graphic posters, such as these designed by Edward McKnight Kauffer in 1934–6, became a powerful tool in communicating the identity of London's transport network, and indeed of the British capital as a whole. Many of the posters included constant features such as Edward Johnston's Underground typeface and the LT roundel, which helped distinguish them from surrounding commercial advertising.

Pick often commissioned work from young contemporary artists, while designs frequently featured commercial takes on international avant-garde styles such as Cubism and Futurism. The striking modernity of the posters might have chimed well with other features of London Transport identity, such as Holden's brick-and-concrete stations, but in reality there was very little joined-up thinking.

EPPING FOREST
BY MOTOR BUS
ROUTE NO.

CHEAP
RETURN TICKETS

TO
Aldwych
Holborn
Covent Garden
Leicester Square

6 D

Piccadilly Circus
Dover Street
Down Street
Trafalgar Square
Oxford Circus
Strand
Charing Cross

8 D

Issued on Weekdays, available on forward journey by any
train after 10 a.m.   Return by any train on day of issue.

FROM
UNDERGROUND
THIS
STATION

E. McKnight   Kauffer '27.

This page: Work by F H K Henrion, one of the pioneers of corporate identity in post-war Britain. During World War I, Henrion worked for the Ministry of Information, designing posters for the Dig for Victory campaign, among others, as well as for smaller projects such as this poster (above) for 'Artists Aid Russia' (1940). Immediately after the war, Henrion lent his talents to national organizations such as the Post Office (top and right).

environments. Advertising agencies produced advertising – communication material aimed at persuading customers and potential customers to buy ... and buy again.

So the notion that an organization as a whole could develop a clear concept of what it stood for and what it did, and then encapsulate that concept through all of its visual manifestations – its products, environments and communications, let alone the behaviour of its staff – hardly existed. That's why, within large companies, the property department looked after buildings; the engineers and a few 'stylists' looked after product design; and the advertising agencies looked after communications. Simple, perhaps ... but wrong.

Identity rediscovered

Around the late 1950s and early 1960s a few very large organizations in the UK began to play around with the idea that they needed a distinctive and coordinated visual identity. Some of these were transport companies – airlines, the steamship line Cunard, British Rail and so on. Tentatively, they began to see that if they could find a way to coordinate their visual presence – their graphics, uniforms and environments – they would make a powerful impact on the outside world and even on their own staff. In the mid-1960s George Williams, in the newly created position of design manager at British Rail, commissioned the Design Research Unit to create a comprehensive design programme that included not only the groundbreaking logo designed by Gerald Barney but also a range of uniforms for railway staff. Unfortunately, it has to be added, the caps for the uniforms closely resembled the forage caps used by the German Wehrmacht in World War II and were pretty soon abandoned, although the logo stayed around for years.

At the same time, other design consultants were also waking up to the idea that a coordinated approach to design could bring them hitherto unimaginable opportunities. In 1967 Henrion cooperated with his former assistant Alan Parkin (born 1934) to write *Design Coordination and Corporate Image*. I quote from the blurb:

This is the first authoritative book on an important new subject. *Design Coordination and Corporate Image* is the title chosen by the authors to describe the activity which creates a house style, and yet goes a great deal further and deeper. It is an activity which can only be initiated by a corporation's top management as a long-term policy. Its planning and implementation must be accepted as an important managerial responsibility. Success can only be achieved by close collaboration between management and designer.

Design coordination is the concerted and related planning of all activities which can be seen. Buildings, products, packaging, transport, stationery, publications, signs, uniforms and all kinds of promotion. These constitute the design items which have to be coordinated.

By today's standards these observations may seem both obvious and platitudinous, but in the Britain of that time they were both unusual and inspirational. Henrion, it turned out, was very far-sighted.

In retrospect, it is also clear that the example of the United States was an influential factor. During the 1950s and 1960s, Eliot Noyes (1910–77) was bringing a vigorous corporate identity to both IBM and Mobil, collaborating with luminaries

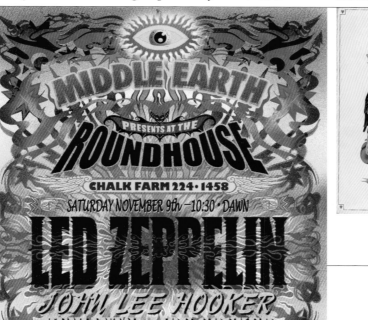

Right: Alan Aldridge (1943–) and his graphic design agency, INK, were largely responsible for creating the image of Swinging London – a world of bold colour, retro lettering and surreal, *Alice in Wonderland*-like imagery. Among his projects were logos for the Hard Rock Café and The House of Blues, together with numerous posters for the contemporary music scene.

Above: Aldridge became especially closely associated with the Beatles and their record label, Apple, and helped to create the Fab Four's particular 'brand identity' of hallucinogenic zaniness. Book cover for *The Beatles Illustrated Lyrics* (1969), together with the illustration for the 1966 song 'Tomorrow Never Knows'.

such as Saul Bass (1920–96) and other great designers of the day to produce work that was truly inspirational. There were a number of other high-profile successful designers in the United States, including Walter Dorwin Teague (1883–1960), Henry Dreyfuss (1904–72) and, particularly, Raymond Loewy (1893–1986), all of whom came from an earlier generation, and none of whom was shy about self-promotion. They designed industrial products, exhibitions, publications and graphics, and they even tackled house styles – or identities, as they were now beginning to be called.

But the US company that shouted loudest about identity was Lippincott & Margulies, founded in 1943. The phrase 'corporate identity' is attributed to the company's co-founder Walter Margulies (1914–86) himself; at least, he claimed to have coined it. Margulies made it his personal mission to put identity consultancy into the mainstream of US business, and over 20 or so years produced a plethora of publications, all dedicated to showing US corporations how a significant identity programme could make their businesses more profitable. It isn't too much to say that Margulies was the single most important voice in putting identity back on the map.

This is a typical piece of Lippincott & Margulies promotional blurb from the 1970s, but it could have been written earlier – or later:

Achieving a competitive advantage. Aside from solving specific business problems, identity management is a competitive tool. To negotiate successfully for the human, technological and financial resources, and for the distribution networks and new technology needed to create value and competitive advantage – in short, to attract the favourable attention of key audiences – all businesses must find ways to differentiate themselves from all others. A strong corporate identity supports that primary objective.

At the time, this kind of stuff was dramatically different from anything anyone else was saying. Phrases such as 'value creation' and 'competitive advantage' that lit up the pages of Lippincott & Margulies publications had never been used by the design world before. It was an attempt to make design relevant to business. And it worked.

Swinging London

But there was another factor at play in the UK – a dramatic change in the Zeitgeist, and more specifically the emergence of what was called 'Swinging London'. So much has been written about the change from austerity to hedonism, from self-restraint and quiet deference to self-publicity and noisy independence, that it seems otiose to go through it all again. But there is no doubt that the mood in post-war Britain – and in London particularly – between the 1950s and 1960s changed almost beyond recognition, at least in the world of fashion, music, the arts, and of course design. And, as the mood changed, the design business changed with it.

Quite suddenly a number of very ambitious, very young people came into design. Many of them seemed to feel intuitively that there was a big opportunity somewhere, although they might not have known exactly what or where it was. They were optimistic, iconoclastic, imaginative and, in a way, quite brave. Perhaps, though, they – I should say we – were just foolhardy. We didn't exactly know what we were doing, but whatever it was we wanted to do it.

This page and opposite:
In 1964 Britain's nationalized railway company, British Rail, commissioned a far-reaching and innovative identity programme. The programme included the famous red-and-white 'double arrow' logo by Gerald Barney, a Rail Alphabet typeface by typographic legends Jock Kinneir and Margaret Calvert, and even cutlery by David Mellor.

Above: The power of the logo –
the old British Rail logo has burned
itself deeply into the national psyche.
Although the company has long
since been broken up and privatized,
the logo survives as a generic street
sign for a railway station.

This page: Then and now – Habitat shopping bags from the 1960s and now. Terence Conran's chain of household furnishing stores, Habitat – founded in 1964 – marketed the pared-down, Scandinavian style to Britain's newly affluent middle classes. The distinctive lower-case typographic style has helped to make the Habitat brand a long-lived one.

Making Marks_Identity

We didn't know quite what the opportunities were, but we wanted to find them.

Design hit the high street in a big way and quite soon it became public property. While Terence Conran (1931–) was busy launching Habitat, a store that encapsulated, promoted and sold the modern lifestyle to the young, increasingly affluent middle class, Mary Quant and her contemporaries were introducing an entirely new London fashion scene in Chelsea. Design became interesting, noisy, exciting, groundbreaking and everyone noticed it, so eventually even big businesses began to sit up a bit.

Suddenly, in the field of identity consultancy – almost as it seemed from nowhere – extremely talented and ambitious individual designers and consultants came together to form groups that embraced a number of design disciplines. Many of these groups developed an idea that design could be used to help solve significant commercial problems. Design, they felt, could become important, even mainstream.

Sir Paul Reilly, later Lord Reilly, director of the Council of Industrial Design (now the Design Council), noticed the changing atmosphere and strongly supported it in influential government and senior business circles. He and his successors continually lobbied the various governments of the day to take design seriously and to support it ... and sometimes – not often, but from time to time – they did. Occasionally a junior minister would appear from somewhere, such as John Butcher (who, as it happened was a Tory), who really understood the power of design and was very supportive. Usually, however, these junior ministers lasted just a year or two and were replaced by bewildered nonentities, so one has to say that government support was at best partial and fragmentary.

Nonetheless, and for a variety of reasons, quite suddenly in the 1960s corporate design – or corporate identity as it began to be called – began to emerge. Identities – that is, full-scale, major corporate identities – began to be commissioned.

Identity takes off

In the early and mid-1960s a whole raft of design consultancy businesses sprang to life more or less at the same time. Wolff Olins – founded by myself and the designer Michael Wolff, and operating out of Camden Town, a rather less fashionable and less glamorous part of London than Mary Quant's Chelsea – started getting business from many sizeable companies, including Hadfield Paints, English Electric and even Norton, the motorcycle company. At that time I was chairman of the company, and we always liked to claim that we helped to put the final nail in the coffin of the British motorcycle industry. In 1966 the British Oxygen Company, one of the UK's largest companies, appointed Wolff Olins to carry out what was at that time one of the country's biggest identity programmes. We publicized it vigorously, and rather successfully, too.

James Pilditch (1929–95) started Allied International Designers, later to mutate into Aidcom, embracing product design, graphic design and environments. Alan Fletcher (1931–2006), Colin Forbes (1923–) and Bob Gill (1931–), all gifted and very talented graphic designers, came together to form Fletcher/Forbes/Gill, which soon mutated into Pentagram, a multidisciplinary design firm that very rapidly gained immense respect globally, both inside and outside the industry. And there were other companies, many less well known and usually more ephemeral.

Above: The 1960s saw the birth of numerous design consultancies in London. Among them was Fletcher/Forbes/Gill (later Pentagram), responsible for this 1962 advertisement for Pirelli slippers.

Above: The logo for Trees for Cities, designed by the London-based design consultancy Atelier Works. The logo is graphically very simple, yet manages to communicate its message supremely well.

Despite the example of such notable – and honourable – pioneers, throughout the 1960s and early 1970s identity consultancy remained peripheral, if not marginal; it was moreover rickety financially, and for the most part more or less incomprehensible to many people in most potential client businesses. Without overstating the case, it was only the sheer noisy exuberance of this new generation of design consultancies that made a few of the more enlightened members of the British business and industrial community begin to take notice of this strange thing called corporate identity.

Identity goes abroad

It didn't help that advertising agencies were for the most part suspicious of and disdainful towards the new breed of design consultancies. They continued for the most part to believe that if something had anything to do with communication it was their birthright to handle it.

But the identity consultancies, full of bravado and a bit of swagger, felt that if they could find work in the UK, where things weren't easy economically, they might also do well in Europe, where economic growth was much faster and business leaders were thought to be more open-minded. Design consultancies believed they could perhaps exploit the newfound fame – or was it notoriety? – of British design and Swinging London abroad. So, by the end of the 1960s, many of the new identity companies had at least as much work in Europe as in the UK. Thus a 1975 article in the *Sunday Times* entitled 'Designs on Europe' could pronounce: 'As far as Europeans are concerned, British is indisputably best when it comes to design consultancy, the business of using design to solve management as well as marketing problems.'

The journalist, Gwen Nuttall, went on:

That is why a handful of UK firms are now quite literally changing the face of Europe – re-vamping 9,000 petrol stations in Germany, designing the interior of the first self-service department store in Holland, shaping the appearance of three shopping centres in France. 'It is British designers who are getting on planes and going all out to sell their skills,' asserts James Pilditch of Allied International Designers, one of the first companies to set out deliberately for business across the Channel.

'The multi-skilled design office as we know it is very much an Anglo-American phenomenon,' observes Pilditch. 'You won't find a European design group which includes marketing men, sociologists, or architects in its team as a matter of course,' enlarges Wally Olins of Wolff Olins ... The fact that a Swedish multi-national, with timber and earth-moving equipment companies in North America, should come to London for a corporate image underlines Pilditch's argument. 'Europe is far behind us in corporate design.'

As the *Sunday Times* piece underlines, British design, especially identity design, was turning heads in mainland Europe and even in the United States, a development that British design companies exploited with their by now familiar mixture of panache and bravado.

At Wolff Olins we went into Germany. We won a job for Aral, the German petrol retailer, and then for a Dutch–German aircraft company named VFW-Fokker, and this led us eventually into a corporate identity programme for Volkswagen and Audi. We also went into France, where eventually we won Renault. Despite trying very hard, we

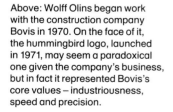

Above: Wolff Olins began work with the construction company Bovis in 1970. On the face of it, the hummingbird logo, launched in 1971, may seem a paradoxical one given the company's business, but in fact it represented Bovis's core values – industriousness, speed and precision.

Another Wolff Olins logo, this one for the venture-capital group Investors in People, or 3i. The logo, launched in 1991, helped to transform what had been a bland, anonymous institution into a dynamic, creative force.

This page: Founded in 1972,
Pentagram has been one of the
powerhouses of contemporary
multidisciplinary design. Two recent
Pentagram visual identities, for
the news agency Reuters and the
noodle-bar chain Wagamama.

never got a UK motor manufacturer as a client, which perhaps says something about the climate of UK industry at that time.

By now there were more than a handful of design or identity consultancies, almost all based in London, doing the same sort of thing. After a few forays into Europe, Pentagram successfully opened in New York, while a few smaller consultancies went into the Netherlands, which seemed friendly and near.

Revolution complete

This success had further repercussions. As the identity business began to take root in the UK, new consultancies started up. It doesn't take much money to form a design consultancy, only a bit of talent, some chutzpah and one or two clients. So younger people broke away from more established companies, themselves only a few years old, and started their own businesses. Many of them included the word 'design' in their titles – Design Bridge, Design House and so on.

By the early 1970s the old, fastidious and rather snooty professional practices that charged in guineas were out, and the small new businesses – a bit shaky financially perhaps, but full of self-confidence, charm and creativity – were in. Brilliant young designers such as Michael Peters and Rodney Fitch were even more ambitious than the previous generation ... and sometimes even more foolhardy. It's not surprising that, in their enthusiasm and ambition to grow, they occasionally tripped over themselves. Putting it another way, some of them simply didn't know when and where to stop.

As the UK identity business began to grow up, the work, which was created mainly in London, began to shock and excite the world. At Wolff Olins we created the Bovis

hummingbird logo, and shortly after this Michael Peters produced a remarkable range of packaging for Winsor & Newton, the ink and paints people. Pentagram produced outstanding design work in almost every category. Identity for commercial corporations, which had been neglected and misunderstood for years, began to be rediscovered, and the phrase 'corporate identity' became familiar.

Some of the most talented designers in Europe and the United States came to work in London, attracted by its success, and this of course made UK design even stronger. At Wolff Olins we had Erik Spiekermann (1947–), who later went on to found MetaDesign in what was then West Germany. For a time Michael Peters was partnered with the notable American designer Lou Klein. Bob Gill of Pentagram was American – and so it went on. London – perhaps slightly to everyone's surprise, and certainly to mine – had emerged as the design capital of Europe.

Once it took root, it seemed as if would never stop. Even when the UK economy got into real difficulties in the 1970s, with the three-day week, power cuts, endemic strikes, and more than a faint whiff of revolution in the air, the identity business continued to grow. Some people in government and elsewhere even began to contrast the success of Britain's creative sector with the decline of its traditional smokestack industries. This was the period when UK advertising led the world, and when some of today's great figures in architecture – Foster, Rogers, Grimshaw and so on – were beginning to shine. Identity consultancies were seen as part of the new world of service business success.

By the late 1970s and early 1980s, the identity business was no longer a misunderstood stepchild or waif. Peter Gorb ,

Above: Peter Saville (1955–) was responsible for creating an especially strong identity for the Manchester record label Factory Records, of which he was a founder member. He designed record sleeves for bands such as Joy Division and New Order, together with a company logo suggestive of the gritty urban scene out of which much of the music arose.

Right: Saville's poster for another iconic Manchester institution, the Haçienda nightclub.

Making Marks_Identity

the design enthusiast and Fellow of the London Business School, began to lecture about the place of design in business. I suspect that most of his fellow academics had absolutely no idea what he was talking about, and I know from personal experience that most of his students didn't either. Nevertheless it was, as he kept on saying, a step in the right direction. Increasingly, when some of us in the identity consultancy business, or profession, as so many of our older colleagues preferred to call it, tried to explain what we did in the wider world beyond smart, professional North London dinner parties, we were no longer met with quite so many blank stares of complete incomprehension.

Just about this time, a few of the more enlightened advertising agencies began to get the idea that design consultancies need not be competitors but could work with them together as part of a team. Then things began to change again...

The next phase
I think of the early 1980s as the time when the identity consultancy business began to take a new shape. We began to recruit people outside the somewhat narrow and specialized world of design. Enterprising graduates of business schools looking for new opportunities and ways of self-expression joined some of the more open-minded identity consultancies, and helped them to talk the language of business more confidently. Identity consultancies even recruited a few people from strategic consultancies such as Bain and McKinsey, usually leading – at least initially – to mutual incomprehension and a fairly rapid parting of the ways.

In recent years Britain's fiercely competitive supermarket chains have focused on creating eye-catching branding, of both their economy and high-end lines. The Co-operative chose a simple, predominantly black styling for its 'truly irresistible' range.

Identity consultancies even began to think about the *internal* world of the client – how, for example, the client's own staff could be convinced that the company's identity was worth believing in. Some of us experimented with recruiting human-resources consultants, because we wanted to make the identity a reality for people who worked inside the client company. At first, this mix of professionals with different backgrounds and disciplines didn't work very well. Designers, like so many other professionals, found it hard to look out from their small world and understand the larger picture – although many tried.

Nevertheless, by the early to mid-1980s identity was an established part of the communication scene, as companies all over Europe and the United States increasingly appointed consultants to work on identity programmes. It even had a flourishing trade press – two present-day stalwarts, *Creative Review* and *Design Week*, were launched in 1980 and 1986, respectively – and a few people wrote books about it. My own, *Corporate Personality*, was published by the Design Council in 1978. Naturally, as the activity became better established, it also attracted more would-be consultants and thus increased competition, too. So those of us who had started back in the 1960s now found that we had to fight hard to stay on top.

For the most part, identity design remained a cottage industry in which individual designers with varying levels of talent worked either on their own or with just an assistant or two. However, there were also quite a number of consultancies employing between 10 and 20 people, and even a few with staffs numbering as many as 70 or 80 and with offices in mainland Europe and the United States.

A few became very ambitious. James Pilditch even went public with his company, Allied International Designers. And so, shortly afterwards, did Michael Peters. Eventually this proved a step too far, or at least a step too early. Design consultancy managements in those early days did not have the expertise, experience or rigorous financial discipline that a publicly quoted company demands.

Additionally, there was a little American invasion. Lippincott & Margulies, Siegel & Gale and Landor – three of the leaders in the US identity business – all made attempts to enter the European market through London. Initially, only Landor was successful. Lippincott & Margulies, having failed to buy Wolff Olins, started a small branch operation but eventually withdrew. Siegel & Gale didn't take root in London either, although in recent years both Lippincott (under a modified name) and Siegel & Gale have tried again, with UK design offices working largely for European businesses.

The American invasion both challenged and heartened the UK-based companies. The US consultancies brought with them a very hard-nosed attitude. They claimed identity made sense for business because it contributed directly to a higher profile, which meant higher profits. The UK design consultancies listened and learned from this. They began to talk about profit, too. Not so much their own, but their clients'.

Attitudes began to change in advertising agencies also, and they became increasingly cooperative. Some of them started little design or identity departments of their own.

The take-off in the 1980s

All this, though, was merely preparation before the real take-off of identity consultancy in the 1980s. Under Margaret

Shelter

This page: Logo and associated 'branded' object for the homeless charity Shelter by Johnson Banks. Housing is here put at the core of the brand, with the *h* with a pitched roof. The doormat says 'Shelter' even without the logo.

The London-based studio North has been responsible for a large number of well-known contemporary branding projects, including the Co-op, BSM and the RAC. What is striking in the case of the RAC branding is not so much the logo, which is blunt and to the point, but the bright-orange company livery – highly visible on vans, motorcycles and uniforms.

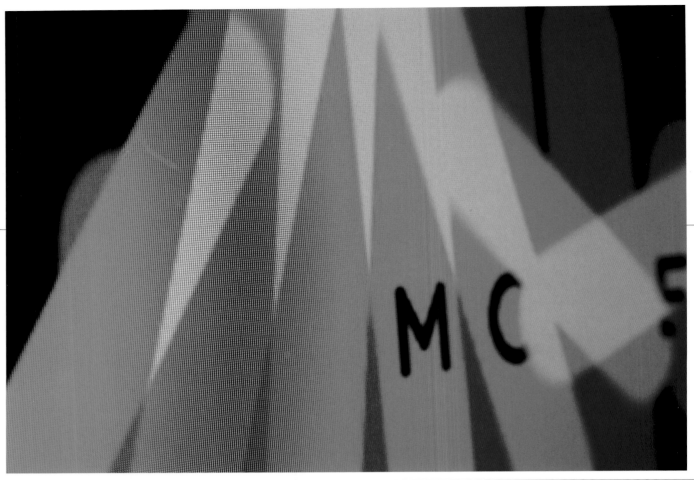

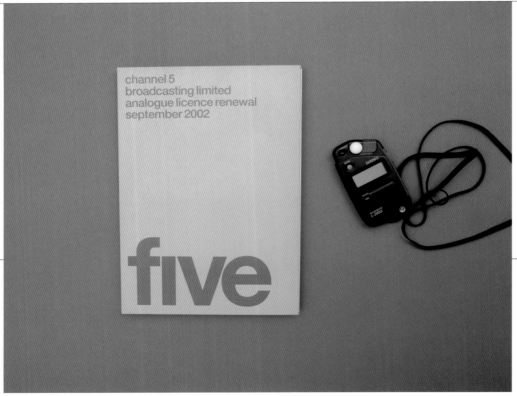

five

This page: In an age of multiple digital channels, branding has become all the more crucial for media companies, both in the private and the public spheres. The British design consultancy Spin – founded in 1992 by Patricia Finegan and Tony Brook – has created innovative identities for five and More4.

Thatcher the UK economy went through a revolution, the reverberations of which are still very much with us. Although manufacturing went into sharp decline, services of every kind took off. Suddenly an entirely new world opened up. The Thatcher government launched a series of privatization programmes, introducing competition in areas of activity that had previously been completely off-limits.

The privatization of Post Office Telecommunications and its transformation into BT were accompanied by dramatic technological change, in which a multiplicity of mobile phone businesses, all with powerful, noisy and occasionally dramatically different identities, emerged – apparently from nowhere. Where in 1970 there had been one telecoms brand with static technology, in 1990 there were about 80 with constantly changing technologies, many of which ultimately morphed into the IT business, which again spawned a proliferation of identity activity.

Telecommunications wasn't the only part of the business world that changed beyond recognition in the 1980s. In financial services, the dramatic deregulation of the market in 1986 – the so-called Big Bang – introduced competition all over the sector. The City of London was restructured more or less overnight. Even high street banks, which hitherto had regarded 'touting' for business as entirely inappropriate for their type of activity, suddenly got the competition bug. They merged, took each other over, launched new activities (some of them, as it transpired, rather risky), and competed in a kind of frenzy, the final outcome of which, according to some, emerged only in the economic crisis of 2008.

Insurance companies and other businesses in the financial sector also underwent dramatic technological and marketing transformations. Building societies demutualized and changed their names, their identities and, above all, their business models – though with unhappy long-term effects for some. Nevertheless, it was a development that brought a flood of new work for identity consultancies. To cite just one example, in 1989 Wolff Olins created the identity of First Direct, an exciting new type of remote banking, for Midland Bank.

Insurance companies with antiquated-sounding names such as Clerical and Medical, Standard Life or Liverpool and Victoria began to feel, well, just a bit out of touch. During the 1990s almost all of them had what was increasingly being billed as a makeover. They began to behave differently, often marketing themselves with considerable flair and appointing identity consultants to work with them. Many of the new identity programmes created primarily for the service sector were groundbreaking. At Wolff Olins, I think it is fair to say, the identities for both 3i and Orange were creative milestones.

Competition increased elsewhere and likewise necessitated strong branding. In broadcasting, Channel 4 commissioned Martin Lambie-Nairn (1945–) to create the new channel's identity. It was seen as a creative breakthrough and much applauded at the time. His company and others like it went on to create TV 'idents', as they are called in the trade, all over Europe.

The wave of new identities had a knock-on effect on other businesses. Retailers who had previously worked on various bits of their organization quite separately, who had treated issues such as packaging and staff behaviour in different silos, now began to look at the whole. Boots, for instance, appointed John McConnell (1940–) of Pentagram to coordinate all their design activity. Waitrose, Tesco,

This page: The BBC is not immune to the marketplace either and has had to create its own distinctive identity. Lambie-Nairn revamped the old BBC TV logo, the globe, by transforming it into a hot-air balloon and filming it in iconic landscapes across the country. Nation and national institution are reunited.

Sainsbury, Asda, all started to look at everything they did holistically – not just their packaging or shop design, but their identity as a whole. They began to realize that their own staff were a key part of their brand.

Enter the communications conglomerates

And as the identity business became much stronger, more important and more mainstream, another development took place.

In retrospect I suppose it was inevitable, but at the time it seemed to come out of the blue. Communications giants appeared on the scene and gobbled up many of the leading advertising agencies, identity consultancies, research companies, PR companies and events companies around the globe, and out of this hotchpotch of mergers and acquisitions there emerged a few very big, publicly quoted organizations with big, impersonal-sounding names like Interpublic, Omnicom, WPP and Publicis. In my opinion, it's impossible to exaggerate the significance of this development for the nature, style and culture of the identity business.

The most aggressive – or, if you prefer, entrepreneurial – of these new vast communications groups was WPP, headed up by the British businessman Martin Sorrell (1945–). Within a few years Sorrell had bought the distinguished US identity consultancy Anspach Grossman Portugal, which he then proceeded to merge with the London-based Sampson Tyrrell to form Enterprise IG (now called Brand Union), one of WPP's global identity consultancies. And that was only for starters. One of Sorrell's other targets was Landor, which under the ownership of Young & Rubicam had already engaged in an aggressive expansion programme.

The other huge communication groups weren't far behind. The London-based Interbrand was bought by Omnicom. Interbrand then marched across the world, buying one identity consultancy after another, many of them with very different cultures and traditions from each other. Each major communication group did the same. Interpublic created FutureBrand out of Diefenbach Elkins and a few other bits and pieces it had bought in various countries. Although many identity consultancies now shared the same name, it took time for them to shrink down into one company based around a single philosophy. Many of them have still not quite managed it. Within a few years during the 1990s, these identity consultancies were operating on a global basis. Some of them had twelve or more offices and five or six hundred staff.

How did the atmosphere and culture inside the new giant identity businesses change? If you run a large people business which is part of a publicly owned, high-profile, profit-hungry communications business, your job is to make the business both easy to understand and attractive to clients, who need continually to be reminded that it will help them make more money and grow. And in order to be very efficient and make good profits itself, the consultancy has to work fast. Is there likely to be a trade-off between the requirements for high levels of both profitability and creativity? Probably. The identity consultancy charges on time spent, so if you do it fast – wrap it up in formulaic deliverables and sell something not too challenging, with the focus firmly on the logo – it doesn't have to be that imaginative or creative. It's easier that way. I may be exaggerating, but only slightly.

This page: The Design Museum itself, of course, has its own branding – commissioned from Graphic Thought Facility in 2003. Fresh, 'friendly' typography combines with intricate line drawings of products that float across both promotional literature and the walls of the building itself.

This doesn't mean that the identity consulting business is entirely dominated by the giants, or even that the giants don't sometimes do interesting or even groundbreaking work. From time to time they do. All over the world, small identity businesses are continually emerging and re-emerging – sometimes in an entirely new form. It's like a self-perpetuating ecosystem.

Saffron, the design consultancy of which I am chairman, employs 60 people in four locations – London, Madrid, Mumbai, New York – and everyone in the company works wherever they are needed, because many of our clients operate globally. There are no separate profit centres, so there are no separate offices – no silos, just places we happen to live and work in. That's a new way of using talent economically and sharing experiences of different markets.

In addition, many of the really large corporate communication businesses own other, smaller identity businesses that they allow to operate quasi-independently. Lambie-Nairn, Coley Porter Bell, The Partners, Fitch and a number of other units are all owned by WPP; Siegel+Gale and Wolff Olins are owned by Omnicom. All of these consultancies compete with each other aggressively and, provided they perform to corporate financial norms, they have complete licence from their owners to be as creative and imaginative as they like.

The arrival of the brand
At about the same time as the communications giants entered and transformed the identity business, something else happened. Over a relatively short time during the 1990s, the word 'brand' overtook and then completely displaced the more woolly and loose term 'corporate identity'.

Identity consultants are no more; we are all brand consultants now. This is much more than a semantic shift: it represents a massive change in perception. Nobody seems to know quite when it happened exactly, but it must have been directly related to an attempt – a successful one at that– to push the identity business even further into the mainstream.

So what's the real difference, then, between identity and branding? Well, branding sounds bigger and more grown-up. It offers much more scope. It's less predominantly visual. It's a curious paradox that, because the identity activity is largely about the management of perceptions, the word 'branding' itself has changed the perceptions of our business.

Brands and branding are from the real world, the commercial world, the world of power and influence and money and profit. Branding is serious. Brands make a real difference to the value of the company. Brand can be used comfortably in conjunction with phrases such as 'perceived value' and 'added value'. Brand strategy is right at the centre. Conceptually, it knocks advertising right off its perch. Advertising is one of the techniques used in branding, not the other way round. The new media have given even more power to brand strategy, just as they have removed it from advertising agencies.

Branding is multidisciplinary. It is about IT, the Web and environmental design; it's about the inside – behavioural issues within the organization – and the outside – the way in which the brand is made visible and palpable externally through the mediums of graphic design and communications.

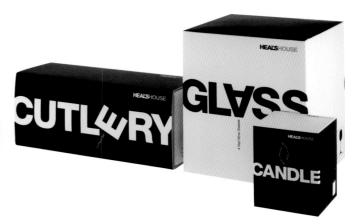

This page: This bold black-on-white or white-on-black branding was carried out by Pentagram for the upmarket furnishings retailer Heal's. Occasional playful notes such as the fallen E to form the shape of a fork or the inverted A to form a glass enliven what might otherwise have been a monotonous scheme.

Established
&SONS
Great Britain

Left: MadeThought is another relatively youthful design studio that concentrates on brand development. Clients have included fashion label Stella McCartney, trend-forecasting company The Future Laboratory and hairdresser James Brown. MadeThought branding often combines graphic purity with a traditionalist twist.

Top left and right: Like many other multidisciplinary design consultancies, MadeThought has embarked on long-term brand strategies with clients — in a fast-changing world, brands need to evolve almost constantly. One such ongoing project is with the British furniture maker Established & Sons.

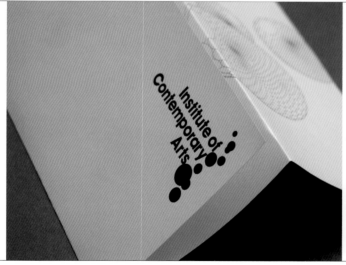

Experimenta:
Under The Radar
16 Nov — 2 Dec 2006
12 — 7.30pm

Theatre

This page: Cultural institutions have also sought to raise their profile by developing strong branding. Spin created a brand for the Institute of Contemporary Arts (ICA), featuring free-floating spheres, which encompassed everything from signage and packaging to website design.

Institute of
Contemporary
Arts

No organization can be a serious player without a clearly articulated brand strategy that is directed at and modulated for all its stakeholders, including the society in which it operates. Above all, branding is about 'adding value' – which is business jargon for making money. This focus on finance has a few interesting knock-on effects.

The brand is taking over the business. As products and services all over the world become similar, and as companies are often outsourcing more and more of what they do, the brand becomes the most important – sometimes the only – significant differentiator. Increasingly, large businesses everywhere in the world are concerned about the value of their brand because the brand is sometimes the most valuable asset the company has. Look at Virgin or Coca-Cola – both companies, like many others, would be worth practically nothing without their brands.

Brand valuation

Naturally enough, clients – who may spend millions of pounds on creating brands – want to know what they're getting for their money. Specifically and unsurprisingly, they often want to know what is the financial value of their brand.

So a new activity has grown up that purports to show, using the most complex econometric of measurements, the specific financial value of any given major brand at any particular point in time. Companies use these figures on their balance sheets where they can, as justification for further brand acquisition and expenditure.

While I am entirely sympathetic to the idea behind brand evaluation, I am also clear that in reality it just can't be done. As the collapse of the stock markets in October 2008 once again confirmed, share prices are governed not by carefully calculated rational evaluation, but by emotion. Brands are volatile and difficult to control – they can be hit by a metaphorical tsunami at any time.

The truth is you don't need an incredibly complex formula to work out the value of a brand. There's often only one way to gauge the value of a brand – see what people will pay for it.

So what about the future?

Brand strategy really is at the heart of most businesses. So branding consultancy is becoming increasingly important and is becoming much broader in scope. Brand consultants are getting closer to the centre of things. They complement and sometimes compete with more traditional strategic consultants. Some consultants even talk about 'designing' businesses.

The opportunities have never been greater. Branding is global. Brands are emerging from India, China, Brazil and Russia and elsewhere. Branding has moved into cities, regions, nations, sport, the arts – it is everywhere you look.

Brand consultancies based in the UK have an extremely high reputation worldwide for standards of excellence. Very many UK-based companies now carry out far more work for clients outside of Britain than inside it.

What excitement ... and my, how it's changed.

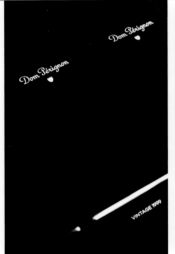

This page: In a world bombarded with over-excitable branding, simplicity and discretion can sometimes work wonders. Discreet branding by Neville Brody for Dom Périganon champagne (left and centre) and by Peter Saville for Kate Moss for Topshop. Sometimes the cachet of the designer's name can be an added bonus, too.

British Council Collection
Whitechapel Gallery

Great Early Buys 5 April
—
14 June 2009

Whitechapel Gallery
77—82 Whitechapel High Street
London E1 7QX
⊖ Aldgate East

BRITISH COUNCIL | 75 YEARS OF CULTURAL RELATIONS

whitechapelgallery.org

This page: The brands of two more great cultural institutions – though at different ends of the scale. Spin created sharply contemporary branding for the Whitechapel Art Gallery in London's East End – primarily a venue for contemporary art; while the London-based Studio Fernando Gutiérrez undertook a careful rebranding of the Prado, launched in 2007.

The View From Outside

Post Script
Paola Antonelli

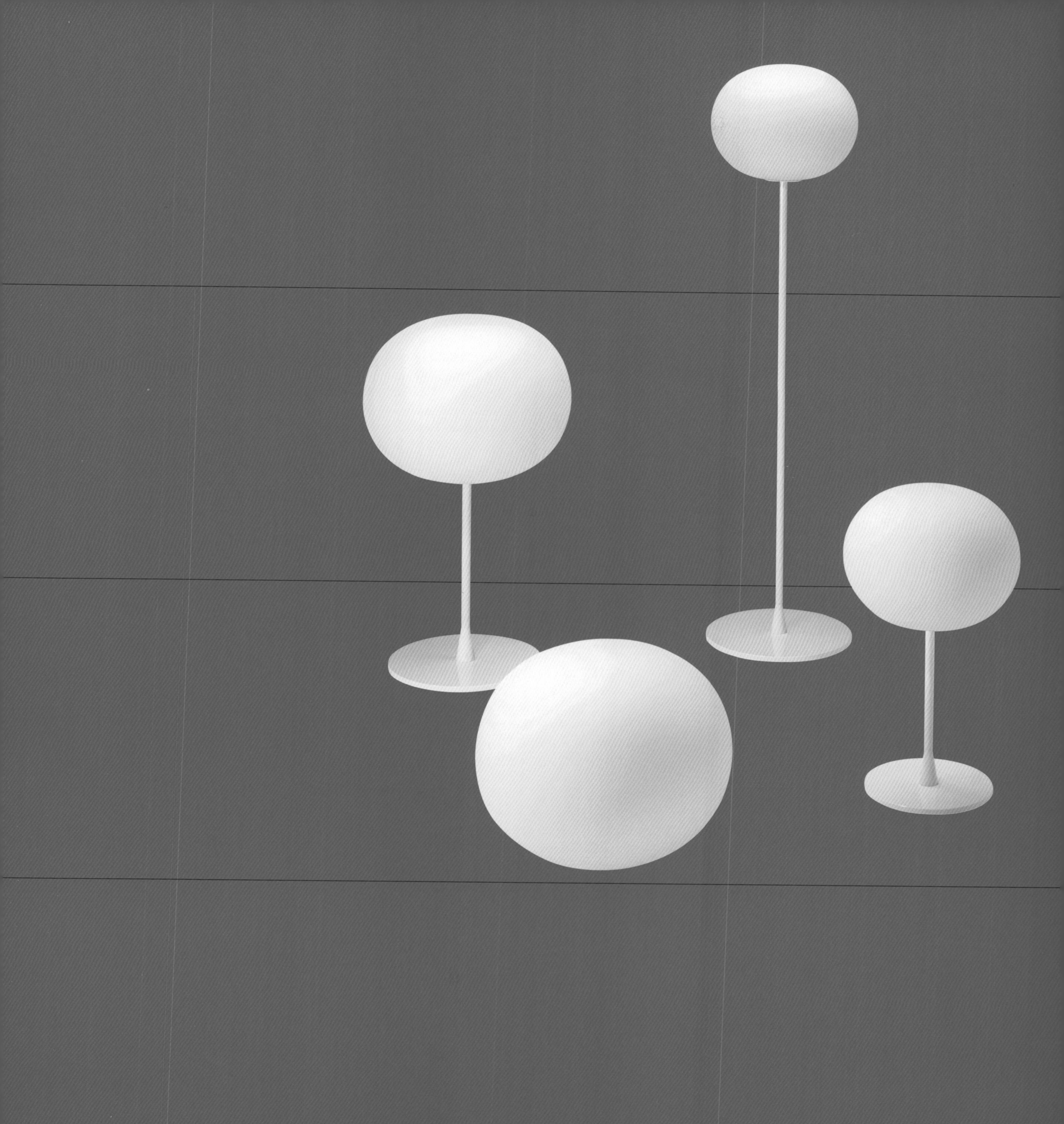

This text is the result of a conversation between Deyan Sudjic and Paola Antonelli, Senior Curator in the Department of Architecture and Design at the Museum of Modern Art, in December 2008, complemented by excerpts from Antonelli's essay for the catalogue of the MoMA exhibition Ron Arad: No Discipline *(The Museum of Modern Art, New York 2009).*

Of the 84 acquisitions made by the Museum of Modern Art (MoMA) between 1995 and 2008 that could in even the most tangential way be described as British design, there are a handful of what might be called the classics. These are the objects conventionally used to represent 'Britishness'.

British classics
At the top of the list is the charismatic E-Type Jaguar Roadster, the most distinctive product ever to emerge from Sir William Lyons' Browns Lane factory in Coventry. Designed in 1961 by Malcolm Sayer (1916–70) and William Heynes (1904–89), the E-Type combined consummate engineering with sleek good looks and, in comparison with its peers, was marketed at a competitive price. MoMA's 1963 example was a gift from the manufacturer in the days when Jaguar was already a subsidiary of US automotive giant Ford, and today the company belongs to Tata of India – a trajectory that says a lot about Britain, let alone the contemporary world. Another recently acquired icon of Britishness in MoMA's collection is a 1949 Vincent Black Shadow motorcycle. Again, interestingly, it was an Anglo-Argentine, Philip Vincent (1908–79), who had founded Vincent-HRD back in 1928, while the Black Shadow itself was designed in collaboration with an Australian engineer, Phil Irving (1903–92). Also in the collection is a 1982 AM2 bicycle, designed by maverick British engineer Alex Moulton (1920–).

Along with these, there are three or four other pieces that hold an iconic place in British, indeed international, design history. A remarkable armchair by Gerald Summers (1899–1967), made from a single sheet of bent, moulded and cut plywood, is a highlight, as are a side table by Baillie Scott (1865–1945), a condiment set by Christopher Dresser (1834–1904) and a striking 1935 poster for Imperial Airways by the great British modernist Ben Nicholson (1894–1982).

Also to be added to the list, perhaps, is the studio pottery made by German émigrés Lucie Rie (1902–85) and Hans Coper (1920–81), objects whose British identity is the result of war and the totalitarian onslaught on Europe, and which, by some definitions, depend on making rather than on design. Natural British modesty prevents anybody from claiming the iPod – another MoMA acquisition – as British design, although the designer, Jonathan Ive (1967–), was born in Chingford, east London, and learned his metier at Newcastle Polytechnic (now Northumbria University).

All of these acquisitions cast light on the nature of Britishness in design. They tell us about its preoccupations, its character and its attractions for newcomers. But perhaps the most striking thing about MoMA's design collection is that almost everything else that the museum has acquired with a connection with Britain since 1995 can trace a link with the Royal College of Art (RCA) – indeed, no less than 75 per cent of the acquisitions depend on that great South Kensington institution in one way or another.

This is nowhere more evident than in the contribution of the Israeli-born designer Ron Arad (1951–), who studied at the Architectural Association in London, after arriving from a year at the Bezalel Academy of Art and Design in Jerusalem, and who went on to have a huge impact on the RCA as the head of Design Products. MoMA has, among other Arad

Paola Antonelli

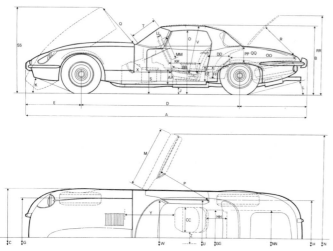

Above and top right: British design, in the historic sense, is represented in the Museum of Modern Art's permanent collection by a series of landmarks, such as the E-Type Jaguar, designed by Sayer and Heynes. This was perhaps the most distinctive and charismatic car ever built in Britain, a machine that combined engineering excellence with a beautiful body.

Above: Hugh Ballie Scott's oak side table from 1901 represents the continuing Arts and Crafts tradition.

Left: Christopher Dresser can be understood as the first design consultant in the modern sense. — MoMA has several of his pieces, among them this electroplated silver cruet set.

Above left: Gerald Summers' remarkable birch plywood bent chair dates from 1934, and represents a brilliant synthesis of form and technique.

Above: MoMA's Design Store also has sold work by Sam Hecht for the Japanese retailer Muji, for whom he has also produced the engaging city in a bag series, reducing London to its essential building blocks.

Above top: More recent aspects of British design at MoMA include Alex Moulton's radical reinvention of the bicycle, with its low centre of gravity, a concept that he has continually refined since the 1960s. This version is from 1983.

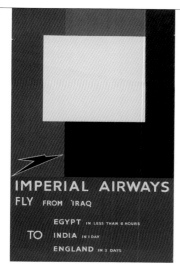

works, the FPE (Fantastic, Plastic, Elastic) stackable chair (1997), the MT3 Rocking Chair (2005), and the PizzaKobra adjustable lamp (2007) – all typically playful and elegant designs. There are pieces, too, by other Royal College graduates – a series of minimalist phones by Sam Hecht (1969–) and chairs by Ross Lovegrove (1958–) and Jasper Morrison (1959–) among them. Another RCA–MoMA connection comes in the form of the experimental work of Anthony Dunne (1964–) and Fiona Raby (1963–), who together pioneered the Design Interactions department at the college.

The concentration of RCA work at MoMA shows how important design schools can be in understanding and documenting the development of design, and demonstrates how significant the college has been to the contemporary evolution of design in Britain.

British connections

Two recent MoMA exhibitions, 'Design and the Elastic Mind' and a retrospective devoted to Ron Arad – staged in 2008 and 2009 respectively and both curated by Paola Antonelli – reflect, though perhaps tangentially, on the nature of design in Britain, and the impact on it of the Royal College of Art.

In 2008 'Design and the Elastic Mind' was an exhibition that was about almost everything *except* the idea of 'Britishness'. Nevertheless, without the contribution of designers from, or trained, or living in Britain, it's an exhibition that could hardly have taken place. 'Design and the Elastic Mind' looked beyond the limits of industrial production and the commercial manufacture of objects, to explore the reciprocal relationship between science and design in the contemporary world. The exhibition brought together design objects and concepts that married the most advanced scientific research with close consideration of human limitations, habits and aspirations.

'Design and the Elastic Mind' highlighted the ability of designers to grasp momentous changes in technology, science and history – changes that demand or reflect major adjustments in human behaviours – and translate them into objects that people can actually understand and use. Over the past 25 years, people have weathered dramatic changes in their experience of time, space, matter and identity. Individuals cope daily with a multitude of changes in scale and pace – working across several time zones, travelling with relative ease between satellite maps and nano-scale images, and being inundated with information. Adaptability is an ancestral distinction of intelligence, but today instant variations in rhythm call for something even stronger – elasticity, 'the product of adaptability *plus* acceleration' (from the exhibition wall text).

'Design and the Elastic Mind' featured new and challenging work from all over the world, but at the core of the exhibition were contributions from a generation of designers from Britain, or at least designers who were educated there. Many of them were not yet in their thirties. Some had come under the influence of Anthony Dunne and Fiona Raby and the RCA's Design Interactions programme. Others had been attracted to Ron Arad and his school of Design Products at the college. Some were already relatively well known.

Dunne and Raby themselves contributed a number of projects, notably several hypothetical pieces sourced from their collaboration with the Cypriot-born industrial designer (and RCA graduate) Michael Anastassiades (1967–) (this project was entitled 'Do you want to replace the existing normal?'; 2007–8). These included the Risk Watch – a device that 'measures' the probability of a plane crashing or a dirty bomb going off in your vicinity – and the Perfect Alignment –

Above: MoMA's holdings include Ben Nicholson's lithograph from 1935 for Imperial Airways, a commission that came from Marcus Brumwell, who went on to establish the Design Research Unit. It is a reminder of a period when the line between art and design was less sharp than it has since become.

This page and opposite: Philip Worthington put a series of software packages together to create Shadow Monsters, which allows viewers to interact with their shadow projection in unpredictable and engaging ways. The software makes its own mildly sinister additions to turn the familiar into surprising forms.

a horoscope device that periodically exudes a bright-pink pink mass that then subsequently deflates. (The latter did in fact have an inescapably British aspect, in that it was made from English oak, albeit with the addition of pink RipStock fabric.) Like all the pieces in the MoMA exhibition, the Dunne–Raby–Anastassiades collaboration set out to provide an insight into the future definitions of design, and its impact on our understanding of the world around us.

Looking at the exhibition checklist, it is perhaps surprising to see so many British-based designers – from Crispin Jones and Mat Hunter at the UK outpost of the Californian design consultancy IDEO, to British designer Synnøve Fredericks, who produced the gently humorous Doffing Headphone – a device 'designed to bring elegance and manners to an everyday technology' – while still at Central Saint Martins. There was Philip Worthington's Shadow Monsters – which literally adds teeth (and growls!) to the conventional shadow puppet show – and Peter Marigold and Beta Tank's Mind Chair, which transmits moving imagery to the sitter's brain via electronic impulses sent through the skin.

Such playful and exploratory designs are far removed indeed from the historical idea of what constitutes British design, as represented by the 1851 Great Exhibition, the Victoria and Albert Museum, and even the iconic classics acquired by MoMA. Together these tell the familiar, heroic narrative of Britain's contribution to industrial design, taking in William Morris, Arts and Crafts, Christopher Dresser and Charles Rennie Mackintosh's version of Art Nouveau. This was a period in which the tidal wave of the industrial revolution demanded the creation of the modern profession of design, but also triggered a reaction against it. William Morris was horrified by the machine age; Christopher Dresser embraced it.

The work in 'Design and the Elastic Mind' offers another and different kind of definition. Design is all about material culture; it serves to define a place in the multiple meanings that UK design critic Hugh Aldersey-Williams employed to discuss globalization and nationalism in the 'Design and the Elastic Mind' catalogue. Design can suggest not only a sense of distinctive difference, but also a kind of banal placelessness. Industrial production is important, of course. But as this generation's work shows, there are other things going on in design, too. There is an interest in dematerialization, in the potential for design to become a kind of storytelling, and in using design to explore the impact on contemporary life of the new directions that science is taking, from nano technology to bio engineering.

In 2009 the Museum of Modern Art staged a very different kind of exhibition – a monographic exhibition on the work of Ron Arad that included a very large new sculptural installation as well as sample pieces of his industrial production, along with illustrations of his architecture. It's been quite a time since the museum has done a monograph on a single designer: in the last 20 years Achille Castiglioni, Ingo Maurer and the Campana brothers have been the only other subjects granted this honour.

Design in the headlines

Taken together, *Ron Arad* and *Design and the Elastic Mind* offer clues in understanding just what it is about Britain that at this particular moment makes it a compelling place to begin thinking about design. First of all, as Paola Antonelli points out, design occupies a very different place in the cultural landscape of Britain as compared with the United States. In America, there is simply no public discussion of the subject. The country's largest metropolitan newspaper,

Opposite page: Designs from the Do You Want to Replace the Existing Normal? project created by Tony Dunne, Fiona Raby and Michael Anastassiades. In these experimental works, the designers look beyond narrow definitions of function and purpose to imagine intellectually more complex objects that do not as yet exist.

Left: Put the Risk Watch to your ear and the rubber nipple deflates, triggering an internal monitor that givers you a threat level based on the political instability of your location.

Top left: In an age of anxiety, the Statistical Clock monitors the BBC for news of disasters – fatal plane crashes, car crashes and so on – and provides an audible count. Each variety of disaster gets its own channel, allowing for individual phobias to be catered for.

Above: Perfect Alignment – an inexplicable explosive detonation like an airbag in a car, triggered by planetary alignment and offering a sign or warning.

This page: Peter Marigold and Beta Tank worked together on the Mind Chair that was exhibited by Paola Antonelli at MoMA. It postulates a practical application in the classroom context of the phenomenon known as sensory substitution. The chair allows moving imagery to be perceived in the mind, through nerve endings in the skin. The standard polypropylene chair would be retrofitted with a pixelated monitor inset in the back.

Above: New reproductive technologies have almost succeeded in severing the connection between fertility and natural cycles. Revital Cohen's Artificial Body Clock seeks to reconnect women with an instinctive response. Or rather, it seeks to remind us of what may have happened to humans struggling to adapt to rapid change. The clock responds to online data from the owner's doctor, therapist and bank manager to signal optimum periods at which to conceive.

The New York Times, has a dance critic, an architecture critic, and several art, theatre, literature and film critics; it even has a perfume critic. Extraordinarily, however, there is no design critic, and even when the subject is covered it is corralled in the 'House and Home' or even the 'Business' pages. It's a situation that's replicated in publications across the whole country – from *The New Yorker* to most other general-interest dailies, weeklies and monthlies. Interestingly, the *International Herald Tribune*, which is part of the New York Times Company, features a high-profile design critic, Alice Rawsthorn.

There are, Antonelli laments, simply no design critics in America with a public platform. That's a gigantic difference from the UK and Italy, where there is a sense of normality about design that is entirely absent in America. 'People in London discuss design,' the MoMA curator says, 'it's part of the cultural environment. The RCA annual graduation design show is visited as if it were an art show and attracts the same kind of curious and engaged visitors that an art show would.' According to Antonelli:

Design is misplaced in American culture. It is seen either as decoration or as business, as market, as a commodity. When Paul Thompson was appointed to become the Rector of the Royal College that was discussed in the press in Britain. But in New York there has not been a word about him leaving the Cooper-Hewitt National Design Museum to go back to Britain, or anything about who might replace him. It's simply not that way in Britain, or in Italy (although I would say that design in Italy is on some kind of life-support system). The impact of a company like Established & Sons, the recently founded British furniture manufacturer, has put the fear of God into some of the Italians – becoming so renowned and respected, so quickly. It's scary to them. They see the UK as a formidable competitor, despite also providing an important source of design ideas for Italian production – from Sebastian Bergne to Jasper Morrison and James Irvine.

Britain, Antonelli points out, is not the only country with a flourishing design culture – far from it. The Netherlands, for example, has an especially rich and idiosyncratic scene, while in the Far East, Japan is moving beyond what has been its characteristic interest in mechanical perfection towards a more poetic marriage between technological advances and aesthetics. China and Taiwan look set to become the next places to look for an emergent design culture. South Korea is already doing impressive things — witness the Korea Advanced Institute of Science and Technology (more commonly known by its acronym, KAIST), which is aspiring to be the MIT of Asia as it seeks to fuse science and technology with design and art. At present, KAIST may be embryonic, but the model that they are following is one that has partly been put forward by Britain and partly by California. The places with the most potential are those where craft weds high technology – something long since pioneered in Britain.

The centrality of the design school

It's the design schools, of course, that have defined the geography of design. It's a geography marked out by where the key schools are. It's something, Antonelli is particularly keen to stress, that plays a central role in her appreciation of British design:

[In Britain] design is about its popular culture as well as its strong schools. Ron Arad, of course, was born in Israel, and he now lives and works in Britain. One could argue that

This page: Revital Cohen is one of a number of students at the Royal College of Art who has used design as the starting point for a series of reflections on the nature of man's relationship with technology. Ventilator Dog asks us if we would feel more or less comfortable relying on an animal, rather than an anonymous machine, to keep us alive on a life-support system.

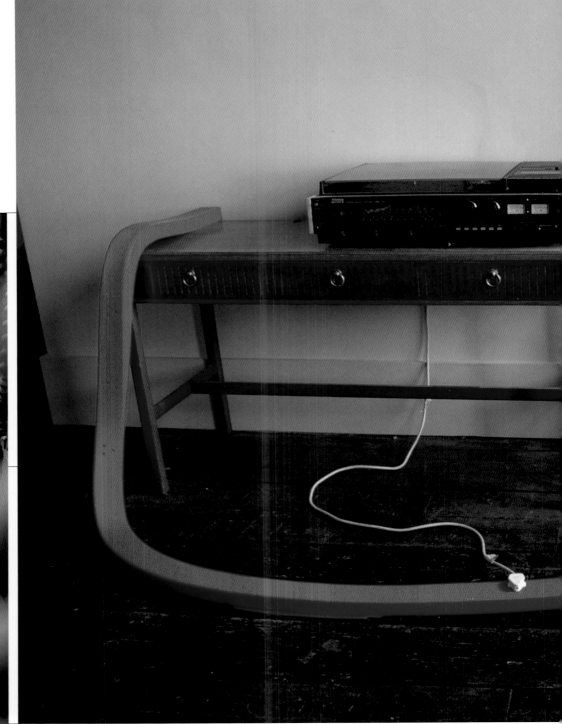

This page and opposite: David Cameron and Toby Hadden work together under the name of &Made. Their Standby Extension project was fabricated for the Museum of Modern Art's 'Design and the Elastic Mind' exhibition. It postulated an extruded power source that could provide sockets where needed, and which would also allow for intelligent switches to ensure that power was not wasted.

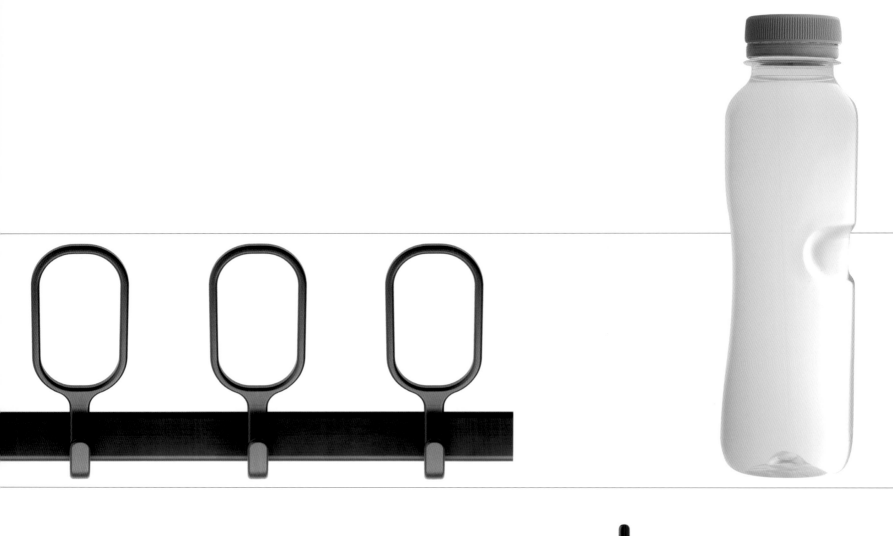

This page: BarberOsgerby mix architecture with product and furniture design. As with most successful British designers, most of their work is made outside Britain. Birds on a Wire (above), their coat storage system in extruded aluminium, and the Tab table lamp (right) are both made in Italy. The PET bottle (top right) was a project for Coca-Cola that aimed at an increased sense of tactility.

The View From Outside_Post Script

his placement is simple happenstance, but I do not believe that he would have blossomed quite the same way anywhere else. Britain is a place where you can do anything you like, and be what you want to be. There is apparently *no discipline* – the title Ron prefers for his show. If you are exciting, you will be cherished.

Christopher Frayling [the outgoing Rector at the RCA] saw this at the Royal College, and it's how best to make use of Ron. At the RCA, Ron did much to provide a route for the graduates of the Bezalel School in Jerusalem into London. Another interesting aspect about the way that the Royal College is organized (or the Architectural Association for that matter) is the way in which the departments are allowed to cross-pollinate and contaminate each other. That is something that does not happen in the USA, and the Italians also have some difficulty with it ...

Building on the success of places like the Royal College of Art, Britain has been able to achieve a critical mass of extraordinarily talented and well-educated designers who are willing to take an innovative, even conceptual approach to their craft. These are exactly the kind of designers who will be important in the future, especially as the significance of the production of material possessions begins to dwindle.

The future of design, Antonelli believes, is one in which physical objects are not the only or necessary end of a design process. They can be just accessories, access routes to services and networks, and their importance as objects to possess and cherish will weaken. New solutions will be found – some material, some immaterial. In this context, the most important designers will be those who teach curiosity and those who are omnivorous for expertise. Designers of the future will be not so much 'makers' but *synthesizers,* and in this regard Britain is already at the forefront of a new and revolutionary model of design.

Design schools are today the most important centres for the production of ideas, having earned pre-eminence over the research and development departments of corporations and other think tanks by progressively shedding the focus on immediate production of finite artifacts in order to privilege experimentation. The trajectory of design education since the second half of the nineteenth century is a fascinating but somewhat unexplored subject. Much of this has to do with the difficulty in capturing a precise definition of something so fleeting, so mercurial as design – that vague noun that always seems to be in need of some qualifier in order to make complete its cultural meaning – *graphic* design, *furniture* design, *fashion* design, and so on ... When it comes to education, moreover, examples of schools entirely devoted to design are rare, as design often figures as a division of schools devoted to the arts, or of polytechnic schools founded on architecture and engineering.

In a sweeping timeline of design history since the second half of the nineteenth century, different schools have reached their creative and influential zenith at different times, each becoming the beacon of international design for that particular period. Naturally enough, this dynamic has closely followed the wider path of social, economical and political history, with schools blossoming when supported by the right patrons and exploited by the most receptive industries, or inspired and defined by intense political circumstances. Each high moment coincides with the tenure of enlightened rectors, directors, chairs, or tutors, and sometimes with the construction of new departments or buildings to celebrate fervour and intellectual splendour. The RCA is no exception.

This page and opposite: James Auger and Jimmy Loizeau explored the idea of telepresence before the 3G wireless technologies became available. They postulated a range of scenarios: by equipping a dog with a small camera and a micro-phone (top), connected wirelessly to a pair of TV glasses that would transmit head movements in real time (opposite), the elderly could experience window-shopping, or a walk in the country without leaving their armchair …

… Similarly, those afflicted by pathological shyness could use it to go on a date without embarrassment (opposite). Auger and Loizeau also speculated about other less benign applications. If a public figure was anxious about being discovered in a massage parlour, he could adopt a similar arrangement with a human surrogate (opposite middle).

The RCA – focus British design

The Royal College of Art is, as its Rector until September 2009 Christopher Frayling reminds us, 'the longest continuous experiment in publicly funded art and design education anywhere in the world'. It currently features six schools – Applied Art, Architecture & Design, Communications, Fashion & Textiles, Fine Art, Humanities – and no fewer than 19 academic departments, ranging from Painting, Conservation, Photography and Architecture to the aforementioned Design Interactions and Design Products. (The unusual titles of these last two return us once again to Ron Arad's key role at the RCA.) The academic structure currently hosts about 850 students and 100 teachers, all of whom are renowned practitioners in their field. The fact that it is a postgraduate school certainly helps its record, but so does the echo created by well-known alumni such as David Hockney, Tracey Emin and the Chapman Brothers from the Fine Art school; Philip Treacy and Zandra Rhodes from the Fashion & Textiles school; and Alan Fletcher, Ridley Scott and Jonathan Barnbrook from the Communications school.

The Government School of Design, set up in 1837 to train practitioners for careers in an industrial context, was heavily influenced by London's Great Exhibition of 1851, which also led to the founding of the Victoria and Albert Museum. The first famous graduate was Christopher Dresser (1834–1904) – often touted as Britain's first industrial designer – who began his studies there in 1847, aged just 15, and became a student lecturer in 1852, giving an articulate and motivated push towards the technical knowledge that he deemed necessary to form designers for the industry. Among the educators was also the German architect Gottfried Semper (1803–79), who, having fled Germany in 1849 after the May Uprising in Dresden, coordinated all the technical workshops for a while.

In the twentieth century the design curricula followed different directions until the courses of Furniture and Industrial design became separate – the former ensconced in a safe and solid Scandinavian tradition, the latter in a Ulm-inflected functionalism. In 1990 the school inaugurated a course dedicated to Computer-Related Design, run by Gillian Crampton-Smith and upholding the RCA's longstanding tradition of attention to the latest technologies. Christopher Frayling became Rector in 1996, after having tutored students in the Humanities Department and taught Cultural History over the previous 23 years. He cites 1981 as a milestone in the history of design at RCA, when at the end-of-year show the then student Daniel Weil (1953–) – an Argentine, incidentally – presented his famous deconstructed radio sealed inside transparent plastic:

Within a very traditional design culture, he did an exhibit of all those see-through radios hanging in a polythene tent, and he called it *Homage to Duchamp*. The examiners stood there and did not know what to make of it – was it art, was it design, was it culture, was it technical? They did not know what was going on … That was the moment when postmodernism started here.

Thereafter, in the early to mid-1980s, the RCA became home to a generation of great students – including Jasper Morrison, Ross Lovegrove, Anthony Dunne – who defined a very different approach to industrial design. At the same time a separate department of Design Engineering arose to cover the traditional discipline of industrial design.

Frayling's first real encounter with Ron Arad was in 1994, when he had to introduce him in the context of a master class in furniture that he was to teach. On that occasion, Frayling announced him by using a contemporary TV commercial for a lager showing a 'designer' throwing away

Left and top left: Jasper Morrison's refined and undemonstrative aesthetic sensibility has been translated far beyond the furniture that he designed in his early days. He was responsible for a range of consumer electronics for Rowenta, including this jug kettle.

Above: After projects for Sony, Morrison is now a consultant to the Korean electronics group Samsung, and travels regularly to Seoul to work inside the organization, rather than simply as an external consultant. He has led a group that has transformed the image of Samsung's products, from telephones to refrigerators.

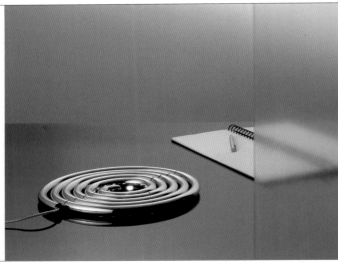

This page: Ron Arad has pursued a career on multiple levels that has taken him from provocative, surreal projects such as his stereo system from the 1980s (above top), which mixed raw concrete with delicate electronics, to more mainstream product design. The PizzaKobra adjustable desk light (above and above right) has a carefully designed mechanism that allows the lamp to unfold gradually.

a Memphis-like chair to replace it with a Rover-like one. ('Oh for a culture where design can sell beer!' Antonelli interpolates.) Arad was at that time a professor of Product Design at the Hochschule für Angewandte Kunst in Vienna – a title that he would hold for three more years. Then, in 1997, Arad 'interviewed' for the position of Head of the Furniture department. Somewhat typically for the RCA, it was a non-interview in which Arad initially formed part of the committee searching for a new head, but then found the tables turned on him and ended up being offered the job.

At this time, as we've seen, the Furniture and the Industrial Design departments were separate, and the absence of the word 'design' after 'furniture', as Arad has explained, meant that it was 'almost like running a craft course'. Frayling and Arad together pushed to have the departments joined under one header, and in 1998 Arad coined a new name for the new division – 'Design Products'. 'Interestingly, the BBC was here at that time,' recalls Frayling, 'filming a documentary about a year in the life of the College, a five-parter. So it all got filmed for posterity, the cameras were there ... The documentary was a big gamble but it kind of positioned the College as the Oxbridge of design, which is what I wanted.'

The subtlety of the new department name, Design Products, becomes momentous, Antonelli reminds us, when we consider the implication of moving the focus from physical things meant to enter the commercial system of the world – the meaning normally associated with the word 'products' – to any concept, idea or construction stemming from a design attitude. The product is first and foremost the idea, supported by an object, a performance, or perhaps a video. To some industrial designers from the old establishment, the change was plain traumatic. A few years later Tony Dunne would carry out the same change in the department that he heads

today – established in 1989 under the direction of Gillian Crampton-Smith as Computer-Related Design, now Design Interactions. That was only the first of the lessons Arad carried over from the Architectural Association (AA), which he attended in the 1970s.

Ron Arad – a pivotal figure

For Paola Antonelli, Ron Arad is one of the undoubted stars of British design – a pivotal figure who not only has had a profound influence on contemporary practice but in whom many of the concerns and tensions of today's global design culture vibrate with special intensity. Moreover, his experience as foreign student at the Architectural Association has much to tell us about the particular strengths of the British design education system and, indeed, of British design culture in general.

As we've seen, Arad first came to London in 1973, after one year of art school at the Bezalel Academy in Jerusalem. At that time the AA, then directed by Alvin Boyarsky (1928–90), was a lively forum for the most interesting, autonomous and atypical approaches to architecture. Arad recalls

It was a period when pre-1968 optimistic modernism was being abandoned amid economic uncertainty and cultural conservatism. In architecture, too, democratic modernism was perceived to have failed and there was a swing towards historicist postmodernism and conservation. The AA's theorists did the opposite. They rejected kitsch postmodernism to become still more modernist.

As the Design Museum's website puts it,

Like snakes shedding their skins, they discarded the failed utopian projects of 'first' modernism to think up a new modernism with a more sophisticated idea of history and

Above: Ron Arad's Fantastic Plastic Elastic chair has been produced in large numbers ever since it was first launched in 1997. It is fabricated from an ingenious aluminium extrusion held firmly in place by the polypropylene membrane that forms the seat and back.

human identity, an architecture embodying modernity's chaos and disjuncture in its very shape.

The record of Arad's admission interview echoes that of his job offer at the RCA, as he recalled in an interview with Paola Antonelli in May 2008:

> I joined the queue for the interview. Alvin [Boyarsky] was there, ... looking at huge portfolios. I didn't have a portfolio. I walk into the room and they ask me, 'Why do you want to be an architect?' And I said, 'I don't want to be an architect. My mother wants me to be an architect.' Which was true, because she was worried that I might want to be an artist instead, and architecture is more respectable and safer. 'Let's see your portfolio.' I said, 'I don't have one, but I have a pencil here.' What do you want me to do? I was cocky and stupid. And the same day after my interview, there was election night in London and it was a party and some guy from the panel said to me: 'Don't do it again. Don't go to your interview like that. We decided to give you a place, but it was a big argument and you nearly didn't get in.' ... I was a reluctant architect most of the time at the AA.

Boyarsky was, says Arad,

> ... pluralist to the point of being indifferent ... you could never know what he really thought. He had established a teaching system based on 'Units', inspired by the eight autonomous *unités pédagogiques* that the École des Beaux-Arts in Paris had set up after the events of May 1968. Each Unit had its own expertise and focus and each Unit Master was free to teach it however he or she pleased. The school was diverse and continuously changing, collegial and yet competitive. There were cliques and ways to belong to them; there were star teachers and star students; there was brilliance and rivalry. And above all, there was a comfortably dangerous atmosphere of anarchy and freedom that was the perfect turf for visionary ideas.

'Pluralism' remains one of Ron's favourite words – and it's a quality, incidentally, that Antonelli especially admires in British design. Arad brought into the Royal College his experience at the AA – everything from the idea of conceptual architecture (and design) and the feeling for pluralism and managed freedom, to the pedagogical structure of the autonomous Unit, which at the RCA he rechristened the 'Platform'. In the newly united departments of Furniture and Industrial Design, Platforms were crucial in order to safeguard difference of interests and directions. To achieve this goal, Arad assigned each Platform to the strongest, most opinionated tutors that he could find. Proceeding on the assumption that graduate students know what they want to do, the Platforms and their leaders were to provide them with what was in effect a sophisticated intellectual and technological trampoline. Frayling has written admiringly of the Arad ethos, in an interview with Antonelli in July 2008:

> He does actually I think have a quite strong philosophy, which is this kind of postmodernist idea of [acting] in a social world. Design is the creation of visual meaning in a responding context ... Also, he was completely at home with digital technology very early on. [He has] no religion, no formula, if you ask Ron what is his philosophy he will say something very relativistic like, 'A good designer is someone who fulfils his promise.'

The Frayling–Arad tenure also coincided with design moving centre-stage politically; Frayling, who was also Chairman of

Right: Troika is a group started by Conny Freyer, Eva Rucki and Sébastien Noël, whose interests encompass art and design, but who also have the engineering and software skills to realize their ambitious installations. *Cloud*, which hangs outside the access escalators for the British Airways lounge at Terminal 5 in Heathrow, is their best-known work to date.

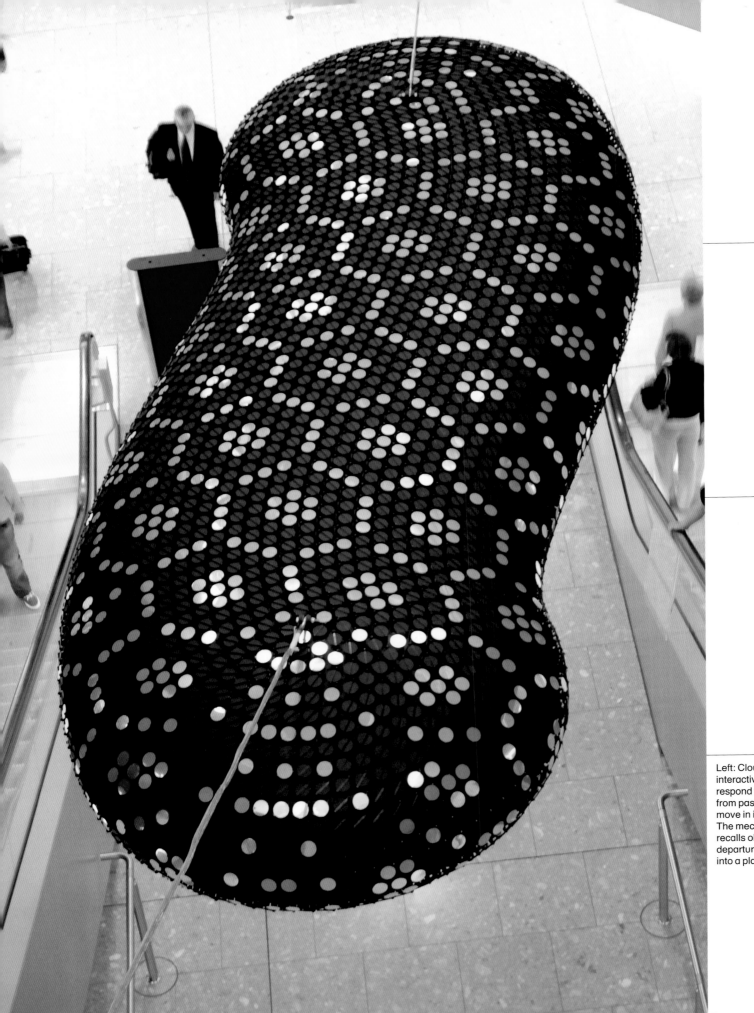

Left: Cloud is not really an interactive work – it does not respond to movement, or input from passers-by. However, it does move in intriguing, engaging ways. The mechanism of flipping discs recalls old-fashioned mechanical departure boards, here transformed into a playful sculptural object.

the UK Design Council in the late 1990s, and then later became Chairman of the Arts Council in 2003, has reflected on how this shift affected the whole design industry:

When New Labour came in in 1997, they were very keen to re-present Britain. I was on several government think tanks [working] on how we could emphasize the creative industry. We realized that ... what we were strong at was design and design education ... The effect that it had on the College was that it made designers feel much more confident. They felt that society wanted them. When I first came to the College in the 1970s, a whole lot of designers were ... sticking two fingers up at the world because they thought the world hated them, so they hated the world.

What has made the RCA so important is that it has been able to continue to attract gifted students from around the world. Both its position will not stay unchallenged. There are other British schools, notably Central Saint Martins, which is relocating from its Lethaby-designed home to a new building in King's Cross. But there is also a procession of other schools in Asia that are eager to invest in their own students.

A reflection on British design

In the economic crisis that began in 2007 with the run on the Northern Rock, Britain has been hit particularly hard. The financial services that, for one booming decade, sustained Britain are now clinging to the life raft of taxpayers' money. Politicians of every persuasion now talk about the creative industries as the future hope of the British economy. Despite the attention these industries have received, and the undoubted talent they contain, there are no grounds to be complacent about their hopes for success.

The same thought about the creative industries has occurred to every other government, from China to Brazil to India, that is not asleep at the wheel. And at this difficult moment, the paradox at the heart of British design that began with William Morris is even more acute. Now as then there is a tension between those who see design as a means of engineering desire, and those who see it as a reflection of a utopian vision of what the world might be. And a generation of designers who saw their work as critical of the world of design and as a means for self-expression are now the very people who are expected to rescue factories on short time and tottering banks.

Index

The publisher would like to thank the following photographers and agencies for their kind permission to reproduce the following photographs: 1 Paul Smith; 9 David Mellor; 11 above & centre V&A Images/Victoria & Albert Museum; 11 below Private Collection/The Stapleton Collection/The Bridgeman Art Library; 13 above left Phil Talbot/Rex Features; 13 above right Courtesy of the Royal College of Art; 13 below left Keystone/Getty Images; 13 below right Science Museum; 14 above left Ercol; 14 above right David Mellor; 14 below left V&A Images/Victoria & Albert Museum; 14 below right Hille; 15 Supporto; 16 above Jim Winkley/Ecoscene/Corbis; 16 below Kodak; 17 left Science Museum; 17 right Kartell; 18 Conran Octopus; 19 above left & right V&A Images/Victoria & Albert Museum; 19 below left Ron Arad; 19 below right Seymour Powell; 20 SCP; 21 above left Science Museum; 21 right & below Dyson; 22 left Ross Lovegrove; 22 right Pearson Lloyd; 23 left Jason Evans; 23 right Edra; 24 above left and right Pearson Lloyd; 24 below Dunne & Raby; 25 left Vitra; 25 right Jasper Morrison; 26 left Industrial Facility; 26 right & 27 left Michael Young; 27 right Sebastian Bergne; 28 Barber Osgerby; 29 left Sebastian Conran Studio; 29 right El Ultimo Grito; 30 Shay Alkalay; 31 left Peter Marigold; 31 right Omlet; 32 Steve Speller; 33 left Jan Kaplicky; 33 right Zaha Hadid; 34 & 35 left Industrial Facility; 35 above Marc Newson; 35 below Konstantin Grcic; 36 Christoph Behling Design; 37 Sebastian

Bergne; 38 Konstantin Grcic; 41 Peter Cook/VIEW; 43 Richard Bryant/Arcaid; 44 Wilkinson Eyre Architects; 46 Adam Parker/Alamy; 47, 48 & 49 Grant Smith/VIEW; 50 Hufton+Crow/VIEW; 51 Chris Brink/VIEW; 52–53 Paul Riddle/ VIEW; 55 Chris Gascoigne/VIEW; 56–57 Will Alsop; 58–59 Edmund Sumner/VIEW; 60 left Anthony Weller/VIEW; 60 right Edmund Sumner/VIEW; 61 Peter Cook/VIEW; 63 & 64–65 Barbara Sax/AFP/Getty Images; 66 & 67 Peter Cook/VIEW; 68–69 & 70–71 Werner Huthmacher, Berlin; 72 above Werner Huthmacher, Berlin; 72 below Helene Binet; 73 Werner Huthmacher, Berlin; 74–75 Richard Brine/VIEW; 75 right Satoru Mishima; 76 & 77 Peter Mackinven/VIEW; 78 Lyndon Douglas; 79 Edmund Sumner/VIEW; 80–81 Richard Glover/VIEW; 82 Drive Images/ Alamy; 84 National Motor Museum/ MPL; 85 Bentley Motors; 86 & 87 Julian Anderson; 88 above right BMW; 88 top left and below British Motor Industry Heritage Trust; 89 Paramount/The Kobal Collection; 90 & 91 BMW; 92 & 93 above & centre National Motor Museum/MPL; 93 below British Motor Industry Heritage Trust; 94–97 National Motor Museum/ MPL; 98 left Percy Lawman/Action Library; 98 right National Motor Museum/MPL; 99 Bauer/Action Library; 100 & 101 Richard Thompson; 102–105 Flow Images/Alamy; 106 Gus Gregory/ Action Library; 107 Stuart Collins/ Action Library; 108 & 109 Jaguar Daimler Heritage Trust; 110 & 111 Morgan Motor Co; 114 left David Gentleman; 114 right Pentagram;

115 above Graphic Thought Facility; 115 below Peter Saville; 116 Jonathan Barnbrook; 117 left Tomato; 117 right Blah Blah Blah; 118 Why Not Associates; 119 Graphic Thought Facility; 120 left A Practise For Everyday Life; 120 right James Goggin; 121 above Kerr Noble; 121 below Sara de Bondt; 122 & 123 Daniel Eatock; 124 Made Thought; 125 left Bibliotheque; 125 right SEA; 126 Bibliotheque; 127 above Spin; 127 below The Wire; 128 A2/SW/HK; 129 left Village Green; 129 right Tom Hingston; 130 above left and right Frost Design; 130 below left Jonathan Gray; 131 left David Pearson; 131 right Jamie Keenan; 132 Jon Wozencroft; 133 Julian House © Ghost Box; 135 Mark Porter; 136 & 137 left Fuel Design; 137 right Dot Dot Dot; 138 Ace Jet 170; 139 Michael Johnson/Johnson Banks; 140 Tate; 141 North Design; 142 left Reuters/Dylan Martinez; 142 right Reuters/Luke MacGregor; 143 John Greenway/Alamy; 145 Anthea Simms; 147 above left Central Press/Getty Images; 147 right David Dagley/Rex Features; 147 below Topical Press Agency/Getty Images; 148 above left Lichfield/Getty Images; 148 above right Terry O'Neill/Hulton Archive/Getty Images; 148 below left V&A Images/Victoria & Albert Museum; 148–149 Colin Davey/ Camera Press London; 150 above Popperfoto/Getty Images; 150 below Hulton Deutsch Collection/Corbis; 151 above and below left Nils Jorgensen/Rex Features; 151 right Nick Knight/NK Images; 153 above left Central Press/Getty Images;

153 above right Marilyn Stafford/ Camera Press London; 153 below left Jim Gray/Keystone/Getty Images; 153 below right John Young/ Camera Press London; 154 Courtesy of The Advertising Archives; 155 & 156 left Niall McInerney; 156 right & 157 Vivienne Westwood; 158 & 159 left Chris Moore/Catwalking; 159 right & 160 Anthea Simms; 161 Nick Knight/ NK Images; 163 left Chris Moore/ Catwalking; 163 right Anthea Simms; 164 & 165 below right Paul Smith; 165 above Press Association Images; 166 Chris Moore/ Catwalking; 167–169 Anthea Simms; 170–173 Chris Moore/ Catwalking; 173 below right VinMag Archives Ltd; 174–181 Chris Moore/ Catwalking; 182 & 183 Anthea Simms; 186 Science Museum; 187 left MaRoDee Photography/ Alamy; 187 right Science Museum; 189 above Jamaway/Alamy; 190–191 www.jodi.org; 192 above www.dopplr.com; 192 below left www.ted.com; 192 below right www.google.com; 193 www.vimeo .com; 194–195 Wang Wei/Haque; 196 www.agentprovocateur.com; 197 www.flickr.com; 198–199 www.alexandermcqueen.com; 200–201 Kurt Riedi & Stefanie Gloor www.kurtli.com; 202–203 Karsten Schmidt/http://postspectacular.com; 204 www.WeFail.com; 205 above www.rathergood.com; 205 below www.itsnicethat.com; 206–207 Media Molecule; 208–209 www.orangeunlimited.com; 210–211 www.cobrabeer.com; 214 left akg-images; 214 right Florian Profitlich/ akg-images; 215 Archivio Storico Olivetti, Ivrea, Italy; 216–219 TfL

from the London Transport Museum Collection; 220 Digital Images, The Museum of Modern Art New York/ Scala, Florence; 221 Alan Aldridge; 222 Colin Underhill/Alamy; 223 Department for Transport; 224 left V&A Images/Victoria & Albert Museum; 225 left Pentagram; 225 right Atelier Works; 226 left Bovis; 226 right 3i; 227 Pentagram; 228 Peter Saville; 229 Pentagram; 230 Michael Johnson/Johnson Banks; 230 Fi McGhee/North Design; 232 Spin; 233 Lambie Nairn; 234 Graphic Thought Facility; 235 Pentagram; 236 Made Thought; 237 Spin; 238 left Neville Brody; 238 right Peter Saville; 239 above Spin; 239 below Fernando Gutierrez; 241 Studio Morrison; 243 above & left Jaguar Daimler Heritage Trust; 243 right & below Digital Images, The Museum of Modern Art, New York/Scala, Florence; 244 left Alivar; 244 above Conran Octopus; 244 below Industrial Facility; 245 Digital Image, The Museum of Modern Art, New York/Scala, Florence; 246–247 Philip Worthington; 249 Francis Ware; 250 Peter Marigold; 251 & 253 Revital Cohen; 254–255 &Made; 256 Barber Osgerby; 258–259 Auger-Loizeau; 261 left Christoph Licherer; 261 right Nicola Tree; 262–263 Ron Arad; 265 & 266 Alex Delfanne/ Artwise Curators © Troika 2008.

Every effort has been made to trace the copyright holders. We apologise in advance for any unintentional omissions and would be pleased to insert the appropriate acknowledgement in any subsequent publication.

Acknowledgements

Daniel Charny is a curator, designer and tutor with an industrial design background. He is a strategic consultant and a guest curator for the Design Museum, London, and Senior Tutor at the Royal College of Art in London where he has been a leading member of the Design Products department for the past ten years. In 2002 he established for Zeev Aram, the Aram Gallery, a unique design gallery in central London dedicated to experimental and new work, where he curates exhibitions that offer insights into the design process. In 2009 he co-founded the creative projects consultancy From Now On.

Deyan Sudjic is Director of the Design Museum in London, UK. Previously, he was the design and architecture critic for the *Observer*, the Dean of the Faculty of Art, Design and Architecture at Kingston University and Co-Chair of the Urban Age Advisory Board. He founded and was Editorial Director of *Blueprint*, the monthly architecture magazine, and has also been the Editor of *Domus* magazine. Alongside these roles, he was the Director of the Glasgow UK City of Architecture and Design programme and the Director of the Venice Architecture Biennale. His last book was *The Language of Things*. He is now working on a biography of Ettore Sottsass.

Andrew Nahum is Principal Curator of Technology and Engineering at the Science Museum. He is also a research tutor, and formerly Visiting Professor in vehicle design at the Royal College of Art, London. He recently led the curatorial team which created the acclaimed special exhibitions *Dan Dare and the Birth of Hi-tech Britain* and *Inside the Spitfire*. He has written extensively on the history of technology, aviation and transport for both scholarly and popular journals. His books include *Issigonis and the Mini*, *Flying Machine* and *Frank Whittle: Invention of the Jet*.

Rick Poynor is a writer on design, media and visual culture. He was the founding Editor of *Eye* magazine, and is a Contributing Editor and columnist of *Print* magazine in New York. In 2003 he co-founded *Design Observer*, which rapidly became a leading design weblog. He lectures internationally on design matters and has been a Visiting Professor and a Research Fellow at the Royal College of Art, London. Poynor's books include *Obey the Giant*, an essay collection, *No More Rules*, a critical study of graphic design and postmodernism, *Typographica*, and *Communicate: Independent British Graphic Design since the Sixties*. He curated the 'Communicate' exhibition at the Barbican Art Gallery, London in 2004.

Susannah Frankel has been Fashion Editor of the *Independent* since 1999 and is Fashion Features Director of *AnOther* magazine. Having studied English at Goldsmiths College, London, she went on to work as a Junior Editor at Academy Editions, publishers of books on art and architecture. In 1989 Frankel moved to *BLITZ* Magazine, becoming Deputy Editor. She was Fashion Editor of the *Guardian* from 1996–9. Her first book, *Visionaries: Interviews With Fashion Designers*, was published by V&A Enterprises in 2001. In 2007 she co-wrote the catalogue for 'The House of Viktor & Rolf' at the Barbican, published by Merrell, and has just completed an essay for a monograph on the work of Martin Margiela to be published by Rizzoli.

Simon Waterfall started his first company 20 years ago, designing games for the Commodore 64 when he was 16. Over the next two decades he helped form the digital industry we know today. He and his partners set up Deepend in the early Nineties which expanded to nine offices around the globe, and was the leading Internet consultancy in 2001 before bursting into flames in the dot com crash. He went on to form Poke in London and New York where he won his second BAFTA for Alexander McQueen's website. Poke has been voted the number one agency twice in the past seven years, and in 2008 he became the youngest and first digital President of the D&AD. In September 2008 he was made a Royal Designer for Industry (RDI).

Wally Olins is one of the world's most respected and experienced practitioners of corporate identity and branding. He was co-founder and Chairman of Wolff Olins and is currently the Chairman and co-founder of Saffron Brand Consultants. He has advised many of the world's leading commercial organizations, including 3i, Renault, Repsol, BT, Volkswagen, Tata and Lloyd's of London, and has also worked with a number of countries on branding issues, among them Portugal and Poland. Olins is the author of several books, including the seminal *Corporate Identity* and *Wally Olins. On B®and*. He has also been Visiting Fellow at Said Business School in Oxford and the London Business School, and Visiting Professor at Lancaster University and Copenhagen Business School. He was awarded a CBE in 1999.

Paola Antonelli is Senior Curator in the Department of Architecture and Design at the Museum of Modern Art in New York, USA, and one of the world's foremost design experts. She has lectured on design and architecture in Europe and the United States and has served on several international architecture and design juries. She has been a Contributing Editor for *Domus* magazine, the Design Editor for *Abitare* and has contributed to many other publications, including *Metropolis*, the *Harvard Design Magazine*, *I.D.*, *Harper's Bazaar*, and *Nest*, as well as to the BBC series *Building Sights*. She has also written two books: *Objects of Design* and *Safe: Design Takes on Risk*.

Contributors